D1429744

Kawasaki EX500 (GPZ500S) Owners Workshop Manual

**by Alan Ahlstrand
and John H Haynes**

Member of the Guild of Motoring Writers

Models covered:
USA: Kawasaki EX500-A1 through A-7
     498cc. 1987 through 1993
UK: Kawasaki EX500-A1 through A-6 (GPZ500S)
     498cc. January 1987 through 1993

ABCDE
FGHIJ
KLMNO
PQRST

Haynes Publishing Group
Sparkford Nr Yeovil
Somerset BA22 7JJ England

Haynes North America, Inc
861 Lawrence Drive
Newbury Park
California 91320 USA

Acknowledgements

Our thanks to Kawasaki Motors (UK) Ltd for permission to re-produce certain illustrations used in this manual. We would also like to thank NGK Spark Plugs (UK) Ltd for supplying the color spark plug condition photos, the Avon Rubber Company for supplying information on tire fitting, and Kevin Wood, who did the mechanical work and provided numerous technical tips.

© **Haynes North America, Inc.   1993**

With permission from J.H. Haynes & Co. Ltd.

A book in the Haynes Owners Workshop Manual Series

Printed in the U.S.A.

ISBN 1 56392 052 2

Library of Congress Catalog Card Number 93-77136

British Library Cataloguing in Publication Data
A catalogue record for this book is available from the British Library

We take great pride in the accuracy of information given in this manual, but motorcycle manufacturers make alterations and de-sign changes during the production run of a particular motorcycle of which they do not inform us. No liability can be accepted by the authors or publishers for loss, damage or injury caused by any er-rors in, or omissions from, the information given.

Contents

Right front view of the Kawasaki EX500/GPZ500S

Left front view of the Kawasaki EX500/GPZ500S

About this manual

Its purpose

The purpose of this manual is to help you get the best value from your motorcycle. It can do so in several ways. It can help you decide what work must be done, even if you choose to have it done by a dealer service department or a repair shop; it provides information and procedures for routine maintenance and servicing; and it offers diagnostic and repair procedures to follow when trouble occurs.

We hope you use the manual to tackle the work yourself. For many simpler jobs, doing it yourself may be quicker than arranging an appointment to get the vehicle into a shop and making the trips to leave it and pick it up. More importantly, a lot of money can be saved by avoiding the expense the shop must pass on to you to cover its labor and overhead costs. An added benefit is the sense of satisfaction and accomplishment that you feel after doing the job yourself.

Using the manual

The manual is divided into Chapters. Each Chapter is divided into numbered Sections, which are headed in bold type between horizontal lines. Each Section consists of consecutively numbered paragraphs.

At the beginning of each numbered Section you will be referred to any illustrations which apply to the procedures in that Section. The reference numbers used in illustration captions pinpoint the pertinent Section and the Step within that Section. That is, illustration 3.2 means the illustration refers to Section 3 and Step (or paragraph) 2 within that Section.

Procedures, once described in the text, are not normally repeated. When it's necessary to refer to another Chapter, the reference will be given as Chapter and Section number. Cross references given without use of the word "Chapter" apply to Sections and/or paragraphs in the same Chapter. For example, "see Section 8" means in the same Chapter.

References to the left or right side of the vehicle assume you are sitting on the seat, facing forward.

Motorcycle manufacturers continually make changes to specifications and recommendations, and these, when notified, are incorporated into our manuals at the earliest opportunity.

Even though we have prepared this manual with extreme care, neither the publisher nor the author can accept responsibility for any errors in, or omissions from, the information given.

NOTE

A **Note** provides information necessary to properly complete a procedure or information which will make the procedure easier to understand.

CAUTION

A **Caution** provides a special procedure or special steps which must be taken while completing the procedure where the Caution is found. Not heeding a Caution can result in damage to the assembly being worked on.

WARNING

A **Warning** provides a special procedure or special steps which must be taken while completing the procedure where the Warning is found. Not heeding a Warning can result in personal injury.

Introduction to the Kawasaki EX500 (GPZ500S)

The Kawasaki EX500 is a best-selling lightweight sport bike.

The engine, derived from the center two cylinders of the ZX600 Ninja/GPX, is a double overhead camshaft design with four valves per cylinder. Fuel is delivered through two 34 mm Keihin carbutrtors.

The front suspension is a conventional telescopic fork design. The rear end uses Kawasaki's proven Uni-trak suspension, which employs a shock absorber/spring unit mounted ahead of the swingarm, close to the center of gravity of the machine. The Uni-trak linkage provides a progressive damping effect.

The front brake is a dual-piston hydraulic disc design, with drum brakes at the rear.

Identification numbers

The frame serial number is stamped into the right side of the steering head and the engine serial number is stamped into the right engine case. Both of these numbers should be recorded and kept in a safe place so they can be furnished to law enforcement officials in the event of theft.

The frame serial number, engine serial number and carburetor identification number should also be kept in a handy place (such as with your driver's license) so they are always available when purchasing or ordering parts for your machine.

The models covered by this manual are as follows:
- EX500-A1 (GPZ500S) - 1987
- EX600-A2 (GPZ500S) - 1988
- EX500-A3 (GPZ500S) - 1989
- EX500-A4 (GPZ500S) - 1990
- EX500-A5 (GPZ500S) - 1991
- EX500-A6 (GPZ500S) - 1992*
- EX500-A7 (GPZ500S) - 1993

The following table is a breakdown of the engine and frame numbers by model and year of production:

Year	Model Code	Frame number range	Engine number range
1987	EX500-A1	US JKAEXA1*HA000001-010500 UK EX500A-000001 to 010500	US, UK EX500AE-000001 to 008000
1988	EX500-A2	US JKAEXA1*JA010501 UK EX500A-010501 to 020500	US EX500AE008001-on UK EX500AE008001 to 018000
1989	EX500-A3	US JKAEXVA1*KA020501-on UK EX500A-020501-on	US, UK EX500AE-018001-on
1990	EX500-A4	US JKAEXVA1*LA020501 to 035336/ 036501 to 048000 UK EX500A-033001 to 035336/ 036501 to 048000	US, UK EX500AE-018001-on
1991	EX500-A5	US KKAEXVA1*MA048001 to 060000 UK EX500A-048001-on	US, UK EX500AE-018001-on
1992	EX500-A6*	US JKAEXVA1*NA060001-on UK EX500A-060001-on	US, UK EX500AE-018001-on
1993	EX500-A7	US JKAEXVA1-PA075001-on UK same as 1992	US EX500AE-018001-on UK same as 1992

The UK A6 model continues unchanged for 1993.

The frame serial number is stamped on the right side of the steering head

The engine serial number is located on the right side of the engine case

Buying parts

Once you have found all the identification numbers, record them for reference when buying parts. Since the manufacturers change specifications, parts and vendors (companies that manufacture various components on the machine), providing the ID numbers is the only way to be reasonably sure that you are buying the correct parts.

Whenever possible, take the worn part to the dealer so direct comparison with the new component can be made. Along the trail from the manufacturer to the parts shelf, there are numerous places that the part can end up with the wrong number or be listed incorrectly.

The two places to purchase new parts for your motorcycle - the accessory store and the franchised dealer - differ in the type of parts

they carry. While dealers can obtain virtually every part for your motorcycle, the accessory dealer is usually limited to normal high wear items such as shock absorbers, tune-up parts, various engine gaskets, cables, chains, brake parts, etc. Rarely will an accessory outlet have major suspension components, cylinders, transmission gears, or cases.

Used parts can be obtained for roughly half the price of new ones, but you can't always be sure of what you're getting. Once again, take your worn part to the wrecking yard (breaker) for direct comparison.

Whether buying new, used or rebuilt parts, the best course is to deal directly with someone who specializes in parts for your particular make.

General specifications

Frame and suspension

Wheelbase	83.46 in (2120 mm)
Overall length	
1987	
US	83.66 in (2125 mm)
UK	80.70 in (2050 mm)
1988-on	83.07 in (2110) mm
Overall width	26.57 in (675 mm)
Overall height	45.86 in (1165 mm)
Seat height	30.81 in (770 mm)
Dry weight	
Except California	373 lbs (169 kg)
California	374 lbs (170 kg)
Front suspension	Telescopic fork
Rear suspension	Uni-trak
Front brake	Hydraulic disc
Rear brake	Mechanical drum
Fuel capacity	4.7 US gal, 4.0 Imp gal (18 liters)

Engine

Type	Liquid cooled, 4-stroke, DOHC parallel twin
Displacement	498 cc
Ignition system	Transistorized
Fuel system	Two 34 mm Keihin carburetors
Clutch	Wet, multi-plate
Transmission	6-speed, constant mesh

Maintenance techniques, tools and working facilities

Basic maintenance techniques

There are a number of techniques involved in maintenance and repair that will be referred to throughout this manual. Application of these techniques will enable the amateur mechanic to be more efficient, better organized and capable of performing the various tasks properly, which will ensure that the repair job is thorough and complete.

Fastening systems

Fasteners, basically, are nuts, bolts and screws used to hold two or more parts together. There are a few things to keep in mind when working with fasteners. Almost all of them use a locking device of some type (either a lock washer, locknut, locking tab or thread adhesive). All threaded fasteners should be clean, straight, have undamaged threads and undamaged corners on the hex head where the wrench fits. Develop the habit of replacing all damaged nuts and bolts with new ones.

Rusted nuts and bolts should be treated with a penetrating oil to ease removal and prevent breakage. Some mechanics use turpentine in a spout type oil can, which works quite well. After applying the rust penetrant, let it -work" for a few minutes before trying to loosen the nut or bolt. Badly rusted fasteners may have to be chiseled off or removed with a special nut breaker, available at tool stores.

If a bolt or stud breaks off in an assembly, it can be drilled out and removed with a special tool called an E-Z out (or screw extractor). Most dealer service departments and motorcycle repair shops can perform this task, as well as others (such as the repair of threaded holes that have been stripped out).

Flat washers and lock washers, when removed from an assembly, should always be replaced exactly as removed. Replace any damaged washers with new ones. Always use a flat washer between a lock washer and any soft metal surface (such as aluminum), thin sheet metal or plastic. Special locknuts can only be used once or twice before they lose their locking ability and must be replaced.

Tightening sequences and procedures

When threaded fasteners are tightened, they are often tightened to a specific torque value (torque is basically a twisting force). Over-tightening the fastener can weaken it and cause it to break, while under-tightening can cause it to eventually come loose. Each bolt, depending on the material it's made of, the diameter of its shank and the material it is threaded into, has a specific torque value, which is noted in the Specifications. Be sure to follow the torque recommendations closely.

Fasteners laid out in a pattern (i.e. cylinder head bolts, engine case bolts, etc.) must be loosened or tightened in a sequence to avoid warping the component. Initially, the bolts/nuts should go on finger tight only. Next, they should be tightened one full turn each, in a criss-cross or diagonal pattern. After each one has been tightened one full turn, return to the first one tightened and tighten them all one half turn, following the same pattern. Finally, tighten each of them one quarter turn at a time until each fastener has been tightened to the proper torque. To loosen and remove the fasteners the procedure would be reversed.

Disassembly sequence

Component disassembly should be done with care and purpose to help ensure that the parts go back together properly during reassembly. Always keep track of the sequence in which parts are removed. Take note of special characteristics or marks on parts that can be installed more than one way (such as a grooved thrust washer on a shaft). It's a good idea to lay the disassembled parts out on a clean surface in the order that they were removed. It may also be helpful to make sketches or take instant photos of components before removal.

When removing fasteners from a component, keep track of their locations. Sometimes threading a bolt back in a part, or putting the washers and nut back on a stud, can prevent mixups later. If nuts and bolts can't be returned to their original locations, they should be kept in a compartmented box or a series of small boxes. A cupcake or muffin tin is ideal for this purpose, since each cavity can hold the bolts and nuts from a particular area (i.e. engine case bolts, valve cover bolts, engine mount bolts, etc.). A pan of this type is especially helpful when working on assemblies with very small parts (such as the carburetors and the valve train). The cavities can be marked with paint or tape to identify the contents.

Whenever wiring looms, harnesses or connectors are separated, it's a good idea to identify the two halves with numbered pieces of masking tape so they can be easily reconnected.

Gasket sealing surfaces

Throughout any motorcycle, gaskets are used to seal the mating surfaces between components and keep lubricants, fluids, vacuum or pressure contained in an assembly.

Many times these gaskets are coated with a liquid or paste type gasket sealing compound before assembly. Age, heat and pressure can sometimes cause the two parts to stick together so tightly that they are very difficult to separate. In most cases, the part can be loosened by striking it with a soft-faced hammer near the mating surfaces. A regular hammer can be used if a block of wood is placed between the hammer and the part. Do not hammer on cast parts or parts that could be easily damaged. With any particularly stubborn part, always recheck to make sure that every fastener has been removed.

Avoid using a screwdriver or bar to pry apart components, as they can easily mar the gasket sealing surfaces of the parts (which must remain smooth). If prying is absolutely necessary, use a piece of wood, but keep in mind that extra clean-up will be necessary if the wood splinters.

After the parts are separated, the old gasket must be carefully scraped off and the gasket surfaces cleaned. Stubborn gasket material can be soaked with a gasket remover (available in aerosol cans) to soften it so it can be easily scraped off. A scraper can be fashioned from a piece of copper tubing by flattening and sharpening one end. Copper is recommended because it is usually softer than the surfaces to be scraped, which reduces the chance of gouging the part. Some gaskets can be removed with a wire brush, but regardless of the method used, the mating surfaces must be left clean and smooth. If for some reason the gasket surface is gouged, then a gasket sealer thick enough to fill scratches will have to be used during reassembly of the components. For most applications, a non-drying (or semi-drying) gasket sealer is best.

Hose removal tips

Hose removal precautions closely parallel gasket removal precautions. Avoid scratching or gouging the surface that the hose mates against or the connection may leak. Because of various chemical reactions, the rubber in hoses can bond itself to the metal spigot that the hose fits over. To remove a hose, first loosen the hose clamps that secure it to the spigot. Then, with slip joint pliers, grab the hose at the clamp and rotate it around the spigot. Work it back and forth until it is completely free, then pull it off (silicone or other lubricants will ease removal if they can be applied between the hose and the outside of the spigot). Apply the same lubricant to the inside of the hose and the outside of the spigot to simplify installation.

If a hose clamp is broken or damaged, do not reuse it. Also, do not reuse hoses that are cracked, split or torn.

Spark plug gap adjusting tool

Feeler gauge set

Control cable pressure luber

Hand impact screwdriver and bits

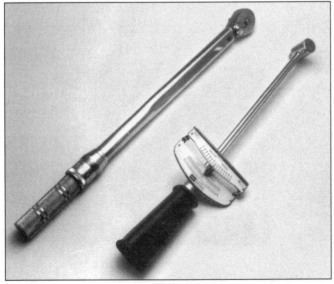

Torque wrenches (left - click type; right - beam type)

Tools

A selection of good tools is a basic requirement for anyone who plans to maintain and repair a motorcycle. For the owner who has few tools, if any, the initial investment might seem high, but when compared to the spiraling costs of routine maintenance and repair, it is a wise one.

To help the owner decide which tools are needed to perform the tasks detailed in this manual, the following tool lists are offered: Maintenance and minor repair, Repair and overhaul and Special. The newcomer to practical mechanics should start off with the Maintenance and minor repair tool kit, which is adequate for the simpler jobs. Then, as confidence and experience grow, the owner can tackle more difficult tasks, buying additional tools as they are needed. Eventually the basic kit will be built into the Repair and overhaul tool set. Over a period of time, the experienced do-it-yourselfer will assemble a tool set complete enough for most repair and overhaul procedures and will add tools from the Special category when it is felt that the expense is justified by the frequency of use.

Maintenance and minor repair tool kit

The tools in this list should be considered the minimum required for performance of routine maintenance, servicing and minor repair work. We recommend the purchase of combination wrenches (box

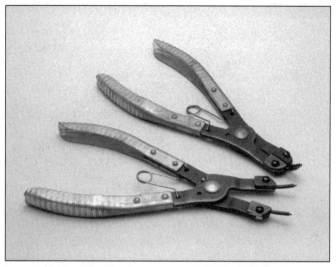

Snap-ring pliers (top - external; bottom - internal)

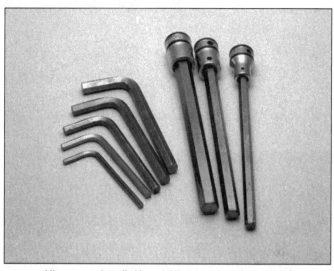

Allen wrenches (left) and Allen head sockets (right)

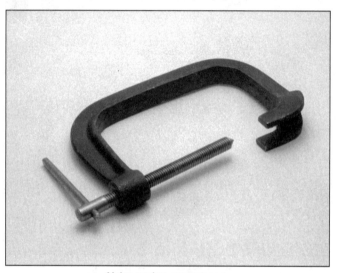

Valve spring compressor

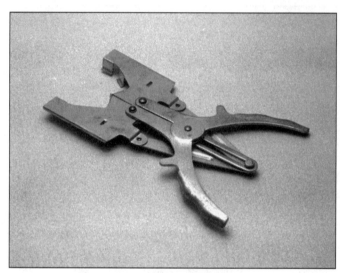

Piston ring removal/installation tool

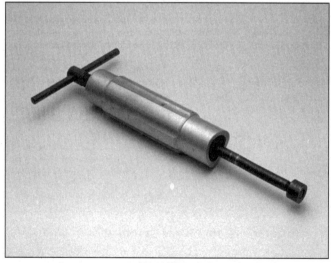

Piston pin puller

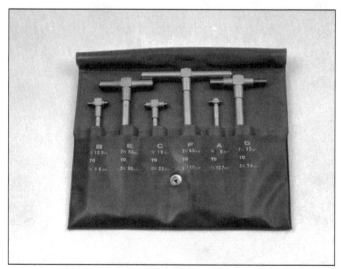

Telescoping gauges

0-to1-inch micrometer

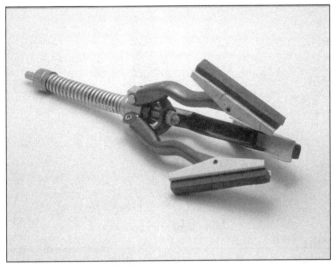

Cylinder surfacing hone

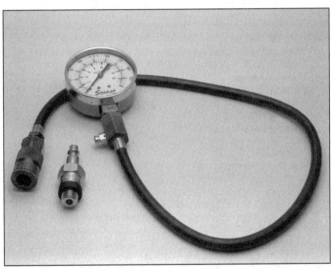

Cylinder compression gauge

Dial indicator set

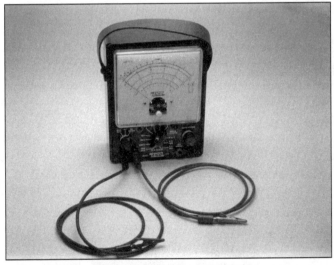

Multimeter (volt/ohm/ammeter)

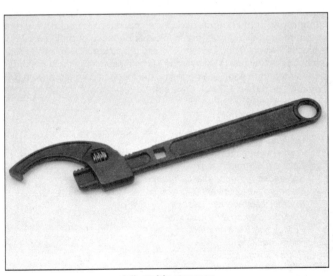

Adjustable spanner

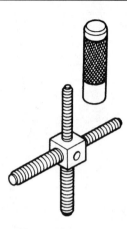

Alternator rotor puller

end and open end combined in one wrench); while more expensive than open-ended ones, they offer the advantages of both types of wrench.

  Combination wrench set (6 mm to 22 mm)
  Adjustable wrench - 8 in
  Spark plug socket (with rubber insert)
  Spark plug gap adjusting tool
  Feeler gauge set
  Standard screwdriver (5/16 in x 6 in)
  Phillips screwdriver (No. 2 x 6 in)
  Allen (hex) wrench set (4 mm to 12 mm)
  Combination (slip-joint) pliers - 6 in
  Hacksaw and assortment of blades
  Tire pressure gauge
  Control cable pressure luber
  Grease gun
  Oil can
  Fine emery cloth
  Wire brush
  Hand impact screwdriver and bits
  Funnel (medium size)
  Safety goggles
  Drain pan
  Work light with extension cord

Repair and overhaul tool set

These tools are essential for anyone who plans to perform major repairs and are intended to supplement those in the Maintenance and minor repair tool kit. Included is a comprehensive set of sockets which, though expensive, are invaluable because of their versatility (especially when various extensions and drives are available). We recommend the 3/8 inch drive over the 1/2 inch drive for general motorcycle maintenance and repair (ideally, the mechanic would have a 3/8 inch drive set and a 1/2 inch drive set).

  Socket set(s)
  Reversible ratchet
  Extension - 6 in
  Universal joint
  Torque wrench (same size drive as sockets)
  Ball pein hammer - 8 oz
  Soft-faced hammer (plastic/rubber)
  Standard screwdriver (1/4 in x 6 in)
  Standard screwdriver (stubby - 5/16 in)
  Phillips screwdriver (No. 3 x 8 in)
  Phillips screwdriver (stubby - No. 2)
  Pliers - locking
  Pliers - lineman's
  Pliers - needle nose
  Pliers - snap-ring (internal and external)
  Cold chisel - 1/2 in

  Scriber
  Scraper (made from flattened copper tubing)
  Center punch
  Pin punches (1/16, 1/8, 3/16 in)
  Steel rule/straightedge - 12 in
  Pin-type spanner wrench
  A selection of files
  Wire brush (large)

Note: Another tool which is often useful is an electric drill with a chuck capacity of 3/8 inch (and a set of good quality drill bits).

Special tools

The tools in this list include those which are not used regularly, are expensive to buy, or which need to be used in accordance with their manufacturer's instructions. Unless these tools will be used frequently, it is not very economical to purchase many of them. A consideration would be to split the cost and use between yourself and a friend or friends (i.e. members of a motorcycle club).

This list primarily contains tools and instruments widely available to the public, as well as some special tools produced by the vehicle manufacturer for distribution to dealer service departments. As a result, references to the manufacturer's special tools are occasionally included in the text of this manual. Generally, an alternative method of doing the job without the special tool is offered. However, sometimes there is no alternative to their use. Where this is the case, and the tool can't be purchased or borrowed, the work should be turned over to the dealer service department or a motorcycle repair shop.

  Valve spring compressor
  Piston ring removal and installation tool
  Piston pin puller
  Telescoping gauges
  Micrometer(s) and/or dial/Vernier calipers
  Cylinder surfacing hone
  Cylinder compression gauge
  Dial indicator set
  Multimeter
  Adjustable spanner
  Alternator rotor holder
  Alternator rotor puller
  Manometer or vacuum gauge set
  Small air compressor with blow gun and tire chuck

Buying tools

For the do-it-yourselfer who is just starting to get involved in motorcycle maintenance and repair, there are a number of options available when purchasing tools. If maintenance and minor repair is the extent of the work to be done, the purchase of individual tools is satisfactory. If, on the other hand, extensive work is planned, it would be a good idea to purchase a modest tool set from one of the large retail chain stores. A set can usually be bought at a substantial savings over the individual tool prices (and they often come with a tool box). As additional tools are needed, add-on sets, individual tools and a larger tool box can be purchased to expand the tool selection. Building a tool set gradually allows the cost of the tools to be spread over a longer period of time and gives the mechanic the freedom to choose only those tools that will actually be used.

Tool stores and motorcycle dealers will often be the only source of some of the special tools that are needed, but regardless of where tools are bought, try to avoid cheap ones (especially when buying screwdrivers and sockets) because they won't last very long. There are plenty of tools around at reasonable prices, but always aim to purchase items which meet the relevant national safety standards. The expense involved in replacing cheap tools will eventually be greater than the initial cost of quality tools.

It is obviously not possible to cover the subject of tools fully here. For those who wish to learn more about tools and their use, there is a book entitled *Motorcycle Workshop Practice Manual* (Book no. 1454) available from the publishers of this manual. It also provides an introduction to basic workshop practice which will be of interest to a home mechanic working on any type of motorcycle.

Care and maintenance of tools

Good tools are expensive, so it makes sense to treat them with respect. Keep them clean and in usable condition and store them properly when not in use. Always wipe off any dirt, grease or metal chips before putting them away. Never leave tools lying around in the work area.

Some tools, such as screwdrivers, pliers, wrenches and sockets, can be hung on a panel mounted on the garage or workshop wall, while others should be kept in a tool box or tray. Measuring instruments, gauges, meters, etc. must be carefully stored where they can't be damaged by weather or impact from other tools.

When tools are used with care and stored properly, they will last a very long time. Even with the best of care, tools will wear out if used frequently. When a tool is damaged or worn out, replace it; subsequent jobs will be safer and more enjoyable if you do.

Working facilities

Not to be overlooked when discussing tools is the workshop. If anything more than routine maintenance is to be carried out, some sort of suitable work area is essential.

It is understood, and appreciated, that many home mechanics do not have a good workshop or garage available and end up removing an engine or doing major repairs outside (it is recommended, however, that the overhaul or repair be completed under the cover of a roof).

A clean, flat workbench or table of comfortable working height is an absolute necessity. The workbench should be equipped with a vise that has a jaw opening of at least four inches.

As mentioned previously, some clean, dry storage space is also required for tools, as well as the lubricants, fluids, cleaning solvents, etc. which soon become necessary.

Sometimes waste oil and fluids, drained from the engine or cooling system during normal maintenance or repairs, present a disposal problem. To avoid pouring them on the ground or into a sewage system, simply pour the used fluids into large containers, seal them with caps and take them to an authorized disposal site or service station. Plastic jugs (such as old antifreeze containers) are ideal for this purpose.

Always keep a supply of old newspapers and clean rags available. Old towels are excellent for mopping up spills. Many mechanics use rolls of paper towels for most work because they are readily available and disposable. To help keep the area under the motorcycle clean, a large cardboard box can be cut open and flattened to protect the garage or shop floor.

Whenever working over a painted surface (such as the fuel tank) cover it with an old blanket or bedspread to protect the finish.

Safety first

Professional mechanics are trained in safe working procedures. However enthusiastic you may be about getting on with the job at hand, take the time to ensure that your safety is not put at risk. A moment's lack of attention can result in an accident, as can failure to observe simple precautions.

There will always be new ways of having accidents, and the following is not a comprehensive list of all dangers; it is intended rather to make you aware of the risks and to encourage a safe approach to all work you carry out on your bike.

Essential DOs and DON'Ts

DON'T start the engine without first ascertaining that the transmission is in neutral.

DON'T suddenly remove the filler cap from a hot cooling system - cover it with a cloth and release the pressure gradually first, or you may get scalded by escaping coolant.

DON'T attempt to drain oil until you are sure it has cooled sufficiently to avoid scalding you.

DON'T grasp any part of the engine or exhaust system without first ascertaining that it is cool enough not to burn you.

DON'T allow brake fluid or antifreeze to contact the machine's paint work or plastic components.

DON'T siphon toxic liquids such as fuel, hydraulic fluid or antifreeze by mouth, or allow them to remain on your skin.

DON'T inhale dust - it may be injurious to health (see *Asbestos* heading).

DON'T allow any spilled oil or grease to remain on the floor - wipe it up right away, before someone slips on it.

DON'T use ill fitting wrenches or other tools which may slip and cause injury.

DON'T attempt to lift a heavy component which may be beyond your capability - get assistance.

DON'T rush to finish a job or take unverified short cuts.

DON'T allow children or animals in or around an unattended vehicle.

DON'T inflate a tire to a pressure above the recommended maximum. Apart from over stressing the carcase and wheel rim, in extreme cases the tire may blow off forcibly.

DO ensure that the machine is supported securely at all times. This is especially important when the machine is blocked up to aid wheel or fork removal.

DO take care when attempting to loosen a stubborn nut or bolt. It is generally better to pull on a wrench, rather than push, so that if you slip, you fall away from the machine rather than onto it.

DO wear eye protection when using power tools such as drill, sander, bench grinder etc.

DO use a barrier cream on your hands prior to undertaking dirty jobs - it will protect your skin from infection as well as making the dirt easier to remove afterwards; but make sure your hands aren't left slippery. Note that long-term contact with used engine oil can be a health hazard.

DO keep loose clothing (cuffs, ties etc. and long hair) well out of the way of moving mechanical parts.

DO remove rings, wristwatch etc., before working on the vehicle- especially the electrical system.

DO keep your work area tidy - it is only too easy to fall over articles left lying around.

DO exercise caution when compressing springs for removal or installation. Ensure that the tension is applied and released in a controlled manner, using suitable tools which preclude the possibility of the spring escaping violently.

DO ensure that any lifting tackle used has a safe working load rating adequate for the job.

DO get someone to check periodically that all is well, when working alone on the vehicle.

DO carry out work in a logical sequence and check that everything is correctly assembled and tightened afterwards.

DO remember that your vehicle's safety affects that of yourself and others. If in doubt on any point, get professional advice.

IF, in spite of following these precautions, you are unfortunate enough to injure yourself, seek medical attention as soon as possible.

Asbestos

Certain friction, insulating, sealing and other products - such as brake pads, clutch linings, gaskets, etc. - contain asbestos. *Extreme care must be taken to avoid inhalation of dust from such products since it is hazardous to health.* If in doubt, assume that they *do* contain asbestos.

Fire

Remember at all times that gasoline (petrol) is highly flammable. Never smoke or have any kind of naked flame around, when working on the vehicle. But the risk does not end there - a spark caused by an electrical short-circuit, by two metal surfaces contacting each other, by careless use of tools, or even by static electricity built up in your body under certain conditions, can ignite gasoline (petrol) vapor, which in a confined space is highly explosive. Never use gasoline (petrol) as a cleaning solvent. Use an approved safety solvent.

Always disconnect the battery ground (earth) terminal before working on any part of the fuel or electrical system, and never risk spilling fuel on to a hot engine or exhaust.

It is recommended that a fire extinguisher of a type suitable for fuel and electrical fires is kept handy in the garage or workplace at all times. Never try to extinguish a fuel or electrical fire with water.

Fumes

Certain fumes are highly toxic and can quickly cause unconsciousness and even death if inhaled to any extent. Gasoline (petrol) vapor comes into this category, as do the vapors from certain solvents such as trichloroethylene. Any draining or pouring of such volatile fluids should be done in a well ventilated area.

When using cleaning fluids and solvents, read the instructions carefully. Never use materials from unmarked containers - they may give off poisonous vapors.

Never run the engine of a motor vehicle in an enclosed space such as a garage. Exhaust fumes contain carbon monoxide which is extremely poisonous; if you need to run the engine, always do so in the open air or at least have the rear of the vehicle outside the workplace.

The battery

Never cause a spark, or allow a naked light near the vehicle's battery. It will normally be giving off a certain amount of hydrogen gas, which is highly explosive.

Always disconnect the battery ground (earth) terminal before working on the fuel or electrical systems (except where noted).

If possible, loosen the filler plugs or cover when charging the battery from an external source. Do not charge at an excessive rate or the battery may burst.

Take care when topping up, cleaning or carrying the battery. The acid electrolyte, even when diluted, is very corrosive and should not be allowed to contact the eyes or skin. Always wear rubber gloves and goggles or a face shield. If you ever need to prepare electrolyte yourself, always add the acid slowly to the water; never add the water to the acid.

Electricity

When using an electric power tool, inspection light etc., always ensure that the appliance is correctly connected to its plug and that, where necessary, it is properly grounded (earthed). Do not use such appliances in damp conditions and, again, beware of creating a spark or applying excessive heat in the vicinity of fuel or fuel vapor. Also ensure that the appliances meet national safety standards.

A severe electric shock can result from touching certain parts of the electrical system, such as the spark plug wires (HT leads), when the engine is running or being cranked, particularly if components are damp or the insulation is defective. Where an electronic ignition system is used, the secondary (HT) voltage is much higher and could prove fatal.

Motorcycle chemicals and lubricants

A number of chemicals and lubricants are available for use in motorcycle maintenance and repair. They include a wide variety of products ranging from cleaning solvents and degreasers to lubricants and protective sprays for rubber, plastic and vinyl.

Contact point/spark plug cleaner is a solvent used to clean oily film and dirt from points, grime from electrical connectors and oil deposits from spark plugs. It is oil free and leaves no residue. It can also be used to remove gum and varnish from carburetor jets and other orifices.

Carburetor cleaner is similar to contact point/spark plug cleaner but it usually has a stronger solvent and may leave a slight oily reside. It is not recommended for cleaning electrical components or connections.

Brake system cleaner is used to remove grease or brake fluid from brake system components (where clean surfaces are absolutely necessary and petroleum-based solvents cannot be used); it also leaves no residue.

Silicone-based lubricants are used to protect rubber parts such as hoses and grommets, and are used as lubricants for hinges and locks.

Multi-purpose grease is an all purpose lubricant used wherever grease is more practical than a liquid lubricant such as oil. Some multipurpose grease is colored white and specially formulated to be more resistant to water than ordinary grease.

Gear oil (sometimes called gear lube) is a specially designed oil used in transmissions and final drive units, a s well as other areas where high friction, high temperature lubrication is required. It is available in a number of viscosities (weights) for various applications.

Motor oil, of course, is the lubricant specially formulated for use in the engine. It normally contains a wide variety of additives to prevent corrosion and reduce foaming and wear. Motor oil comes in various weights (viscosity ratings) of from 5 to 80. The recommended weight of the oil depends on the seasonal temperature and the demands on the engine. Light oil is used in cold climates and under light load conditions; heavy oil is used in hot climates and where high loads are encountered. Multi-viscosity oils are designed to have characteristics of both light and heavy oils and are available in a number of weights from 5W-20 to 20W-50.

Gas (petrol) additives perform several functions, depending on their chemical makeup. They usually contain solvents that help dissolve gum and varnish that build up on carburetor and intake parts. They also serve to break down carbon deposits that form on the inside surfaces of the combustion chambers. Some additives contain upper cylinder lubricants for valves and piston rings.

Brake fluid is a specially formulated hydraulic fluid that can withstand the heat and pressure encountered in brake systems. Care must be taken that this fluid does not come in contact with painted surfaces or plastics. An opened container should always be resealed to prevent contamination by water or dirt.

Chain lubricants are formulated especially for use on motorcycle final drive chains. A good chain lube should adhere well and have good penetrating qualities to be effective as a lubricant inside the chain and on the side plates, pins and rollers. Most chain lubes are either the foaming type or quick drying type and are usually marketed as sprays.

Degreasers are heavy duty solvents used to remove grease and grime that may accumulate on engine and frame components. They can be sprayed or brushed on and, depending on the type, are rinsed with either water or solvent.

Solvents are used alone or in combination with degreasers to clean parts and assemblies during repair and overhaul. The home mechanic should use only solvents that are non-flammable and that do not produce irritating fumes.

Gasket sealing compounds may be used in conjunction with gaskets, to improve their sealing capabilities, or alone, to seal metal-to-metal joints. Many gasket sealers can withstand extreme heat, some are impervious to gasoline and lubricants, while others are capable of filling and sealing large cavities. Depending on the intended use, gasket sealers either dry hard or stay relatively soft and pliable. They are usually applied by hand, with a brush, or are sprayed on the gasket sealing surfaces.

Thread cement is an adhesive locking compound that prevents threaded fasteners from loosening because of vibration. It is available in a variety of types for different applications.

Moisture dispersants are usually sprays that can be used to dry out electrical components such as the fuse block and wiring connectors. Some types can also be used as treatment for rubber and as a lubricant for hinges, cables and locks.

Waxes and polishes are used to help protect painted and plated surfaces from the weather. Different types of paint may require the use of different types of wax polish. Some polishes utilize a chemical or abrasive cleaner to help remove the top layer of oxidized (dull) paint on older vehicles. In recent years, many non-wax polishes (that contain a wide variety of chemicals such as polymers and silicones) have been introduced. These non-wax polishes are usually easier to apply and last longer than conventional waxes and polishes.

Troubleshooting

Contents

Engine doesn't start or is difficult to start

1 Starter motor does not rotate

1   Engine stop switch Off.
2   Fuse blown. Check fuse block under the seat (Chapter 9).
3   Battery voltage low. Check and recharge battery (Chapter 9).
4   Starter motor defective. Make sure the wiring to the starter is secure. Make sure the starter solenoid (relay) clicks when the start button is pushed. If the solenoid clicks, then the fault is in the wiring or motor.
5   Starter solenoid (relay) faulty. It is located behind the left side cover. Check it according to the procedure in Chapter 9.
6   Starter button not contacting. The contacts could be wet, corroded or dirty. Disassemble and clean the switch (Chapter 9).
7   Wiring open or shorted. Check all wiring connections and harnesses to make sure that they are dry, tight and not corroded. Also check for broken or frayed wires that can cause a short to ground (see wiring diagram, Chapter 9).
8   Ignition switch defective. Check the switch according to the procedure in Chapter 9. Replace the switch with a new one if it is defective.
9   Engine stop switch defective. Check for wet, dirty or corroded contacts. Clean or replace the switch as necessary (Chapter 9).
10 Faulty starter lockout switch. Check the wiring to the switch and the switch itself according to the procedures in Chapter 9.

2 Starter motor rotates but engine does not turn over

1   Starter motor clutch defective. Inspect and repair or replace (Chapter 2).
2   Damaged idler or starter gears. Inspect and replace the damaged parts (Chapter 2).

3 Starter works but engine won't turn over (seized)

Seized engine caused by one or more internally damaged components. Failure due to wear, abuse or lack of lubrication. Damage can include seized valves, valve lifters, camshaft, pistons, crankshaft, connecting rod bearings, or transmission gears or bearings. Refer to Chapter 2 for engine disassembly.

4 No fuel flow

1   No fuel in tank.
2   Fuel tap vacuum hose broken or disconnected.
3   Tank cap air vent obstructed. Usually caused by dirt or water. Remove it and clean the cap vent hole.
4   Fuel tap clogged. Remove the tap and clean it and the filter (Chapter 4).
5   Fuel line clogged. Pull the fuel line loose and carefully blow through it.
6   Inlet needle valves clogged. For both the valves to be clogged, either a very bad batch of fuel with an unusual additive has been used, or some other foreign object has entered the tank. Many times after a machine has been stored for many months without running, the fuel turns to a varnish-like liquid and forms deposits on the inlet needle valves and jets. The carburetors should be removed and overhauled if draining the float bowls does not alleviate the problem.

5 Engine flooded

1   Float level too high. Check and adjust as described in Chapter 4.
2   Inlet needle valve worn or stuck open. A piece of dirt, rust or other debris can cause the inlet needle to seat improperly, causing excess fuel to be admitted to the float bowl. In this case, the float chamber should be cleaned and the needle and seat inspected. If the needle and seat are worn, then the leaking will persist and the parts should be replaced with new ones (Chapter 4).
3   Starting technique incorrect. Under normal circumstances (i.e., if all the carburetor functions are sound) the machine should start with little or no throttle. When the engine is cold, the choke should be operated and the engine started without opening the throttle. When the engine is at operating temperature, only a very slight amount of throttle should be necessary. On this model, an accelerator pump is fitted and repeated opening and closing of the throttle with the engine off, will cause flooding. If the engine is flooded, turn the fuel tap off and hold the throttle open while cranking the engine. This will allow additional air to reach the cylinders. Remember to turn the gas back on after the engine starts.

6 No spark or weak spark

1   Ignition switch Off.
2   Engine stop switch turned to the Off position.
3   Battery voltage low. Check and recharge battery as necessary (Chapter 9).
4   Spark plug dirty, defective or worn out. Locate reason for fouled plug(s) using spark plug condition chart and follow the plug maintenance procedures in Chapter 1.
5   Spark plug cap or high-tension wiring faulty. Check condition. Replace either or both components if cracks or deterioration are evident (Chapter 5).
6   Spark plug cap not making good contact. Make sure that the plug cap fits snugly over the plug end.
7   IC igniter defective. Check the unit, referring to Chapter 5 for details.
8   Pickup coil defective. Check the unit, referring to Chapter 5 for details.
9   Ignition coil(s) defective. Check the coils, referring to Chapter 5.
10 Ignition or stop switch shorted. This is usually caused by water, corrosion, damage or excessive wear. The switches can be disassembled and cleaned with electrical contact cleaner. If cleaning does not help, replace the switches (Chapter 9).
11 Wiring shorted or broken between:
  a) Ignition switch and engine stop switch
  b) IC igniter and engine stop switch
  c) IC igniter and ignition coil
  d) Ignition coil and plug
  e) IC igniter and pickup coils
Make sure that all wiring connections are clean, dry and tight. Look for chafed and broken wires (Chapters 5 and 8).

7 Compression low

1   Spark plug loose. Remove the plug and inspect the threads. Reinstall and tighten to the specified torque (Chapter 1).
2   Cylinder head not sufficiently tightened down. If the cylinder head is suspected of being loose, then there's a chance that the gasket or head is damaged if the problem has persisted for any length of time. The head bolts should be tightened to the proper torque in the correct sequence (Chapter 2).
3   Improper valve clearance. This means that the valve is not closing completely and compression pressure is leaking past the valve. Check and adjust the valve clearances (Chapter 1).
4   Cylinder and/or piston worn. Excessive wear will cause compression pressure to leak past the rings. This is usually accompanied by worn rings as well. A top end overhaul is necessary (Chapter 2).
5   Piston rings worn, weak, broken, or sticking. Broken or sticking piston rings usually indicate a lubrication or carburetion problem that causes excess carbon deposits or seizures to form on the pistons and rings. Top end overhaul is necessary (Chapter 2).
6   Piston ring-to-groove clearance excessive. This is caused by ex-

cessive wear of the piston ring lands. Piston replacement is necessary (Chapter 2).

7   Cylinder head gasket damaged. If the head is allowed to become loose, or if excessive carbon build-up on the piston crown and combustion chamber causes extremely high compression, the head gasket may leak. Retorquing the head is not always sufficient to restore the seal, so gasket replacement is necessary (Chapter 2).

8   Cylinder head warped. This is caused by overheating or improperly tightened head bolts. Machine shop resurfacing or head replacement is necessary (Chapter 2).

9   Valve spring broken or weak. Caused by component failure or wear; the spring(s) must be replaced (Chapter 2).

10   Valve not seating properly. This is caused by a bent valve (from over-revving or improper valve adjustment), burned valve or seat (improper carburetion) or an accumulation of carbon deposits on the seat (from carburetion, lubrication problems). The valves must be cleaned and/or replaced and the seats serviced if possible (Chapter 2).

8   Stalls after starting

1   Improper choke action. Make sure the choke rod is getting a full stroke and staying in the "out" position. Adjustment of the cable slack is covered in Chapter 1.

2   Ignition malfunction. See Chapter 5.

3   Carburetor malfunction. See Chapter 4.

4   Fuel contaminated. The fuel can be contaminated with either dirt or water, or can change chemically if the machine is allowed to sit for several months or more. Drain the tank and float bowls (Chapter 4).

5   Intake air leak. Check for loose carburetor-to-intake manifold connections, loose or missing vacuum gauge access port cap or hose, or loose carburetor top (Chapter 4).

6   Idle speed incorrect. Turn idle speed adjuster screw until the engine idles at the specified rpm (Chapters 1 and 4).

9   Rough idle

1   Ignition malfunction. See Chapter 5.

2   Idle speed incorrect. See Chapter 1.

3   Carburetors not synchronized. Adjust carburetors with vacuum gauge set or manometer as outlined in Chapter 1.

4   Carburetor malfunction. See Chapter 4.

5   Fuel contaminated. The fuel can be contaminated with either dirt or water, or can change chemically if the machine is allowed to sit for several months or more. Drain the tank and float bowls. If the problem is severe, a carburetor overhaul may be necessary (Chapters 1 and 4).

6   Intake air leak.

7   Air cleaner clogged. Service or replace air filter element (Chapter 1).

Poor running at low speed

10   Spark weak

1   Battery voltage low. Check and recharge battery (Chapter 9).

2   Spark plug fouled, defective or worn out. Refer to Chapter 1 for spark plug maintenance.

3   Spark plug cap or high tension wiring defective. Refer to Chapters 1 and 5 for details on the ignition system.

4   Spark plug cap not making contact.

5   Incorrect spark plug. Wrong type, heat range or cap configuration. Check and install correct plugs listed in Chapter 1. A cold plug or one with a recessed firing electrode will not operate at low speeds without fouling.

6   IC igniter defective. See Chapter 5.

7   Pickup coil defective. See Chapter 5.

8   Ignition coil(s) defective. See Chapter 5.

11   Fuel/air mixture incorrect

1   Pilot screw(s) out of adjustment (Chapters 1 and 4).

2   Pilot jet or air passage clogged. Remove and overhaul the carburetors (Chapter 4).

3   Air bleed holes clogged. Remove carburetor and blow out all passages (Chapter 4).

4   Air cleaner clogged, poorly sealed or missing.

5   Air cleaner-to-carburetor boot poorly sealed. Look for cracks, holes or loose clamps and replace or repair defective parts.

6   Fuel level too high or too low. Adjust the floats (Chapter 4).

7   Fuel tank air vent obstructed. Make sure that the air vent passage in the filler cap is open.

8   Carburetor intake manifolds loose. Check for cracks, breaks, tears or loose clamps or bolts. Repair or replace the rubber boots.

12   Compression low

1   Spark plug loose. Remove the plug and inspect the threads. Reinstall and tighten to the specified torque (Chapter 1).

2   Cylinder head not sufficiently tightened down. If the cylinder head is suspected of being loose, then there's a chance that the gasket and head are damaged if the problem has persisted for any length of time. The head bolts should be tightened to the proper torque in the correct sequence (Chapter 2).

3   Improper valve clearance. This means that the valve is not closing completely and compression pressure is leaking past the valve. Check and adjust the valve clearances (Chapter 1).

4   Cylinder and/or piston worn. Excessive wear will cause compression pressure to leak past the rings. This is usually accompanied by worn rings as well. A top end overhaul is necessary (Chapter 2).

5   Piston rings worn, weak, broken, or sticking. Broken or sticking piston rings usually indicate a lubrication or carburetion problem that causes excess carbon deposits or seizures to form on the pistons and rings. Top end overhaul is necessary (Chapter 2).

6   Piston ring-to-groove clearance excessive. This is caused by excessive wear of the piston ring lands. Piston replacement is necessary (Chapter 2).

7   Cylinder head gasket damaged. If the head is allowed to become loose, or if excessive carbon build-up on the piston crown and combustion chamber causes extremely high compression, the head gasket may leak. Retorquing the head is not always sufficient to restore the seal, so gasket replacement is necessary (Chapter 2).

8   Cylinder head warped. This is caused by overheating or improperly tightened head bolts. Machine shop resurfacing or head replacement is necessary (Chapter 2).

9   Valve spring broken or weak. Caused by component failure or wear; the spring(s) must be replaced (Chapter 2).

10   Valve not seating properly. This is caused by a bent valve (from over-revving or improper valve adjustment), burned valve or seat (improper carburetion) or an accumulation of carbon deposits on the seat (from carburetion, lubrication problems). The valves must be cleaned and/or replaced and the seats serviced if possible (Chapter 2).

13   Poor acceleration

1   Carburetors leaking or dirty. Overhaul the carburetors (Chapter 4).

2   Timing not advancing. The pickup coil unit or the IC igniter may be defective. If so, they must be replaced with new ones, as they cannot be repaired.

3   Carburetors not synchronized. Adjust them with a vacuum gauge set or manometer (Chapter 1).

4   Engine oil viscosity too high. Using a heavier oil than that recommended in Chapter 1 can damage the oil pump or lubrication system and cause drag on the engine.

5   Brakes dragging. Usually caused by debris which has entered the brake piston sealing boot, or from a warped disc or bent axle. Repair as necessary (Chapter 7).

Poor running or no power at high speed

14   Firing incorrect

1   Air filter restricted. Clean or replace filter (Chapter 1).
2   Spark plug fouled, defective or worn out. See Chapter 1 for spark plug maintenance.
3   Spark plug cap or high tension wiring defective. See Chapters 1 and 5 for details on the ignition system.
4   Spark plug cap not in good contact. See Chapter 5.
5   Incorrect spark plug. Wrong type, heat range or cap configuration. Check and install correct plugs listed in Chapter 1. A cold plug or one with a recessed firing electrode will not operate at low speeds without fouling.
6   IC igniter defective. See Chapter 5.
7   Ignition coil(s) defective. See Chapter 5.

15   Fuel/air mixture incorrect

1   Main jet clogged. Dirt, water and other contaminants can clog the main jets. Clean the fuel tap filter, the float bowl area, and the jets and carburetor orifices (Chapter 4).
2   Main jet wrong size. The standard jetting is for sea level atmospheric pressure and oxygen content.
3   Throttle shaft-to-carburetor body clearance excessive. Refer to Chapter 4 for inspection and part replacement procedures.
4   Air bleed holes clogged. Remove and overhaul carburetors (Chapter 4).
5   Air cleaner clogged, poorly sealed or missing.
6   Air cleaner-to-carburetor boot poorly sealed. Look for cracks, holes or loose clamps, and replace or repair defective parts.
7   Fuel level too high or too low. Adjust the float(s) (Chapter 4).
8   Fuel tank air vent obstructed. Make sure the air vent passage in the filler cap is open.
9   Carburetor intake manifolds loose. Check for cracks, breaks, tears or loose clamps or bolts. Repair or replace the rubber boots (Chapter 2).
10   Fuel tap clogged. Remove the tap and clean it and the filter (Chapter 1).
11   Fuel line clogged. Pull the fuel line loose and carefully blow through it.

16   Compression low

1   Spark plug loose. Remove the plug and inspect the threads. Reinstall and tighten to the specified torque (Chapter 1).
2   Cylinder head not sufficiently tightened down. If the cylinder head is suspected of being loose, then there's a chance that the gasket and head are damaged if the problem has persisted for any length of time. The head bolts should be tightened to the proper torque in the correct sequence (Chapter 2).
3   Improper valve clearance. This means that the valve is not closing completely and compression pressure is leaking past the valve. Check and adjust the valve clearances (Chapter 1).
4   Cylinder and/or piston worn. Excessive wear will cause compression pressure to leak past the rings. This is usually accompanied by worn rings as well. A top end overhaul is necessary (Chapter 2).
5   Piston rings worn, weak, broken, or sticking. Broken or sticking piston rings usually indicate a lubrication or carburetion problem that causes excess carbon deposits or seizures to form on the pistons and rings. Top end overhaul is necessary (Chapter 2).

6   Piston ring-to-groove clearance excessive. This is caused by excessive wear of the piston ring lands. Piston replacement is necessary (Chapter 2).
7   Cylinder head gasket damaged. If the head is allowed to become loose, or if excessive carbon build-up on the piston crown and combustion chamber causes extremely high compression, the head gasket may leak. Retorquing the head is not always sufficient to restore the seal, so gasket replacement is necessary (Chapter 2).
8   Cylinder head warped. This is caused by overheating or improperly tightened head bolts. Machine shop resurfacing or head replacement is necessary (Chapter 2).
9   Valve spring broken or weak. Caused by component failure or wear; the spring(s) must be replaced (Chapter 2).
10   Valve not seating properly. This is caused by a bent valve (from over-revving or improper valve adjustment), burned valve or seat (improper carburetion) or an accumulation of carbon deposits on the seat (from carburetion, lubrication problems). The valves must be cleaned and/or replaced and the seats serviced if possible (Chapter 2).

17   Knocking or pinging

1   Carbon build-up in combustion chamber. Use of a fuel additive that will dissolve the adhesive bonding the carbon particles to the crown and chamber is the easiest way to remove the build-up. Otherwise, the cylinder head will have to be removed and decarbonized (Chapter 2).
2   Incorrect or poor quality fuel. Old or improper grades of gasoline can cause detonation. This causes the piston to rattle, thus the knocking or pinging sound. Drain old gas and always use the recommended fuel grade.
3   Spark plug heat range incorrect. Uncontrolled detonation indicates the plug heat range is too hot. The plug in effect becomes a glow plug, raising cylinder temperatures. Install the proper heat range plug (Chapter 1).
4   Improper air/fuel mixture. This will cause the cylinder to run hot, which leads to detonation. Clogged jets or an air leak can cause this imbalance. See Chapter 4.

18   Miscellaneous causes

1   Throttle valve doesn't open fully. Adjust the cable slack (Chapter 1).
2   Clutch slipping. Caused by a cable that is improperly adjusted or snagging or damaged, loose or worn clutch components. Refer to Chapters 1 and 2 for adjustment and overhaul procedures.
3   Timing not advancing.
4   Engine oil viscosity too high. Using a heavier oil than the one recommended in Chapter 1 can damage the oil pump or lubrication system and cause drag on the engine.
5   Brakes dragging. Usually caused by debris which has entered the brake piston sealing boot, or from a warped disc or bent axle. Repair as necessary.

Overheating

19   Cooling system not operating properly

1   Coolant level low. Check coolant level as described in Chapter 1. If coolant level is low, the engine will overheat.
2   Leak in cooling system. Check cooling system hoses and radiator for leaks and other damage. Repair or replace parts as necessary (Chapter 3).
3   Thermostat sticking open or closed. Check and replace as described in Chapter 3.
4   Faulty radiator cap. Remove the cap and have it pressure

checked at a service station.

5   Coolant passages clogged. Have the entire system drained and flushed, then refill with new coolant.

6   Water pump defective. Remove the pump and check the components.

7   Clogged radiator fins. Clean them by blowing compressed air through the fins from the back side.

20   Firing incorrect

1   Spark plug fouled, defective or worn out. See Chapter 1 for spark plug maintenance.

2   Incorrect spark plug.

3   Faulty ignition coils (Chapter 5).

21   Fuel/air mixture incorrect

1   Main jet clogged. Dirt, water and other contaminants can clog the main jets. Clean the fuel tap filter, the float bowl area and the jets and carburetor orifices (Chapter 4).

2   Main jet wrong size. The standard jetting is for sea level atmospheric pressure and oxygen content.

3   Air cleaner poorly sealed or missing.

4   Air cleaner-to-carburetor boot poorly sealed. Look for cracks, holes or loose clamps and replace or repair.

5   Fuel level too low. Adjust the float(s) (Chapter 4).

6   Fuel tank air vent obstructed. Make sure that the air vent passage in the filler cap is open.

7   Carburetor intake manifolds loose. Check for cracks, breaks, tears or loose clamps or bolts. Repair or replace the rubber boots (Chapter 2).

22   Compression too high

1   Carbon build-up in combustion chamber. Use of a fuel additive that will dissolve the adhesive bonding the carbon particles to the piston crown and chamber is the easiest way to remove the build-up. Otherwise, the cylinder head will have to be removed and decarbonized (Chapter 2).

2   Improperly machined head surface or installation of incorrect gasket during engine assembly. Check Specifications (Chapter 2).

23   Engine load excessive

1   Clutch slipping. Caused by an out of adjustment or snagging cable or damaged, loose or worn clutch components. Refer to Chapters 1 and 2 for adjustment and overhaul procedures.

2   Engine oil level too high. The addition of too much oil will cause pressurization of the crankcase and inefficient engine operation. Check Specifications and drain to proper level (Chapter 1).

3   Engine oil viscosity too high. Using a heavier oil than the one recommended in Chapter 1 can damage the oil pump or lubrication system as well as cause drag on the engine.

4   Brakes dragging. Usually caused by debris which has entered the brake piston sealing boot, or from a warped disc or bent axle. Repair as necessary.

24   Lubrication inadequate

1   Engine oil level too low. Friction caused by intermittent lack of lubrication or from oil that is "overworked" can cause overheating. The oil provides a definite cooling function in the engine. Check the oil level

(Chapter 1).

2   Poor quality engine oil or incorrect viscosity or type. Oil is rated not only according to viscosity but also according to type. Some oils are not rated high enough for use in this engine. Check the Specifications section and change to the correct oil (Chapter 1).

25   Miscellaneous causes

Modification to exhaust system. Most aftermarket exhaust systems cause the engine to run leaner, which make them run hotter. When installing an accessory exhaust system, always rejet the carburetors.

Clutch problems

26   Clutch slipping

1   No clutch lever play. Adjust clutch lever free play according to the procedure in Chapter 1.

2   Friction plates worn or warped. Overhaul the clutch assembly (Chapter 2).

3   Steel plates worn or warped (Chapter 2).

4   Clutch springs broken or weak. Old or heat-damaged (from slipping clutch) springs should be replaced with new ones (Chapter 2).

5   Clutch release not adjusted properly. See Chapter 1.

6   Clutch inner cable hanging up. Caused by a frayed cable or kinked outer cable. Replace the cable. Repair of a frayed cable is not advised.

7   Clutch release mechanism defective. Check the shaft, cam, actuating arm and pivot. Replace any defective parts (Chapter 2).

8   Clutch hub or housing unevenly worn. This causes improper engagement of the discs. Replace the damaged or worn parts (Chapter 2).

27   Clutch not disengaging completely

1   Clutch lever play excessive. Adjust at bars or at engine (Chapter 1).

2   Clutch plates warped or damaged. This will cause clutch drag, which in turn causes the machine to creep. Overhaul the clutch assembly (Chapter 2).

3   Clutch spring tension uneven. Usually caused by a sagged or broken spring. Check and replace the springs (Chapter 2).

4   Engine oil deteriorated. Old, thin, worn out oil will not provide proper lubrication for the discs, causing the clutch to drag. Replace the oil and filter (Chapter 1).

5   Engine oil viscosity too high. Using a heavier oil than recommended in Chapter 1 can cause the plates to stick together, putting a drag on the engine. Change to the correct weight oil (Chapter 1).

6   Clutch housing seized on shaft. Lack of lubrication, severe wear or damage can cause the housing to seize on the shaft. Overhaul of the clutch, and perhaps transmission, may be necessary to repair damage (Chapter 2).

7   Clutch release mechanism defective. Worn or damaged release mechanism parts can stick and fail to apply force to the pressure plate. Overhaul the clutch cover components (Chapter 2).

8   Loose clutch hub nut. Causes housing and hub misalignment putting a drag on the engine. Engagement adjustment continually varies. Overhaul the clutch assembly (Chapter 2).

Gear shifting problems

28   Doesn't go into gear or lever doesn't return

1   Clutch not disengaging. See Section 26.

2 Shift fork(s) bent or seized. Often caused by dropping the machine or from lack of lubrication. Overhaul the transmission (Chapter 2).

3 Gear(s) stuck on shaft. Most often caused by a lack of lubrication or excessive wear in transmission bearings and bushings. Overhaul the transmission (Chapter 2).

4 Shift drum binding. Caused by lubrication failure or excessive wear. Replace the drum and bearings (Chapter 2).

5 Shift lever return spring weak or broken (Chapter 2).

6 Shift lever broken. Splines stripped out of lever or shaft, caused by allowing the lever to get loose or from dropping the machine. Replace necessary parts (Chapter 2).

7 Shift mechanism pawl broken or worn. Full engagement and rotary movement of shift drum results. Replace shaft assembly (Chapter 2).

8 Pawl spring broken. Allows pawl to "float", causing sporadic shift operation. Replace spring (Chapter 2).

29 Jumps out of gear

1 Shift fork(s) worn. Overhaul the transmission (Chapter 2).

2 Gear groove(s) worn. Overhaul the transmission (Chapter 2).

3 Gear dogs or dog slots worn or damaged. The gears should be inspected and replaced. No attempt should be made to service the worn parts.

30 Overshifts

1 Pawl spring weak or broken (Chapter 2).

2 Shift drum stopper lever not functioning (Chapter 2).

3 Overshift limiter broken or distorted (Chapter 2).

Abnormal engine noise

31 Knocking or pinging

1 Carbon build-up in combustion chamber. Use of a fuel additive that will dissolve the adhesive bonding the carbon particles to the piston crown and chamber is the easiest way to remove the build-up. Otherwise, the cylinder head will have to be removed and decarbonized (Chapter 2).

2 Incorrect or poor quality fuel. Old or improper fuel can cause detonation. This causes the piston to rattle, thus the knocking or pinging sound. Drain the old gas and always use the recommended grade fuel (Chapter 4).

3 Spark plug heat range incorrect. Uncontrolled detonation indicates that the plug heat range is too hot. The plug in effect becomes a glow plug, raising cylinder temperatures. Install the proper heat range plug (Chapter 1).

4 Improper air/fuel mixture. This will cause the cylinder to run hot and lead to detonation. Clogged jets or an air leak can cause this imbalance. See Chapter 4.

32 Piston slap or rattling

1 Cylinder-to-piston clearance excessive. Caused by improper assembly. Inspect and overhaul top end parts (Chapter 2).

2 Connecting rod bent. Caused by over-revving, trying to start a badly flooded engine or from ingesting a foreign object into the combustion chamber. Replace the damaged parts (Chapter 2).

3 Piston pin or piston pin bore worn or seized from wear or lack of lubrication. Replace damaged parts (Chapter 2).

4 Piston ring(s) worn, broken or sticking. Overhaul the top end (Chapter 2).

5 Piston seizure damage. Usually from lack of lubrication or overheating. Replace the pistons and bore the cylinders, as necessary (Chapter 2).

6 Connecting rod bearing and/or piston pin-end clearance excessive. Caused by excessive wear or lack of lubrication. Replace worn parts.

33 Valve noise

1 Incorrect valve clearances. Adjust the clearances by referring to Chapter 1.

2 Valve spring broken or weak. Check and replace weak valve springs (Chapter 2).

3 Camshaft or cylinder head worn or damaged. Lack of lubrication at high rpm is usually the cause of damage. Insufficient oil or failure to change the oil at the recommended intervals are the chief causes. Since there are no replaceable bearings in the head, the head itself will have to be replaced if there is excessive wear or damage (Chapter 2).

34 Other noise

1 Cylinder head gasket leaking. This will cause compression leakage into the cooling system (which may show up as air bubbles in the coolant in the radiator). Also, coolant may get into the oil (which will turn the oil gray). In either case, have the cooling system checked by a dealer service department.

2 Exhaust pipe leaking at cylinder head connection. Caused by improper fit of pipe(s) or loose exhaust flange. All exhaust fasteners should be tightened evenly and carefully. Failure to do this will lead to a leak.

3 Crankshaft runout excessive. Caused by a bent crankshaft (from over-revving) or damage from an upper cylinder component failure. Can also be attributed to dropping the machine on either of the crankshaft ends.

4 Engine mounting bolts loose. Tighten all engine mount bolts to the specified torque (Chapter 2).

5 Crankshaft bearings worn (Chapter 2).

6 Camshaft chain tensioner defective. Replace according to the procedure in Chapter 2.

7 Camshaft chain, sprockets or guides worn (Chapter 2).

8 Loose alternator rotor. Tighten the mounting bolt to the specified torque (Chapter 2).

Abnormal driveline noise

35 Clutch noise

1 Clutch housing/friction plate clearance excessive (Chapter 2).

2 Loose or damaged clutch pressure plate and/or bolts (Chapter 2).

36 Transmission noise

1 Bearings worn. Also includes the possibility that the shafts are worn. Overhaul the transmission (Chapter 2).

2 Gears worn or chipped (Chapter 2).

3 Metal chips jammed in gear teeth. Probably pieces from a broken clutch, gear or shift mechanism that were picked up by the gears. This will cause early bearing failure (Chapter 2).

4 Engine oil level too low. Causes a howl from transmission. Also affects engine power and clutch operation (Chapter 1).

37 Driveshaft or final drive noise

1 Chain not adjusted properly (Chapter 1).
2 Sprocket (primary sprocket or rear sprocket) loose. Tighten fasteners (Chapter 6).
3 Sprocket(s) worn. Replace sprocket(s) (Chapter 6).
4 Rear sprocket warped. Replace (Chapter 6).
5 Wheel coupling worn. Replace coupling (Chapter 6).

Abnormal frame and suspension noise

38 Front end noise

1 Low fluid level or improper viscosity oil in forks. This can sound like "spurting" and is usually accompanied by irregular fork action (Chapter 6).
2 Spring weak or broken. Makes a clicking or scraping sound. Fork oil, when drained, will have a lot of metal particles in it (Chapter 6).
3 Steering head bearings loose or damaged. Clicks when braking. Check and adjust or replace as necessary (Chapter 6).
4 Fork clamps loose. Make sure all fork clamp pinch bolts are tight (Chapter 6).
5 Fork tube bent. Good possibility if machine has been dropped. Replace tube with a new one (Chapter 6).
6 Front axle or axle clamp bolt loose. Tighten them to the specified torque (Chapter 7).

39 Shock absorber noise

1 Fluid level incorrect. Indicates a leak caused by defective seal. Shock will be covered with oil. Replace shock (Chapter 6).
2 Defective shock absorber with internal damage. This is in the body of the shock and cannot be remedied. The shock must be replaced with a new one (Chapter 6).
3 Bent or damaged shock body. Replace the shock with a new one (Chapter 6).

40 Brake noise

1 Squeal caused by pad shim not installed or positioned correctly (Chapter 7).
2 Squeal caused by dust on brake pads. Usually found in combination with glazed pads. Clean using brake cleaning solvent (Chapter 7).
3 Contamination of brake pads. Oil, brake fluid or dirt causing brake to chatter or squeal. Clean or replace pads (Chapter 7).
4 Pads glazed. Caused by excessive heat from prolonged use or from contamination. Do not use sandpaper, emery cloth, carborundum cloth or any other abrasive to roughen the pad surfaces as abrasives will stay in the pad material and damage the disc. A very fine flat file can be used, but pad replacement is suggested as a cure (Chapter 7).
5 Disc warped. Can cause a chattering, clicking or intermittent squeal. Usually accompanied by a pulsating lever and uneven braking. Replace the disc (Chapter 7).
6 Drum brake linings worn or contaminated. Can cause scraping or squealing. Replace the linings (Chapter 7).
7 Drum brake linings warped or worn unevenly. Can cause chattering. Replace the linings (Chapter 7).
8 Brake drum out of round. Can cause chattering. Replace brake drum (Chapter 7).
9 Loose or worn wheel bearings. Check and replace as needed (Chapter 7).

Oil pressure indicator light comes on

41 Engine lubrication system

1 Engine oil pump defective (Chapter 2).
2 Engine oil level low. Inspect for leak or other problem causing low oil level and add recommended lubricant (Chapters 1 and 2).
3 Engine oil viscosity too low. Very old, thin oil or an improper weight of oil used in engine. Change to correct lubricant (Chapter 1).
4 Camshaft or journals worn. Excessive wear causing drop in oil pressure. Replace cam and/or head. Abnormal wear could be caused by oil starvation at high rpm from low oil level or improper oil weight or type (Chapter 1).
5 Crankshaft and/or bearings worn. Same problems as paragraph 4. Check and replace crankshaft and/or bearings (Chapter 2).

42 Electrical system

1 Oil pressure switch defective. Check the switch according to the procedure in Chapter 9. Replace it if it is defective.
2 Oil pressure indicator light circuit defective. Check for pinched, shorted, disconnected or damaged wiring (Chapter 9).

Excessive exhaust smoke

43 White smoke

1 Piston oil ring worn. The ring may be broken or damaged, causing oil from the crankcase to be pulled past the piston into the combustion chamber. Replace the rings with new ones (Chapter 2).
2 Cylinders worn, cracked, or scored. Caused by overheating or oil starvation. The cylinders will have to be rebored and new pistons installed.
3 Valve oil seal damaged or worn. Replace oil seals with new ones (Chapter 2).
4 Valve guide worn. Perform a complete valve job (Chapter 2).
5 Engine oil level too high, which causes oil to be forced past the rings. Drain oil to the proper level (Chapter 1).
6 Head gasket broken between oil return and cylinder. Causes oil to be pulled into combustion chamber. Replace the head gasket and check the head for warpage (Chapter 2).
7 Abnormal crankcase pressurization, which forces oil past the rings. Clogged breather or hoses usually the cause (Chapter 4).

44 Black smoke

1 Air cleaner clogged. Clean or replace the element (Chapter 1).
2 Main jet too large or loose. Compare the jet size to the Specifications (Chapter 4).
3 Choke stuck, causing fuel to be pulled through choke circuit (Chapter 4).
4 Fuel level too high. Check and adjust the float level as necessary (Chapter 4).
5 Inlet needle held off needle seat. Clean float bowl and fuel line and replace needle and seat if necessary (Chapter 4).

45 Brown smoke

1 Main jet too small or clogged. Lean condition caused by wrong size main jet or by a restricted orifice. Clean float bowl and jets and compare jet size to Specifications (Chapter 4).
2 Fuel flow insufficient. Fuel inlet needle valve stuck closed due to chemical reaction with old gas. Float level incorrect. Restricted fuel

line. Clean line and float bowl and adjust floats if necessary (Chapter 4).
3 Carburetor intake manifolds loose (Chapter 4).
4 Air cleaner poorly sealed or not installed (Chapter 1).

Poor handling or stability

46 Handlebar hard to turn

1 Steering stem locknut too tight (Chapter 6).
2 Bearings damaged. Roughness can be felt as the bars are turned from side-to-side. Replace bearings and races (Chapter 6).
3 Races dented or worn. Denting results from wear in only one position (e. g., straight ahead) from impacting an immovable object or hole or from dropping the machine. Replace races and bearings (Chapter 6).
4 Steering stem lubrication inadequate. Causes are grease getting hard from age or being washed out by high pressure car washes. Disassemble steering head and repack bearings (Chapter 6).
5 Steering stem bent. Caused by hitting a curb or hole or from dropping the machine. Replace damaged part. Do not try to straighten stem (Chapter 6).
6 Front tire air pressure too low (Chapter 1).

47 Handlebar shakes or vibrates excessively

1 Tires worn or out of balance (Chapter 7).
2 Swingarm bearings worn. Replace worn bearings by referring to Chapter 6.
3 Rim(s) warped or damaged. Inspect wheels for runout (Chapter 7).
4 Wheel bearings worn. Worn front or rear wheel bearings can cause poor tracking. Worn front bearings will cause wobble (Chapter 7).
5 Handlebar clamp bolts loose (Chapter 6).
6 Steering stem or fork clamps loose. Tighten them to the specified torque (Chapter 6).
7 Motor mount bolts loose. Will cause excessive vibration with increased engine rpm (Chapter 2).

48 Handlebar pulls to one side

1 Frame bent. Definitely suspect this if the machine has been dropped. May or may not be accompanied by cracking near the bend. Replace the frame (Chapter 6).
2 Wheel out of alignment. Caused by improper location of axle spacers or from bent steering stem or frame (Chapter 6).
3 Swingarm bent or twisted. Caused by age (metal fatigue) or impact damage. Replace the arm (Chapter 6).
4 Steering stem bent. Caused by impact damage or from dropping the motorcycle. Replace the steering stem (Chapter 6).
5 Fork leg bent. Disassemble the forks and replace the damaged parts (Chapter 6).
6 Fork oil level uneven.

49 Poor shock absorbing qualities

1 Too hard:
a) Fork oil level excessive (Chapter 6).
b) Fork oil viscosity too high. Use a lighter oil, (see the Specifications in Chapter 6).
c) Fork tube bent. Causes a harsh, sticking feeling (Chapter 6).
d) Shock shaft or body bent or damaged (Chapter 6).
e) Fork internal damage (Chapter 6).

f) Shock internal damage.
g) Tire pressure too high (Chapters 1 and 7).
2 Too soft:
a) Fork or shock oil insufficient and/or leaking (Chapter 6).
b) Fork oil level too low (Chapter 6).
c) Fork oil viscosity too light (Chapter 6).
d) Fork springs weak or broken (Chapter 6).

Braking problems

50 Front brakes are spongy, don't hold

1 Air in brake line. Caused by inattention to master cylinder fluid level or by leakage. Locate problem and bleed brakes (Chapter 7).
2 Pad or disc worn (Chapters 1 and 7).
3 Brake fluid leak. See paragraph 1.
4 Contaminated pads. Caused by contamination with oil, grease, brake fluid, etc. Clean or replace pads. Clean disc thoroughly with brake cleaner (Chapter 7).
5 Brake fluid deteriorated. Fluid is old or contaminated. Drain system, replenish with new fluid and bleed the system (Chapter 7).
6 Master cylinder internal parts worn or damaged causing fluid to bypass (Chapter 7).
7 Master cylinder bore scratched. From ingestion of foreign material or broken spring. Repair or replace master cylinder (Chapter 7).
8 Disc warped. Replace disc (Chapter 7).

51 Brake lever or pedal pulsates

1 Disc warped. Replace disc (Chapter 7).
2 Axle bent. Replace axle (Chapter 6).
3 Brake caliper bolts loose (Chapter 7).
4 Brake caliper shafts damaged or sticking, causing caliper to bind. Lube the shafts and/or replace them if they are corroded or bent (Chapter 7).
5 Wheel warped or otherwise damaged (Chapter 7).
6 Wheel bearings damaged or worn (Chapter 7).
7 Brake drum out of round. Replace brake drum (Chapter 7).

52 Brakes drag

1 Master cylinder piston seized. Caused by wear or damage to piston or cylinder bore (Chapter 7).
2 Lever balky or stuck. Check pivot and lubricate (Chapter 7).
3 Brake caliper binds. Caused by inadequate lubrication or damage to caliper shafts (Chapter 7).
4 Brake caliper piston seized in bore. Caused by wear or ingestion of dirt past deteriorated seal (Chapter 7).
5 Brake pad damaged. Pad material separating from backing plate. Usually caused by faulty manufacturing process or from contact with chemicals. Replace pads (Chapter 7).
6 Pads improperly installed (Chapter 7).
7 Rear brake pedal free play insufficient.
8 Rear brake springs weak. Replace the springs (Chapter 7).

Electrical problems

53 Battery dead or weak

1 Battery faulty. Caused by sulfated plates which are shorted through the sedimentation or low electrolyte level. Also, broken battery terminal making only occasional contact (Chapter 9).

2 Battery cables making poor contact (Chapter 9).

3 Load excessive. Caused by addition of high wattage lights or other electrical accessories.

4 Ignition switch defective. Switch either grounds internally or fails to shut off system. Replace the switch (Chapter 9).

5 Regulator/rectifier defective (Chapter 9).

6 Stator coil open or shorted (Chapter 9).

7 Wiring faulty. Wiring grounded or connections loose in ignition, charging or lighting circuits (Chapter 9).

54 Battery overcharged

1 Regulator/rectifier defective. Overcharging is noticed when battery gets excessively warm or "boils" over (Chapter 9).

2 Battery defective. Replace battery with a new one (Chapter 9).

3 Battery amperage too low, wrong type or size. Install manufacturer's specified amp-hour battery to handle charging load (Chapter 9).

Chapter 1 Tune-up and routine maintenance

Contents

Specifications

Engine

Spark plugs
    Type
        US models .... NGK D9EA or ND X27ES-U
        UK models .... NGK DR8ES or ND X27ESR-U
        Canadian models.. NGK D8ES or ND X24ES-U
    Gap .... 0.024 to 0.028 inch (0.6 to 0.7 mm)
Engine idle speed
    Except California models .... 1200 +/- 50 rpm
    California models .... 1300 +/- 50 rpm

Engine (continued)

Valve clearances (COLD engine)
  Intake .... 0.005 to 0.007 inch (0.13 to 0.18 mm)
  Exhaust .... 0.007 to 0.009 inch (0.18 to 0.23 mm)
Cylinder compression pressure
  Acceptable range .... 128 to 196 psi (8.8 to 13.5 bars)
Carburetor synchronization (vacuum difference
  between cylinders) .... Less than 0.391 inch (2 cm) Hg
Cylinder numbering (from left side to right side of bike)................. 1-2

Cycle parts

Brake pad minimum thickness .... 0.040 inch (1.0 mm)
Brake pedal position.. 0 to 0.8 inch (0 to 20 mm) below the top of the footpeg
Freeplay adjustments
  Throttle grip .... 0.08 to 0.12 inch (2 to 3 mm)
  Clutch lever (gap between lever and lever bracket
    when freeplay is taken up) .... 0.08 to 0.12 inch (2 to 3 mm)
  Brake pedal .... 0.8 to 1.2 inch (20 to 30 mm)
  Choke lever .... 0.08 to 0.12 inch (2 to 3 mm)
Drive chain
  Slack
    Standard .... 1.38 to 1.57 inch (35 to 40 mm)
    Service limit .... 1.77 inch (45 mm)
  20-link length.. 12.73 inch (323 mm) maximum
Battery electrolyte specific gravity .... 1.280 at 68 degrees F (20 degrees C)
Minimum tire tread depth
  Front .... 0.040 inch (1.0 mm)
  Rear .... 0.080 inch (2.0 mm)
Tire pressures (cold)
  Front
    Up to 215 lbs (97.5 kg)... 28 psi (1.9 bars)
    215 to 406 lbs (97.5 to 184 kg) .... 32 psi (2.2 bars)
  Rear
    Up to 215 lbs (97.5 kg)... 32 psi (2.2 bars)
    215 to 406 lbs (97.5 to 184 kg) .... 36 psi (2.5 bars)

Torque specifications

Oil drain plug .... 22 ft-lbs (30 Nm)
Oil filter .... 12.5 ft-lbs (17 Nm)
Coolant drain bolt .... 104 in-lbs (12 Nm)
Spark plugs... 120 in-lbs (14 Nm)
Valve cover bolts .... 87 in-lbs (9.8 Nm)

Recommended lubricants and fluids

Engine/transmission oil
  Type .... API grade SE or SF
  Viscosity
    In cold climates... SAE 10W40 or 10W50
    In warm climates.. SAE 20W40 or 20W50
  Capacity
    With filter change... 3.2 US qt, 5.3 Imp pt (3.0 liters)
    Oil change only .... 3.0 US qt, 4.9 Imp pt (2.8 liters)
Coolant
  Type .... 50/50 mixture of ethylene glycol based antifreeze and soft water
  Capacity .... 2.0 US qt, 3.1 Imp pt (1.8 liters)
Brake fluid.. DOT 4
Fork oil
  Type .... SAE 10W20 - fork oil
  Amount
    Dry fill .... 287 +/- 2.5 mL/cc (14.1 +/- 0.09 Imp fl oz)
    At oil change .... Approximately 245 mL/cc (8.6 Imp fl oz)
  Oil level .... 5.15 +/- 0.08 inch (131 +/- 2 mm) (fully compressed)
Miscellaneous
  Wheel bearings.. Medium weight, lithium-based multi-purpose grease
  Swingarm pivot bearings .... Medium weight, lithium-based multi-purpose grease
  Cables and lever pivots.. Chain and cable lubricant or 10W30 motor oil
  Sidestand/centerstand pivots .... Medium-weight, lithium-based multi-purpose grease
  Brake pedal/shift lever pivots.. Chain and cable lubricant or 10W30 motor oil
  Throttle grip .... Multi-purpose grease or dry film lubricant

1 Kawasaki EX500 (GPZ500S) Routine maintenance intervals

Routine maintenance intervals

Note: *The pre-ride inspection outlined in the owner's manual covers checks and maintenance that should be carried out on a daily basis. It's condensed and included here to remind you of its importance. Always perform the pre-ride inspection at every maintenance interval (in addition to the procedures listed). The intervals listed below are the shortest intervals recommended by the manufacturer for each particular operation during the model years covered in this manual. Your owner's manual may have different intervals for your model.*

Daily or before riding

- Check the engine oil level
- Check the fuel level and inspect for leaks
- Check the engine coolant level and look for leaks
- Check the operation of both brakes - also check the fluid level and look for leakage
- Check the tires for damage, the presence of foreign objects and correct air pressure
- Check the throttle for smooth operation and correct freeplay
- Check the operation of the clutch - make sure the freeplay is correct
- Make sure the steering operates smoothly, without looseness and without binding
- Check for proper operation of the headlight, taillight, brake light, turn signals, indicator lights, speedometer and horn
- Make sure the sidestand and centerstand return to their fully up positions and stay there under spring pressure
- Make sure the engine STOP switch works properly

Every 200 miles (300 km)

- Lubricate the drive chain

After the initial 500 miles (800 km)

Perform all of the daily checks plus:
- Check and adjust the valve clearances
- Clean the air filter element
- Check/adjust the idle speed
- Check/adjust the carburetor synchronization
- Check/adjust the drive chain slack
- Change the engine oil and oil filter
- Check the evaporative emission control system (California models)
- Check the cooling system hoses
- Check the battery electrolyte level
- Check the tightness of all fasteners
- Check the steering
- Check/adjust clutch freeplay
- Check the brake fluid level
- Check/adjust the brake pedal position
- Check the operation of the brake light

Every 500 miles (800 km)

- Check/adjust the drive chain slack

Every 3000 miles (5000 km)

- Clean and gap the spark plugs
- Check the operation of the air suction valve (if equipped)
- Check/adjust the idle speed
- Check/adjust the carburetor synchronization
- Check the evaporative emission control system (California models)
- Adjust the clutch freeplay
- Check the drive chain and sprockets for wear
- Check the brake fluid level
- Check the brake discs, pads, drum and shoes
- Check/adjust the brake pedal position
- Check the operation of the brake light
- Lubricate all cables
- Lubricate the clutch and brake lever pivots
- Lubricate the shift/brake lever pivots and the sidestand/centerstand pivots
- Check the steering
- Check the tires and wheels
- Check the battery electrolyte level

Every 6000 miles (10,000 km)

All of the items above plus:
- Adjust the valve clearance
- Change the engine oil and oil filter
- Clean the air filter element
- Check the cleanliness of the fuel system and the condition of the fuel and vacuum hoses
- Lubricate the swingarm needle bearings and Uni-trak linkage (Chapter 6)
- Replace the spark plugs
- Check the exhaust system for leaks and check the tightness of the fasteners

Every 12,000 miles or two years (20,000 km)

- Change the brake fluid
- Lubricate the steering head bearings

Every 18,000 miles or two years (30,000 km)

- Check the cooling system and replace the coolant

Every 18,000 miles (30,000 km)

- Change the fork oil

Every two years

- Overhaul the brake caliper and master cylinder (Chapter 7)
- Check and lubricate the wheel bearings (Chapter 7)
- Lubricate the speedometer gear

Every four years

- Replace the fuel hoses (Chapter 4)
- Replace the brake hose (Chapter 7)

1

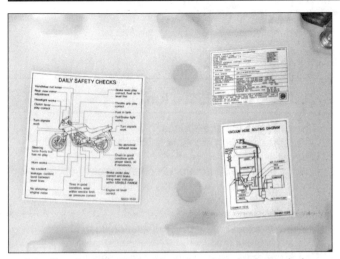

2.3a Decals under the seat include safety checks, emission control and tune-up specifications and a vacuum hose routing diagram

2.3c . . .as well as tire pressures and specifications

2.3b Decals on the chain guard include information about the drive chain. . .

3.3 Check oil level at the inspection window (lower arrow); to add oil, remove the filler cap (upper arrow)

2   Introduction to tune-up and routine maintenance

Refer to illustrations 2.3a, 2.3b and 2.3c

This Chapter covers in detail the checks and procedures necessary for the tune-up and routine maintenance of your motorcycle. Section 1 includes the routine maintenance schedule, which is designed to keep the machine in proper running condition and prevent possible problems. The remaining Sections contain detailed procedures for carrying out the items listed on the maintenance schedule, as well as additional maintenance information designed to increase reliability.

Since routine maintenance plays such an important role in the safe and efficient operation of your motorcycle, it is presented here as a comprehensive check list. For the rider who does all his/her own maintenance, these lists outline the procedures and checks that should be done on a routine basis.

Maintenance information is printed on decals under the seat and on the chain guard **(see illustrations)**. If the information on the decals differs from that included here, use the information on the decal.

Deciding where to start or plug into the routine maintenance schedule depends on several factors. If you have a motorcycle whose warranty has recently expired, and if it has been maintained according to the warranty standards, you may want to pick up routine maintenance as it coincides with the next mileage or calendar interval. If you have owned the machine for some time but have never performed any maintenance on it, then you may want to start at the nearest interval and include some additional procedures to ensure that nothing important is overlooked. If you have just had a major engine overhaul, then you may want to start the maintenance routine from the beginning. If

you have a used machine and have no knowledge of its history or maintenance record, you may desire to combine all the checks into one large service initially and then settle into the maintenance schedule prescribed.

The Sections which outline the inspection and maintenance procedures are written as step-by-step comprehensive guides to the performance of the work. They explain in detail each of the routine inspections and maintenance procedures on the check list. References to additional information in applicable Chapters is also included and should not be overlooked.

Before beginning any maintenance or repair, the machine should be cleaned thoroughly, especially around the oil filter, spark plugs, cylinder head covers, side covers, carburetors, etc. Cleaning will help ensure that dirt does not contaminate the engine and will allow you to detect wear and damage that could otherwise easily go unnoticed.

3   Fluid levels - check

Engine oil

Refer to illustration 3.3

1   Place the motorcycle on the centerstand, then start the engine and allow it to reach normal operating temperature. **Caution:** *Do not run the engine in an enclosed space such as a garage or workshop.*

2   Stop the engine and allow the machine to sit undisturbed on the centerstand for about five minutes.

3   With the engine off, check the oil level in the window located at the lower part of the right crankcase cover. The oil level should be between the Maximum and Minimum level marks next to the window **(see illustration)**.

3.7 With the master cylinder in a level position, check fluid level in the inspection window (arrow)

3.9 To add brake fluid, remove the master cylinder cover screws (arrows) and lift off the cover and diaphragm

3.14 The reservoir is located inside the right fairing; to add coolant, remove the filler cap from the reservoir tank

3.16 The coolant level should be between the marks with the engine cold

4   If the level is below the Minimum mark, remove the oil filler cap from the right crankcase cover (see illustration 3.3) and add enough oil of the recommended grade and type to bring the level up to the Maximum mark. Do not overfill.

Brake fluid

Refer to illustrations 3.7 and 3.9

5   In order to ensure proper operation of the hydraulic disc brakes, the fluid level in the master cylinder reservoir must be properly maintained.

6   With the motorcycle on the centerstand, turn the handlebars until the top of the master cylinder is as level as possible. If necessary, loosen the brake lever clamp bolts and rotate the master cylinder assembly slightly to make it level.

7   Look closely at the inspection window in the master cylinder reservoir. Make sure that the fluid level is above the Lower mark on the reservoir (see illustration).

8   If the level is low, the fluid must be replenished. Before removing the master cylinder cap, cover the fuel tank to protect it from brake fluid spills (which will damage the paint) and remove all dust and dirt from the area around the cap.

9   Remove the screws (see illustration) and lift off the cap and rubber diaphragm. Note: *Do not operate the brake lever with the cap removed.*

10   Add new, clean brake fluid of the recommended type until the level is above the inspection window. Do not mix different brands of brake fluid in the reservoir, as they may not be compatible.

11   Replace the rubber diaphragm and the cover. Tighten the screws evenly, but do not overtighten them.

12   Wipe any spilled fluid off the reservoir body and reposition and tighten the brake lever and master cylinder assembly if it was moved.

13   If the brake fluid level was low, inspect the front brake system for leaks.

Coolant

Refer to illustrations 3.14 and 3.16

14   The engine must be cold for the results to be accurate, so always perform this check before starting the engine for the first time each day. The reservoir is located in the right side of the upper fairing (see illustration).

15   Remove the seat. Detach the fuel tank and move it backward so you can see the reservoir.

16   The coolant level is satisfactory if it is between the Low and Full marks on the reservoir. If the level is at or below the Low mark, remove the reservoir cap and add the recommended coolant mixture (see this Chapter's Specifications) until the Full level is reached (see illustration). If the coolant level seems to be consistently low, check the entire cooling system for leaks.

4   Battery electrolyte level/specific gravity - check

Refer to illustrations 4.3, 4.4, 4.7 and 4.11

Caution: *Be extremely careful when handling or working around the battery. The electrolyte is very caustic and an explosive gas (hydrogen) is given off when the battery is charging.* **Note:** *The first Steps describe battery removal. If the electrolyte level is known to be sufficient it won't be necessary to remove the battery.*

4.3 Lift the junction box and bracket to gain access to the battery - note the position of the battery vent tube (lower arrow) and carburetor vent tube (upper arrow); be sure not pinch either tube or place the end of the carburetor tube near the air intake during installation

4.4 Detach the negative cable (left arrow) from the battery first, then detach the positive cable (right arrow); the plastic cap protects the positive terminal from accidental contact with metal

4.7 Check the specific gravity with a hydrometer

4.11 The clear plastic vent tube supplied with the battery fits inside the motorcycle's drain tube (arrow) when the battery is installed

1　Remove the seat (see Chapter 8).

2　Remove the fuel tank and bracket (see Chapter 4).

3　Unbolt the junction box bracket and lift it off together with the junction box **(see illustration)**. Note the position of the carburetor vent tube and battery vent tube.

4　Remove the bolts securing the battery cables to the battery terminals (remove the negative cable first, positive cable last) **(see illustration)**. Pull the battery straight up to remove it. The electrolyte level will now be visible through the translucent battery case - it should be between the Upper and Lower level marks.

5　If it is low, remove the cell caps and fill each cell to the upper level mark with distilled water. Do not use tap water (except in an emergency), and do not overfill. The cell holes are quite small, so it may help to use a plastic squeeze bottle with a small spout to add the water. If the level is within the marks on the case, additional water is not necessary.

6　Next, check the specific gravity of the electrolyte in each cell with a small hydrometer made especially for motorcycle batteries. These are available from most dealer parts departments or motorcycle accessory stores.

7　Remove the caps, draw some electrolyte from the first cell into the hydrometer **(see illustration)** and note the specific gravity. Compare the reading to the Specifications listed in this Chapter. **Note:** Add 0.004 points to the reading for every 10-degrees F above 68-degrees F (20-degrees C) - subtract 0.004 points from the reading for every 10-

degrees below 68-degrees F (20-degrees C). Return the electrolyte to the appropriate cell and repeat the check for the remaining cells. When the check is complete, rinse the hydrometer thoroughly with clean water.

8　If the specific gravity of the electrolyte in each cell is as specified, the battery is in good condition and is apparently being charged by the machine's charging system.

9　If the specific gravity is low, the battery is not fully charged. This may be due to corroded battery terminals, a dirty battery case, a malfunctioning charging system, or loose or corroded wiring connections. On the other hand, it may be that the battery is worn out, especially if the machine is old, or that infrequent use of the motorcycle prevents normal charging from taking place.

10　Be sure to correct any problems and charge the battery if necessary. Refer to Chapter 9 for additional battery maintenance and charging procedures.

11　Install the battery cell caps, tightening them securely. Reconnect the cables to the battery, attaching the positive cable first and the negative cable last. Make sure to install the plastic cap over the positive terminal. Install the junction box, fuel tank and bracket and the seat. Be very careful not to pinch or otherwise restrict the battery vent tube **(see illustration)**, as the battery may build up enough internal pressure during normal charging system operation to explode.

5.2 The front brake pads (arrows) are visible from the front of the bike (wheel and brake disc removed for clarity)

5.4 If the pointer goes past the Usable Range indicator toward the rear of the bike, the linings are worn and must be replaced

6.6 To adjust the rear brake light switch, hold the switch body and turn the adjusting nut (arrow)

7.2 To adjust the brake pedal position, loosen the locknut (arrow) and turn the adjusting bolt

5   Brake pads and linings - wear check

Refer to illustrations 5.2 and 5.4

1   The front brake pads and rear brake linings should be checked at the recommended intervals and replaced with new ones when worn beyond the limit listed in this Chapter's Specifications.
2   To check the brake pads, position the front wheel so you can see clearly into the front of the brake caliper. The brake pads are visible from this angle and should have at least the specified minimum amount of lining material remaining on the metal backing plate **(see illustration)**.
3   If the pads are worn excessively, they must be replaced with new ones (see Chapter 7).
4   To check the rear brake linings, press the brake pedal firmly and look at the indicator on the brake drum **(see illustration)**. If the pointer is beyond the Usable Range scale, replace the brake shoes (see Chapter 7).

6   Brake system - general check

Refer to illustration 6.6

1   A routine general check of the brakes will ensure that any problems are discovered and remedied before the rider's safety is jeopardized.
2   Check the brake lever and pedal for loose connections, excessive play, bends, and other damage. Replace any damaged parts with new ones (see Chapter 7).

3   Make sure all brake fasteners are tight. Check the brake pads and linings for wear (see Section 5) and make sure the fluid level in the reservoir is correct (see Section 3). Look for leaks at the hose connections and check for cracks in the hoses. If the lever is spongy, bleed the brakes as described in Chapter 7.
4   Make sure the brake light operates when the brake lever is depressed.
5   Make sure the brake light is activated when the rear brake pedal is depressed approximately 15 mm (0.6 inch).
6   If adjustment is necessary, hold the switch and turn the adjusting nut on the switch body **(see illustration)** until the brake light is activated when required. Turning the switch out will cause the brake light to come on sooner, while turning it in will cause it to come on later. If the switch doesn't operate the brake lights, check it as described in Chapter 9.
7   The front brake light switch is not adjustable. If it fails to operate properly, replace it with a new one (see Chapter 9).

7   Brake pedal position and play - check and adjustment

Refer to illustrations 7.2 and 7.5

1   Rear brake pedal position is largely a matter of personal preference. Locate the pedal so that the rear brake can be engaged quickly and easily without excessive foot movement. The recommended factory setting is listed in this Chapter's Specifications.
2   To adjust the position of the pedal, loosen the locknut on the adjusting bolt, turn the bolt to set the pedal position and tighten the locknut **(see illustration)**.

1

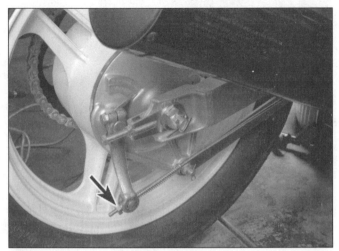

7.5 Turn the adjuster at the rear of the brake rod (arrow) to adjust pedal freeplay

8.4 Use an accurate gauge to check the air pressure in the tires

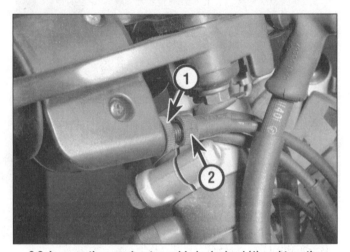

9.3 Loosen the accelerator cable lockwheel (1) and turn the adjuster (2) in or out to obtain the correct throttle freeplay

3   If necessary, adjust the brake light switch (see Section 6).
4   With the pedal position adjusted correctly, check freeplay. Apply the rear brake and compare the pedal travel with that listed in this Chapter's Specifications.
5   To adjust the freeplay, turn the adjuster at the rear end of the brake rod **(see illustration)**.

---

8   Tires/wheels - general check

Refer to illustration 8.4

1   Routine tire and wheel checks should be made with the realization that your safety depends to a great extent on their condition.
2   Check the tires carefully for cuts, tears, embedded nails or other sharp objects and excessive wear. Operation of the motorcycle with excessively worn tires is extremely hazardous, as traction and handling are directly affected. Measure the tread depth at the center of the tire and replace worn tires with new ones when the tread depth is less than specified. **Note:** *In the UK, tread depth must be at least 1 mm over 3/4 of the tread breadth all the way around the tire, with no bald patches.*
3   Repair or replace punctured tires as soon as damage is noted. Do not try to patch a torn tire, as wheel balance and tire reliability may be impaired.
4   Check the tire pressures when the tires are cold and keep them properly inflated **(see illustration)**. Proper air pressure will increase

tire life and provide maximum stability and ride comfort. Keep in mind that low tire pressures may cause the tire to slip on the rim or come off, while high tire pressures will cause abnormal tread wear and unsafe handling.
5   The cast wheels used on this machine are virtually maintenance free, but they should be kept clean and checked periodically for cracks and other damage. Never attempt to repair damaged cast wheels; they must be replaced with new ones.
6   Check the valve stem locknuts to make sure they are tight. Also, make sure the valve stem cap is in place and tight. If it is missing, install a new one made of metal or hard plastic.

---

9   Throttle and choke operation/grip freeplay - check and adjustment

Throttle check

1   With the engine stopped, make sure the throttle grip rotates easily from fully closed to fully open with the front wheel turned at various angles. The grip should return automatically from fully open to fully closed when released. If the throttle sticks, check the throttle cables for cracks or kinks in the housings. Also, make sure the inner cables are clean and well-lubricated.
2   Check for a small amount of freeplay at the grip and compare the freeplay to the value listed in this Chapter's Specifications.

Throttle adjustment

Refer to illustrations 9.3 and 9.5
Note: *These motorcycles use two throttle cables - an accelerator cable and a decelerator cable.*
3   Freeplay adjustments can be made at the throttle end of the cable. Loosen the lockwheel on the cable where it leaves the handlebar **(see illustration)**. Turn the adjuster until the desired freeplay is obtained, then retighten the lockwheel.
4   If the cables can't be adjusted at the grip end, adjust them at the lower ends. To do this, first remove the fuel tank (see Chapter 4).
5   Loosen the locknuts on both throttle cables **(see illustration)**, then turn both adjusting nuts in completely. This will create a large amount of freeplay at the throttle grip.
6   Make sure the throttle grip is in the fully closed position.
7   Turn out the adjusting nut of the decelerator cable until the inner cable just becomes tight, then tighten the locknut.
8   Turn the accelerator cable adjusting nut until the desired freeplay is obtained at the throttle grip, then tighten the locknut.
9   Make sure the throttle linkage lever contacts the idle adjusting screw when the throttle grip is in the closed throttle position. **Warning:** *Turn the handlebars all the way through their travel with the engine*

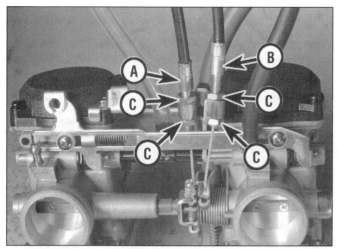

9.5 If freeplay can't be set at the throttle grip, use the adjusters at the carburetors (carburetors removed from engine for clarity)

A   Accelerator cable adjusting nut
B   Decelerator cable adjusting nut
C   Locknuts

9.11 The choke cable adjuster (arrow) is located in the cable (fairing removed for clarity)

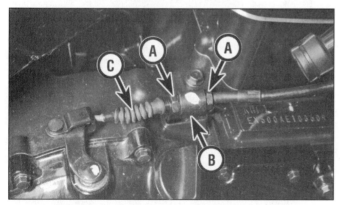

10.4 Details of the lower end of the clutch cable

A)   Adjusting nuts   C)   Dust cover
B)   Bracket

idling. *Idle speed should not change. If it does, the cables may be routed incorrectly. Correct this condition before riding the bike.*

Choke check

Refer to illustrations 9.10 and 9.11

10   Check the freeplay at the choke lever **(see illustration)**. Compare with the value listed in this Chapter's Specifications.

9.10 Check freeplay at the choke lever

10.2 Check clutch freeplay between the lever and bracket; make the initial adjustment at the lever

A)   Check freeplay here   C)   Adjuster
B)   Lockwheel

11   If freeplay is incorrect, locate the cable adjuster inside the left side of the fairing **(see illustration)**. Loosen the locknut, turn the adjusting nut to set freeplay and tighten the locknut.

---

10   Clutch - check and adjustment

Refer to illustrations 10.2, 10.4 and 10.9

1   Correct clutch freeplay is necessary to ensure proper clutch operation and reasonable clutch service life. Freeplay normally changes because of cable stretch and clutch wear, so it should be checked and adjusted periodically.

2   Clutch cable freeplay is checked at the lever on the handlebar. Slowly pull in on the lever until resistance is felt, then note how far the lever has moved away from its bracket at the pivot end **(see illustration)**. Compare this distance with the value listed in this Chapter's Specifications. Too little freeplay may result in the clutch not engaging completely. If there is too much freeplay, the clutch might not release fully.

3   Freeplay adjustments can be made at the clutch lever by loosening the lockwheel and turning the adjuster until the desired freeplay is obtained. Always retighten the lockwheel once the adjustment is complete. If the lever adjuster reaches the end of its travel, try adjusting the cable at its bracket on the engine.

4   Loosen the adjusting nuts at the lower end of the cable completely **(see illustration)**.

1

10.9 This numbered wheel is used to adjust the clutch lever distance from the handlebar to rider preference

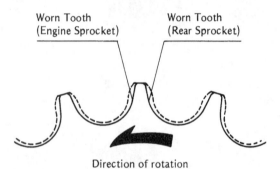

Worn Tooth (Engine Sprocket)   Worn Tooth (Rear Sprocket)

Direction of rotation

11.5 Check the sprockets in the areas indicated to see if they are worn excessively

11.3 Push up on the bottom run of the chain and measure how far it deflects - if it's not within the specified limits, adjust the slack in the chain

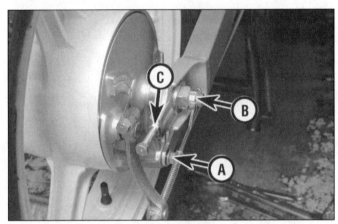

11.7 Loosen the torque link nut and the axle nut, then back-off the chain adjuster locknut

A) Torque link nut   C) Adjuster locknut
B) Axle nut

5   Loosen the knurled lockwheel at the clutch lever and turn the adjuster in or out to expose approximately 5 or 6 mm of threads between the adjuster and the lockwheel.
6   Pull the clutch cable tight to remove all slack, then tighten the adjusting nuts against the bracket at the lower end of the cable.
7   Turn the adjuster at the clutch lever until the correct freeplay is obtained, then tighten the lockwheel.
8   If the proper amount of freeplay still can't be obtained, the cable must be replaced (see Chapter 2).
9   Once the cable is adjusted properly, turn the numbered adjusting wheel to position the clutch lever a comfortable distance from the handlebar **(see illustration)**.

11   Drive chain and sprockets - check, adjustment and lubrication

Check

Refer to illustrations 11.3 and 11.5
1   A neglected drive chain won't last long and can quickly damage the sprockets. Routine chain adjustment and lubrication isn't difficult and will ensure maximum chain and sprocket life.
2   To check the chain, place the bike on its centerstand and shift the transmission into Neutral. Make sure the ignition switch is off.
3   Push up on the bottom run of the chain and measure the slack midway between the two sprockets **(see illustration)**, then compare your measurements to the value listed in this Chapter's Specifications. As wear occurs, the chain will actually stretch, which means adjustment by removing some slack from the chain. In some cases where lubrication has been neglected, corrosion and galling may cause the links to bind and kink, which effectively shortens the chain's length. If

the chain is tight between the sprockets, rusty or kinked, it's time to replace it with a new one. **Note:** *Repeat the chain slack measurement along the length of the chain - ideally, every inch or so. If you find a tight area, mark it with felt pen or paint and repeat the measurement after the bike has been ridden. If the chain's still tight in the same area, it may be damaged or worn. Because a tight or kinked chain can damage the transmission output shaft bearing, it's a good idea to replace it.*
4   Remove the chain guard (it's held on by two bolts). Check the entire length of the chain for damaged rollers, loose links and pins. Hang a 20-lb (9 kg) weight on the bottom run of the chain and measure the length of 20 links along the top run. Rotate the wheel and repeat this check at several places on the chain, since it may wear unevenly. Compare your measurements with the maximum 20-link length listed in this Chapter's Specifications. If any of your measurements exceed the maximum, replace the chain. **Note:** *Never install a new chain on old sprockets, and never use the old chain if you install new sprockets - replace the chain and sprockets as a set.*
5   Remove the shift lever and engine sprocket cover (see Chapter 6). Check the teeth on the engine sprocket and the rear sprocket for wear **(see illustration)**. Refer to Chapter 6 for the sprocket diameter measurement procedure if the sprockets appear to be worn excessively.

Adjustment

Refer to illustrations 11.7 and 11.8
6   Rotate the rear wheel until the chain is positioned with the least amount of slack present.

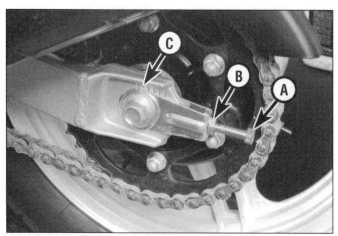

11.8 When the adjuster bolts are set evenly, the adjuster marks on both sides should line up with the same marks in the swingarm, but don't rely completely on this; make a visual check of sprocket alignment as well

A)   Adjuster bolt   C)   Adjuster marks
B)   Locknut

12.4 Remove the oil pan drain plug (arrow)

7   Remove the cotter pin (if equipped) from the torque link nut and loosen the nut **(see illustration)**.
8   Loosen and back-off the locknuts on the adjuster bolts **(see illustration)**.
9   Remove the cotter pin and loosen the axle nut **(see illustration 11.7)**.
10   Turn the axle adjusting bolts on both sides of the swingarm until the proper chain tension is obtained (get the adjuster on the chain side close, then set the adjuster on the opposite side). Be sure to turn the adjusting bolts evenly to keep the rear wheel in alignment. If the adjusting bolts reach the end of their travel, the chain is excessively worn and should be replaced with a new one (see Chapter 6).
11   When the chain has the correct amount of slack, make sure the marks on the adjusters correspond to the same relative marks on each side of the swingarm **(see illustration 11.8)**. Tighten the axle nut to the torque listed in the Chapter 7 Specifications, then install a new cotter pin. If necessary, turn the nut an additional amount to line up the cotter pin hole with the castellations in the nut - don't loosen the nut to do this.
12   Tighten the locknuts and the torque link nut securely.

Lubrication

Refer to illustration 11.13
Note: *If the chain is extremely dirty, it should be removed and cleaned before it's lubricated (see Chapter 6).*

11.13 Apply chain lubricant to the joints between the side plates and the rollers - not in the center of the rollers (with the bike on its centerstand, hold the plastic nozzle near the edge of the chain and turn the wheel by hand as the lubricant sprays out - repeat the procedure on the inside edge of the chain)

13   The best time to lubricate the chain is after the motorcycle has been ridden. When the chain is warm, the lubricant will penetrate the joints between the side plates, pins, bushings and rollers to provide lubrication of the internal load bearing areas. Use a good quality chain lubricant and apply it to the area where the side plates overlap - not the middle of the rollers **(see illustration)**. After applying the lubricant, let it soak in a few minutes before wiping off any excess.

12   Engine oil/filter - change

Refer to illustrations 12.4, 12.5a and 12.5b
1   Consistent routine oil and filter changes are the single most important maintenance procedure you can perform on a motorcycle. The oil not only lubricates the internal parts of the engine, transmission and clutch, but it also acts as a coolant, a cleaner, a sealant, and a protectant. Because of these demands, the oil takes a terrific amount of abuse and should be replaced often with new oil of the recommended grade and type. Saving a little money on the difference in cost between a good oil and a cheap oil won't pay off if the engine is damaged.
2   Before changing the oil and filter, warm up the engine so the oil will drain easily. Be careful when draining the oil, as the exhaust pipes, the engine, and the oil itself can cause severe burns.
3   Put the motorcycle on the centerstand over a clean drain pan. Remove the oil filler cap to vent the crankcase and act as a reminder that there is no oil in the engine.
4   Next, remove the drain plug from the engine **(see illustration)** and allow the oil to drain into the pan. Discard the sealing washer on the drain plug; it should be replaced whenever the plug is removed.
5   As the oil is draining, remove the oil filter **(see illustrations)**. If additional maintenance is planned for this time period, check or service another component while the oil is allowed to drain completely.
6   Wipe any remaining oil off the filter sealing area of the crankcase.
7   Check the condition of the drain plug threads.
8   Coat the gasket on a new filter with clean engine oil. Install the filter and tighten it to the amount listed in this Chapter's Specifications.
9   Slip a new sealing washer over the drain plug, then install and tighten the plug. Tighten the drain plug to the torque listed in this Chapter's Specifications. Avoid overtightening, as damage to the engine case will result.
10   Before refilling the engine, check the old oil carefully. If the oil was drained into a clean pan, small pieces of metal or other material can be easily detected. If the oil is very metallic colored, then the engine is experiencing wear from break-in (new engine) or from insufficient lubrication. If there are flakes or chips of metal in the oil, then

12.5a Remove the oil filter with a filter wrench or a special socket; the special socket is best, since it allows the filter to be tightened accurately with a torque wrench

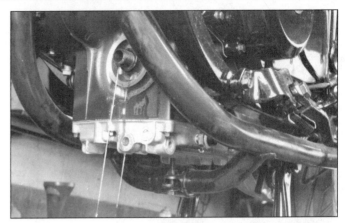

12.5b Let the oil drain completely from the drain plug and filter openings

13.3a Note the location of the carburetor vent tube (arrow); it must be positioned in the groove as shown or it will be pinched when the fuel tank and seat are installed - also make sure the end of the hose is not near the air intake or fuel will be siphoned from the carburetors

13.3b Remove the cover screws, set the harness and vent tube aside. . .

something is drastically wrong internally and the engine will have to be disassembled for inspection and repair.

11   If there are pieces of fiber-like material in the oil, the clutch is experiencing excessive wear and should be checked.

12   If the inspection of the oil turns up nothing unusual, refill the crankcase to the proper level with the recommended oil and install the filler cap. Start the engine and let it run for two or three minutes. Shut it off, wait a few minutes, then check the oil level. If necessary, add more oil to bring the level up to the Maximum mark. Check around the drain plug and filter housing for leaks.

13   The old oil drained from the engine cannot be reused in its present state and should be disposed of. Check with your local refuse disposal company, disposal facility or environmental agency to see whether they will accept the oil for recycling. Don't pour used oil into drains or onto the ground. After the oil has cooled, it can be drained into a suitable container (capped plastic jugs, topped bottles, milk cartons, etc.) for transport to one of these disposal sites.

13   Air filter element - servicing

Refer to illustrations 13.3a, 13.3b and 13.4

1   Remove the seat (see Chapter 8).

2   Remove the fuel tank and its bracket (see Chapter 4).

3   Move the wiring harness and carburetor vent tube aside, then remove the housing cover screws **(see illustrations)**.

4   Lift off the housing cover and remove the air filter element **(see illustration)**. Wipe out the housing with a clean rag.

5   Clean the element with solvent. If compressed air is available, use it to clean the element by blowing from the inside out (from the mesh side toward the foam side). If the foam is extremely dirty or torn, replace the element with a new one.

6   Soak a clean, lint-free cloth in SAE 30 engine oil. Tap the cloth on the foam to oil it.

7   Reinstall the filter by reversing the removal procedure. Make sure the element is seated properly in the filter housing before installing the cover. Make sure the carburetor vent hose is routed correctly so it won't be pinched and so it's not near the air intake **(see illustration 13.3a)**.

8   Reinstall the fuel tank bracket, fuel tank and seat.

14   Cylinder compression - check

Refer to illustration 14.5

1   Among other things, poor engine performance may be caused by leaking valves, incorrect valve clearances, a leaking head gasket, or worn pistons, rings and/or cylinder walls. A cylinder compression check will help pinpoint these conditions and can also indicate the presence of excessive carbon deposits in the cylinder heads.

2   The only tools required are a compression gauge and a spark plug wrench. Depending on the outcome of the initial test, a squirt-type oil can may also be needed.

3   Run the engine until it reaches normal operating temperature. Place the motorcycle on the centerstand, remove the fuel tank, then

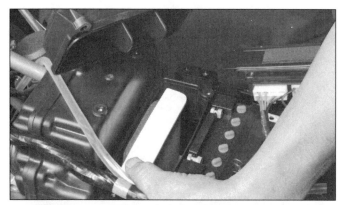

13.4 . . .and lift the cover to expose the element

14.5 A compression gauge with a threaded fitting for the spark plug hole is preferred over the type that requires hand pressure to maintain the seal

15.2a Rotate the spark plug caps back and forth to loosen them. .

15.2c Use an extension and a deep socket (preferably one with a rubber insert to prevent damage to the plug) to remove the spark plugs

15.2b . . .then pull them off the plugs and check them for brittleness and cracking

spins over. Valve and valve seat leakage, or head gasket leakage, is indicated by low initial compression which does not tend to build up.

8   To further confirm your findings, add a small amount of engine oil to each cylinder by inserting the nozzle of a squirt-type oil can through the spark plug holes. The oil will tend to seal the piston rings if they are leaking. Repeat the test for the other cylinder.

9   If the compression increases significantly after the addition of the oil, the piston rings and/or cylinders are definitely worn. If the compression does not increase, the pressure is leaking past the valves or the head gasket. Leakage past the valves may be due to insufficient valve clearances, burned, warped or cracked valves or valve seats, or valves that are hanging up in the guides.

10   If compression readings are considerably higher than specified, the combustion chambers are probably coated with excessive carbon deposits. It is possible (but not very likely) for carbon deposits to raise the compression enough to compensate for the effects of leakage past rings or valves. Remove the cylinder head and carefully decarbonize the combustion chambers (see Chapter 2).

remove the spark plugs (see Section 15, if necessary). Work carefully - don't strip the spark plug hole threads and don't burn your hands.

4   Disable the ignition by unplugging the primary wires from the coils (see Chapter 5). Be sure to mark the locations of the wires before detaching them.

5   Install the compression gauge in one of the spark plug holes **(see illustration)**. Hold or block the throttle wide open.

6   Crank the engine over a minimum of four or five revolutions (or until the gauge reading stops increasing) and observe the initial movement of the compression gauge needle as well as the final total gauge reading. Repeat the procedure for the other cylinder and compare the results to the value listed in this Chapter's Specifications.

7   If the compression in both cylinders built up quickly and evenly to the specified amount, you can assume the engine upper end is in reasonably good mechanical condition. Worn or sticking piston rings and worn cylinders will produce very little initial movement of the gauge needle, but compression will tend to build up gradually as the engine

15 Spark plugs - replacement

Refer to illustrations 15.2a, 15.2b, 15.2c, 15.6a, 15.6b and 15.7

1   This motorcycle is equipped with spark plugs that have 12 mm threads and an 18 mm wrench hex. Make sure your spark plug socket is the correct size before attempting to remove the plugs.

2   Disconnect the spark plug caps from the spark plugs **(see illustrations)**. If available, use compressed air to blow any accumulated

15.6a Spark plug manufacturers recommend using a wire type gauge when checking the gap - if the wire doesn't slide between the electrodes with a slight drag, adjustment is required

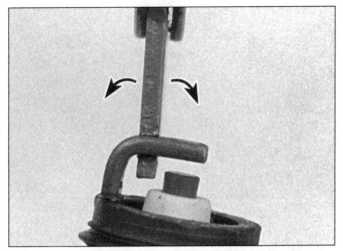

15.6b To change the gap, bend the side electrode only, as indicated by the arrows, and be very careful not to crack or chip the ceramic insulator surrounding the center electrode

15.7 A length of rubber hose will save time and prevent damaged threads when installing the spark plugs

debris from around the spark plugs. Remove the plugs **(see illustration)**.

3   Inspect the electrodes for wear. Both the center and side electrodes should have square edges and the side electrode should be of uniform thickness. Look for excessive deposits and evidence of a cracked or chipped insulator around the center electrode. Compare your spark plugs to the color spark plug reading chart. Check the threads, the washer and the ceramic insulator body for cracks and other damage.

4   If the electrodes are not excessively worn, and if the deposits can be easily removed with a wire brush, the plugs can be regapped and reused (if no cracks or chips are visible in the insulator). If in doubt concerning the condition of the plugs, replace them with new ones, as the expense is minimal.

5   Cleaning spark plugs by sandblasting is permitted, provided you clean the plugs with a high flash-point solvent afterwards.

6   Before installing new plugs, make sure they are the correct type and heat range. Check the gap between the electrodes, as they are not preset. For best results, use a wire-type gauge rather than a flat gauge to check the gap **(see illustration)**. If the gap must be adjusted, bend the side electrode only and be very careful not to chip or crack the insulator nose **(see illustration)**. Make sure the washer is in place before installing each plug.

7   Since the cylinder heads are made of aluminum, which is soft and easily damaged, thread the plugs into the heads by hand. Since the

plugs are quite recessed, slip a short length of hose over the end of the plug to use as a tool to thread it into place **(see illustration)**. The hose will grip the plug well enough to turn it, but will start to slip if the plug begins to cross-thread in the hole - this will prevent damaged threads and the accompanying repair costs.

8   Once the plugs are finger tight, the job can be finished with a socket. If a torque wrench is available, tighten the spark plugs to the torque listed in this Chapter's Specifications. If you do not have a torque wrench, tighten the plugs finger tight (until the washers bottom on the cylinder head) then use a wrench to tighten them an additional 1/4 turn. Regardless of the method used, do not over-tighten them.

9   Reconnect the spark plug caps.

16   Lubrication - general

Refer to illustrations 16.3a, 16.3b, 16.3c and 16.3d

1   Since the controls, cables and various other components of a motorcycle are exposed to the elements, they should be lubricated periodically to ensure safe and trouble-free operation.

2   The footpegs, clutch and brake lever, brake pedal, shift lever and side and centerstand pivots should be lubricated frequently. In order for the lubricant to be applied where it will do the most good, the component should be disassembled. However, if chain and cable lubricant is being used, it can be applied to the pivot joint gaps and will usually work its way into the areas where friction occurs. If motor oil or light grease is being used, apply it sparingly as it may attract dirt (which could cause the controls to bind or wear at an accelerated rate). **Note:** *One of the best lubricants for the control lever pivots is a dry-film lubricant (available from many sources by different names).*

3   The clutch cable should be separated from the handlebar lever and bracket before it is lubricated **(see illustration)**. This is a convenient time to inspect the Teflon bushing at the end of the cable **(see illustration)**. The cable should be treated with motor oil or a commercially available cable lubricant which is specially formulated for use on motorcycle control cables. Small adapters for pressure lubricating the cables with spray can lubricants are available and ensure that the cable is lubricated along its entire length **(see illustration)**. If motor oil is being used, tape a funnel-shaped piece of heavy paper or plastic to the end of the cable, then pour oil into the funnel and suspend the end of the cable upright **(see illustration)**. Leave it until the oil runs down into the cable and out the other end. When attaching the cable to the lever, be sure to lubricate the barrel-shaped fitting at the end with high-temperature grease. **Note:** *While you're lubricating, check the barrel end of the cable for fraying. Replace frayed cables.*

4   To lubricate the throttle and choke cables, disconnect the cable(s) at the lower end, then lubricate the cable with a pressure lube

Spark plug maintenance: Checking plug gap with feeler gauges

Altering the plug gap. Note use of correct tool

Spark plug conditions: A brown, tan or grey firing end is indicative of correct engine running conditions and the selection of the appropriate heat rating plug

White deposits have accumulated from excessive amounts of oil in the combustion chamber or through the use of low quality oil. Remove deposits or a hot spot may form

Black sooty deposits indicate an over-rich fuel/air mixture, or a malfunctioning ignition system. If no improvement is obtained, try one grade hotter plug

Wet, oily carbon deposits form an electrical leakage path along the insulator nose, resulting in a misfire. The cause may be a badly worn engine or a malfunctioning ignition system

A blistered white insulator or melted electrode indicates over-advanced ignition timing or a malfunctioning cooling system. If correction does not prove effective, try a colder grade plug

A worn spark plug not only wastes fuel but also overloads the whole ignition system because the increased gap requires higher voltage to initiate the spark. This condition can also affect air pollution

1

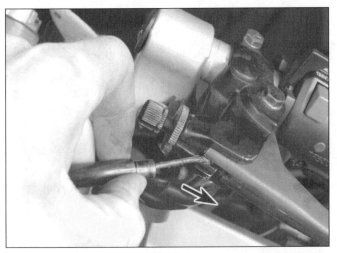

16.3a To disconnect the clutch cable from the lever and bracket, line up the slots in the bracket, lockwheel and adjuster, then pull the cable in the direction of the arrow and slide it through the slots

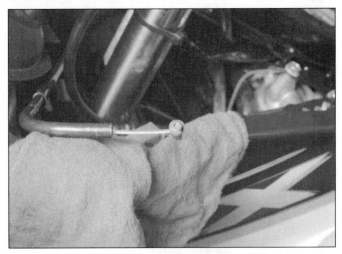

16.3b The bushing at the end of the cable should be checked for wear; lubricate it with high-temperature grease

16.3c Lubricating a cable with a pressure lube adapter (make sure the tool seats around the inner cable)

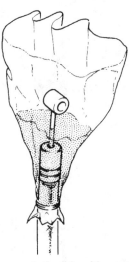

16.3d Lubricating a control cable with a makeshift funnel and motor oil

17.5 Unscrew the covers from the crankshaft rotation bolt and timing window - inspect the cover O-rings and replace them if they're worn or damaged

adapter **(see illustration 16.3c)**. See Chapter 4 for the choke cable removal procedure.

5   The speedometer cable should be removed from its housing and lubricated with motor oil or cable lubricant.

6   Refer to Chapter 6 for the swingarm needle bearing and Uni-trak linkage lubrication procedures.

17   Valve clearances - check and adjustment

Refer to illustrations 17.5, 17.6a, 17.6b, 17.6c, 17.8, 17.9, 17.12a, 17.12b and 17.13

1   The engine must be completely cool for this maintenance procedure, so let the machine sit overnight before beginning.

2   Disconnect the cable from the negative terminal of the battery.

3   Refer to Chapter 4 and remove the fuel tank.

4   Remove the valve cover (see Chapter 2).

5   Remove the covers from the crankshaft rotation bolt and timing inspection holes **(see illustration)**.

6   Position the no. 1 piston (on the left side of the engine) at Top Dead Center (TDC) on the compression stroke. Do this by turning the crankshaft, with a socket placed on the crankshaft bolt, until the T mark on the rotor is aligned with the timing mark on the crankcase

17.6a Turn the crankshaft clockwise with a socket. . .

17.6b . . .until the T mark on the rotor aligns with the timing notch. . .

17.6c . . .and the no. 1 cam lobes point upward

17.8 For the most accurate measurement, use a pair of feeler gauges - because each rocker arm operates two valves, adjusting one valve affects the setting of the other one

1

(see illustrations). Now, check the position of the no. 1 cylinder cam lobes - they should be pointing upward **(see illustration)**. Piston no. 1 is now at TDC compression. **Note:** *Turn the engine in the normal direction of rotation. If you turn it backwards, the starter clutch will make a whining sound.*

7   With the engine in this position, all of the valves for cylinder no. 1 can be checked.

8   Start with the no. 1 intake valve clearance. Insert a feeler gauge of the thickness listed in this Chapter's Specifications between each valve stem and adjuster screw **(see illustration)**. It's best to use "go-no go" (stepped) feeler gauges, which give a positive indication of whether the clearance is correct. If you're using a standard feeler gauge, pull it out slowly - you should feel a slight drag. If there's no drag, the clearance is too loose. If there's a heavy drag, the clearance is too tight.

9   If the clearance is incorrect, loosen the adjuster screw locknut (using Kawasaki valve adjusting screw tool no. 57001 - 1217, or equivalent) **(see illustration)** and turn the adjuster screw in or out, as needed.

10   Hold the adjuster screw with the adjusting screw tool (to keep it from turning) and tighten the locknut. Recheck the clearance to make sure it hasn't changed.

11   Now adjust the no. 1 exhaust valves, following the same procedure you used for the intake valves. Make sure to use feeler gauges of the specified thickness.

12   Rotate the crankshaft to align the C mark on the rotor with the

17.9 A special valve adjusting tool is a good investment, since there's no way to get a box wrench on the locknuts without removing the oil lines - the socket (A) loosens and tightens the locknut while the screwdriver (B) turns the adjusting screw

17.12a Turn the crankshaft until the C mark on the rotor aligns with the timing notch. . .

17.12b . . .and the no. 2 cam lobes point upward. . .

17.13 . . .then adjust the valves for no. 2 cylinder

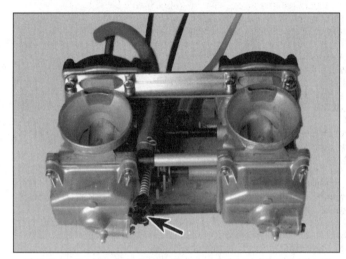

18.3 Turn the idle speed adjusting screw (arrow) in or out until the correct idle speed is obtained (carburetors removed from engine for clarity)

timing mark on the crankcase, which will position piston no. 2 at TDC compression **(see illustration)**. The cam lobes for no. 2 cylinder should now point upward **(see illustration)**.

13   Adjust all four valves on cylinder no. 2, using a pair of feeler gauges and the special tool **(see illustration)**.

14   Install the valve cover and all of the components that had to be removed to get it off.

15   Install the fuel tank and reconnect the cable to the negative terminal of the battery.

---

18   Idle speed - check and adjustment

Refer to illustration 18.3

1   The idle speed should be checked and adjusted after the carburetors are synchronized and when it is obviously too high or too low. Before adjusting the idle speed, make sure the valve clearances and spark plug gaps are correct. Also, turn the handlebars back-and-forth and see if the idle speed changes as this is done. If it does, the accelerator cable may not be adjusted correctly, or it may be worn out. Be sure to correct this problem before proceeding.

2   The engine should be at normal operating temperature, which is usually reached after 10 to 15 minutes of stop and go riding. Place the motorcycle on the centerstand and make sure the transmission is in Neutral.

3   Turn the throttle stop screw, located on the left side of the bike,

just forward of the carburetor for cylinder no. 1 **(see illustration)**, until the idle speed listed in this Chapter's Specifications is obtained.

4   Snap the throttle open and shut a few times, then recheck the idle speed. If necessary, repeat the adjustment procedure.

5   If a smooth, steady idle can't be achieved, the fuel/air mixture may be incorrect. Refer to Chapter 4 for additional carburetor information.

---

19   Carburetor synchronization - check and adjustment

Refer to illustrations 19.9a and 19.9b

Warning: *Gasoline (petrol) is extremely flammable, so take extra precautions when you work on any part of the fuel system. Don't smoke or allow open flames or bare light bulbs near the work area, and don't work in a garage where a natural gas-type appliance (such as a water heater or clothes dryer) is present. If you spill any fuel on your skin, rinse it off immediately with soap and water. When you perform any kind of work on the fuel system, wear safety glasses and have a fire extinguisher suitable for a class B type fire (flammable liquids) on hand.*

1   Carburetor synchronization is simply the process of adjusting the carburetors so they pass the same amount of fuel/air mixture to each cylinder. This is done by measuring the vacuum produced in each cylinder. Carburetors that are out of synchronization will result in decreased fuel mileage, increased engine temperature, less than ideal

19.9a Disconnect the carburetor vacuum lines

**19.9b Turn this screw to synchronize the carburetors
(carburetors removed from engine for clarity)**

A)   *Vacuum line (disconnect*   B)   *Fitting*
     to expose fitting)   C)   *Synchronization screw*

throttle response and higher vibration levels.

2   To properly synchronize the carburetors, you will need some sort of vacuum gauge setup, preferably with a gauge for each cylinder, or a mercury manometer, which is a calibrated tube arrangement that utilizes columns of mercury to indicate engine vacuum.

3   A manometer can be purchased from a motorcycle dealer or accessory shop and should have the necessary rubber hoses supplied with it for hooking into the vacuum hose fittings on the carburetors.

4   A vacuum gauge setup can also be purchased from a dealer or fabricated from commonly available hardware and automotive vacuum gauges.

5   The manometer is the more reliable and accurate instrument, and for that reason is preferred over the vacuum gauge setup; however, since the mercury used in the manometer is a liquid, and extremely toxic, extra precautions must be taken during use and storage of the instrument.

6   Because of the nature of the synchronization procedure and the need for special instruments, most owners leave the task to a dealer service department or a reputable motorcycle repair shop.

7   Start the engine and let it run until it reaches normal operating temperature, then shut it off.

8   Remove the fuel tank (see Chapter 4).

9   Detach the vacuum hoses from the fittings on the carburetors **(see illustrations)**, then hook up the vacuum gauge set or the manometer according to the manufacturer's instructions. Make sure there are no leaks in the setup, as false readings will result.

10   Reconnect the fuel line and vacuum line to the fuel tank (it's not necessary to hook-up the vacuum line to the fuel tap). Have an assistant hold the fuel tank out of the way, but in such a position that fuel can still be delivered and access to the carburetors is unobstructed. Place the fuel tap lever in the On position.

11   Start the engine and make sure the idle speed is correct.

12   The vacuum readings for both of the cylinders should be the same, or at least within the tolerance listed in this Chapter's Specifications. If the vacuum readings vary, adjust as necessary.

13   To perform the adjustment, synchronize the carburetors by turning the butterfly valve adjusting screw, as needed, until the vacuum is identical or nearly identical for both cylinders **(see illustration 19.9b)**.

14   When the adjustment is complete, recheck the vacuum readings and idle speed, then stop the engine. Remove the vacuum gauge or manometer and attach the hoses to the fittings on the carburetors. Reinstall the fuel tank and seat.

20   Cooling system - check

Refer to illustrations 20.7 and 20.8

Warning: *The engine must be cool before beginning this* procedure.

Note: *Refer to Section 3 and check the coolant level before performing this check.*

1   The entire cooling system should be checked carefully at the recommended intervals. Look for evidence of leaks, check the condition

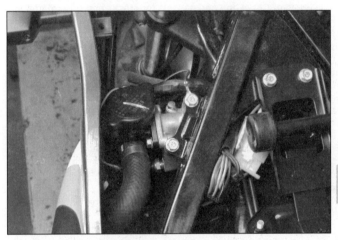

20.7 The cooling system pressure cap is located on the thermostat housing

of the coolant, check the radiator for clogged fins and damage and make sure the fan operates when required.

2   Remove the fuel tank (Chapter 4) and side covers (Chapter 8).

3   Examine each of the rubber coolant hoses along its entire length. Look for cracks, abrasions and other damage. Squeeze each hose at various points. They should feel firm, yet pliable, and return to their original shape when released. If they are dried out or hard, replace them with new ones.

4   Check for evidence of leaks at each cooling system joint. Tighten the hose clamps carefully to prevent future leaks.

5   Check the radiator for evidence of leaks and other damage. Leaks in the radiator leave telltale scale deposits or coolant stains on the outside of the core below the leak. If leaks are noted, remove the radiator (refer to Chapter 3) and have it repaired at a radiator shop or replace it with a new one. **Caution:** *Do not use a liquid leak stopping compound to try to repair leaks.*

6   Check the radiator fins for mud, dirt and insects, which may impede the flow of air through the radiator. If the fins are dirty, force water or low pressure compressed air through the fins from the backside. If the fins are bent or distorted, straighten them carefully with a screwdriver.

7   Remove the pressure cap by turning it counterclockwise (anticlockwise) until it reaches a stop. If you hear a hissing sound (indicating there is still pressure in the system), wait until it stops. Now, press down on the cap with the palm of your hand and continue turning the cap counterclockwise until it can be removed **(see illustration)**. Check the condition of the coolant in the system. If it is rust colored or if accumulations of scale are visible, drain, flush and refill the system with

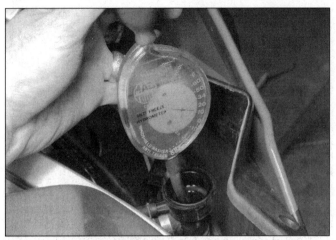

20.8 An antifreeze hydrometer is helpful in determining the condition of the coolant

21.2 The coolant drain bolt is located in the bottom of the water pump cover

new coolant. Check the cap gaskets for cracks and other damage. Have the cap tested by a dealer service department or replace it with a new one. Install the cap by turning it clockwise until it reaches the first stop, then push down on the cap and continue turning until it can turn no further.

8   Check the antifreeze content of the coolant with an antifreeze hydrometer **(see illustration)**. Sometimes coolant may look like it's in good condition, but might be too weak to offer adequate protection. If the hydrometer indicates a weak mixture, drain, flush and refill the cooling system (see Section 21).

9   Start the engine and let it reach normal operating temperature, then check for leaks again. As the coolant temperature increases, the fan should come on automatically and the temperature should begin to drop. If it does not, refer to Chapter 3 and check the fan and fan circuit carefully.

10   If the coolant level is consistently low, and no evidence of leaks can be found, have the entire system pressure checked by a Kawasaki dealer service department, motorcycle repair shop or service station.

---

21 Cooling system - draining, flushing and refilling

Warning: *Allow the engine to cool completely before performing this maintenance operation. Also, don't allow antifreeze to come into contact with your skin or painted surfaces of the motorcycle. Rinse off spills immediately with plenty of water. Antifreeze is highly toxic if ingested. Never leave antifreeze lying around in an open container or in puddles on the floor; children and pets are attracted by its sweet smell and may drink it. Check with local authorities (councils) about disposing of used antifreeze. Many communities have collection centers which will see that antifreeze is disposed of safely. Antifreeze is also combustible, so don't store or use it near open flames.*

Draining

Refer to illustration 21.2

1   Loosen the pressure cap **(see illustration 20.7)**. Place a large, clean drain pan under the right side of the engine.

2   Remove the drain bolt from the bottom of the water pump cover **(see illustration)** and allow the coolant to drain into the pan. **Note:** *The coolant will rush out with considerable force, so position the drain pan accordingly. Remove the pressure cap completely to ensure that all of the coolant can drain.*

3   Drain the coolant reservoir. Refer to Chapter 3 for the reservoir removal procedure. Wash the reservoir out with water.

Flushing

4   Flush the system with clean tap water by inserting a garden hose in the radiator filler neck. Allow the water to run through the system until it is clear when it exits the drain bolt hole. If the radiator is ex-

tremely corroded, remove it by referring to Chapter 3 and have it cleaned at a radiator shop.

5   Check the drain bolt gasket. Replace it with a new one if necessary.

6   Clean the hole, then install the drain bolt and tighten it to the torque listed in this Chapter's Specifications.

7   Fill the cooling system with clean water mixed with a flushing compound. Make sure the flushing compound is compatible with aluminum components, and follow the manufacturer's instructions carefully.

8   Start the engine and allow it to reach normal operating temperature. Let it run for about ten minutes.

9   Stop the engine. Let the machine cool for a while, then cover the pressure cap with a heavy rag and turn it counterclockwise (anticlockwise) to the first stop, releasing any pressure that may be present in the system. Once the hissing stops, push down on the cap and remove it completely.

10   Drain the system once again.

11   Fill the system with clean water, then repeat Steps 8, 9 and 10.

Refilling

12   Fill the system with the proper coolant mixture (see this Chapter's Specifications). When the system is full (all the way up to the top of the radiator cap filler neck), install the cap and start the engine. Allow the engine to reach normal operating temperature, then shut it off.

13   Let the engine cool off for awhile, cover the radiator cap with a heavy rag and loosen it to the first stop to allow any pressure in the system to bleed off before the cap is removed completely. Recheck the coolant level in the radiator filler neck. If it's low, add more coolant until it reaches the top of the filler neck. Reinstall the cap.

14   Allow the engine to cool, then check the coolant level in the reservoir (see Section 3). If the coolant level is low, add the specified mixture until it reaches the Hot mark in the reservoir.

15   Check the system for leaks.

16   Do not dispose of the old coolant by pouring it down a drain. Instead, pour it into a heavy plastic container, cap it tightly and take it to an authorized disposal site or a service station.

---

22 Evaporative emission control system (California models only) - check

Refer to illustrations 22.2, 22.6a through 22.6f and 22.7

1   This system, installed on California models to conform to stringent emission control standards, routes fuel vapors from the fuel system into the engine to be burned, instead of letting them evaporate into the atmosphere. When the engine isn't running, vapors are stored in a carbon canister.

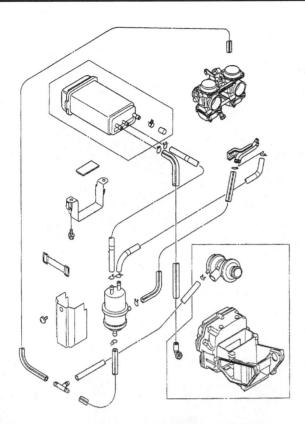

22.2 Emission control system details

22.6c ...follow the vacuum hose from the T-fitting (A) and disconnect its other end; disconnect the air suction hose from each cylinder (B) and from the air box

22.6a To remove the components, unbolt the tank bracket from the frame...

22.6b ...disconnect the purge hose from the canister fitting (arrow) (the other canister hose can be left connected and the canister-to-tank bracket bolts can be left in place)...

22.6d Disconnect the breather hose from the separator...

Hoses

2 To begin the inspection of the system, remove the seat and fuel tank (see Chapters 4 and 8 if necessary). Inspect the hoses from the fuel tank, carburetors and liquid/vapor separator to the canister for cracking, kinks or other signs of deterioration (see illustration).

Liquid/vapor separator test

3 Disconnect the breather hose from the separator and inject about 20 mL of gasoline into the fitting with a syringe.
4 Disconnect the fuel return hose from the tank and place the end of the hose in a container level with the top of the tank.
5 Start the engine and let it idle. If the fuel comes out of the hose, the separator is good; if not, replace it.

Component inspection

6 Label and disconnect the hoses, then remove the separator and canister from the machine. **Note:** *For system inspection, it's easiest to remove the separator, canister, fuel tank bracket and air suction switching valve as a unit* (see illustrations).

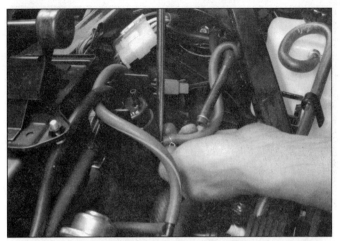

22.6e . . .as well as the fuel tank hose (to disconnect the hoses, squeeze the spring clamps and push the hoses off the fittings with a screwdriver; pulling will cause the hoses to tighten on the fittings)

22.6f Remove the air switching valve, separator, canister and fuel tank bracket

22.7 To replace the separator, disconnect its hoses and remove it from the bracket

23.3a Squeeze the spring clip, slide it back along the hose and detach the hose from the air suction valve

7   Check the separator closely for cracks or other signs of damage. If these are found, replace it **(see illustration)**.

8   Inspect the canister for cracks or other signs of damage. Tip the canister so the nozzles point down. If fuel runs out of the canister, the liquid/vapor separator is probably bad - check it as described above. The fuel inside the canister has probably caused damage, so it would be a good idea to replace it also.

23 Air suction valves - check

Refer to illustrations 23.3a and 23.3b

1   The air suction valves, installed on US models only, are one-way check valves that allow fresh air to flow into the exhaust ports. The suction developed by the exhaust pulses pulls the air from the air cleaner, through a hose to the air switching valve, through a pair of hoses and a pair of reed valves, and finally into the exhaust ports. The introduction of fresh air helps ignite any fuel that may not have been burned by the normal combustion process.

2   Remove the fuel tank (see Chapter 4).

3   Disconnect the hoses from the air suction valves **(see illustration)**. Remove the bolts **(see illustration)** and lift off the covers.

4   Check the valves for cracks, warping, burning or other damage. Check the area where the reeds contact the valve holder for scratches,

23.3b There's an air suction valve mounted on the valve cover above each cylinder

separation and grooves. If any of these conditions are found, replace the valve.

5   Wash the valves with solvent if carbon has accumulated between the reed and the valve holder.

25.6 Loosen the lower pinch bolt on each fork (arrow)

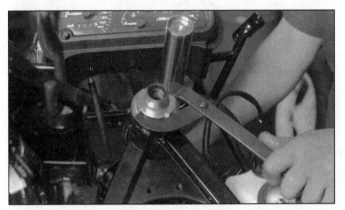

25.8 Use a spanner wrench like this one to loosen or tighten the steering stem locknut (handlebars removed for clarity)

6   Installation of the valves is the reverse of removal. Be sure to use a new gasket.

24   Exhaust system - check

1   Periodically check all of the exhaust system joints for leaks and loose fasteners. The lower fairing (if equipped) will have to be removed to do this properly (see Chapter 8). If tightening the clamp bolts fails to stop any leaks, replace the gaskets with new ones (a procedure which requires disassembly of the system).
2   The exhaust pipe flange nuts at the cylinder heads are especially prone to loosening, which could cause damage to the head. Check them frequently and keep them tight.

25   Steering head bearings - check and adjustment

Refer to illustrations 25.6, 25.7 and 25.8
1   This motorcycle is equipped with ball-and-cone type steering head bearings which can become dented, rough or loose during normal use of the machine. In extreme cases, worn or loose steering head bearings can cause steering wobble that is potentially dangerous.

Check

2   To check the bearings, place the motorcycle on the centerstand and block the machine so the front wheel is in the air.
3   Point the wheel straight ahead and slowly move the handlebars from side-to-side. Dents or roughness in the bearing races will be felt and the bars will not move smoothly.
4   Next, grasp the fork legs and try to move the wheel forward and backward. Any looseness in the steering head bearings will be felt. If play is felt in the bearings, adjust the steering head as follows:

25.7 Loosen the steering stem bolt, but don't remove it or the stem will slip down and bearings may fall out

Adjustment

5   Remove the fuel tank (see Chapter 4).
6   Loosen the fork lower pinch bolts **(see illustration)**. This allows the necessary vertical movement of the steering stem in relation to the fork tubes.
7   Loosen (DO NOT remove) the steering stem bolt **(see illustration)**.
8   Use a spanner wrench to loosen the steering stem locknut **(see illustration)**.
9   Carefully tighten the steering stem locknut until the steering head is tight but does not bind when the forks are turned from side-to-side.
10   Retighten the steering stem bolt and the fork pinch bolts, in that order, to the torque values listed in the Chapter 6 Specifications.
11   Recheck the steering head bearings for play as described above. If necessary, repeat the adjustment procedure. Reinstall all parts previously removed.
12   Refer to Chapter 6 for steering head bearing lubrication and replacement procedures.

26   Fasteners - check

1   Since vibration of the machine tends to loosen fasteners, all nuts, bolts, screws, etc. should be periodically checked for proper tightness.
2   Pay particular attention to the following:
Spark plugs
Engine oil drain plug
Oil filter cover bolt
Gearshift lever
Footpegs and sidestand
Engine mount bolts
Shock absorber mount bolts
Uni-trak linkage bolts
Front axle and clamp bolt
Rear axle nut
3   If a torque wrench is available, use it along with the torque specifications at the beginning of this, or other, Chapters.

27   Fuel system - check and filter cleaning

Refer to illustrations 27.8 and 27.9
Warning: *Gasoline (petrol) is extremely flammable, so take extra precautions when you work on any part of the fuel system. Don't smoke or allow open flames or bare light bulbs near the work area, and don't work in a garage where a natural gas-type appliance (such as a water heater or clothes dryer) is present. If you spill any fuel on your skin, rinse it off immediately with soap and water. When you perform any kind of work on the fuel system, wear safety glasses and have a fire extinguisher suitable for a class B type fire (flammable liquids) on hand.*

1

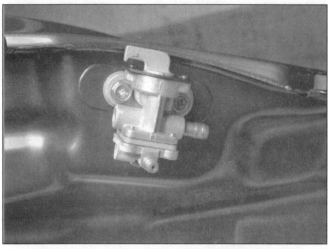

27.8 The fuel tap is secured to the tank by two screws

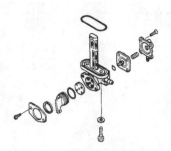

27.9 Fuel tap and filter details

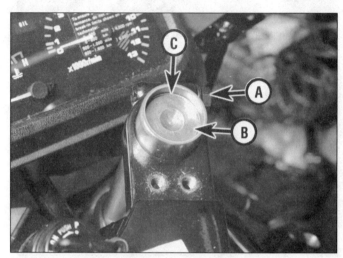

**29.3a Loosen the upper pinch bolt, press down on the top plug
and remove the retaining ring**

| A) | Pinch bolt | C) | Retaining ring |
| B) | Top plug | | |

**28.3 Check above and below the fork seals (arrows) for signs
of oil leakage**

1   Check the fuel tank, the fuel tap, the lines and the carburetors for leaks and evidence of damage.
2   If carburetor gaskets are leaking, the carburetors should be disassembled and rebuilt by referring to Chapter 4.
3   If the fuel tap is leaking, tightening the screws may help. If leakage persists, the tap should be disassembled and repaired or replaced with a new one.
4   If the fuel lines are cracked or otherwise deteriorated, replace them with new ones.
5   Check the vacuum hose connected to the fuel tap. If it is cracked or otherwise damaged, replace it with a new one.
6   The fuel filter, which is attached to the fuel tap, may become clogged and should be removed and cleaned periodically. In order to clean the filter, the fuel tank must be drained and the fuel tap removed.
7   Remove the fuel tank (see Chapter 4). Drain the fuel into an approved fuel container.
8   Once the tank is emptied, loosen and remove the screws that attach the fuel tap to the tank **(see illustration)**. Remove the tap and filter.
9   Clean the filter **(see illustration)** with solvent and blow it dry with compressed air. If the filter is torn or otherwise damaged, replace the entire fuel tap with a new one. Check the mounting flange O-ring and the gaskets on the screws. If they are damaged, replace them with new ones.
10   Install the O-ring, filter and fuel tap on the tank, then install the

tank. Refill the tank and check carefully for leaks around the mounting flange and screws.

---

28   Suspension - check

Refer to illustration 28.3

1   The suspension components must be maintained in top operating condition to ensure rider safety. Loose, worn or damaged suspension parts decrease the vehicle's stability and control.
2   While standing alongside the motorcycle, lock the front brake and push on the handlebars to compress the forks several times. See if they move up-and-down smoothly without binding. If binding is felt, the forks should be disassembled and inspected as described in Chapter 6.
3   Carefully inspect the area around the fork seals for any signs of fork oil leakage **(see illustration)**. If leakage is evident, the seals must be replaced as described in Chapter 6.
4   Check the tightness of all suspension nuts and bolts to be sure none have worked loose.
5   Inspect the rear shock absorber for fluid leakage and tightness of the mounting nuts. If leakage is found, the shock should be replaced.
6   Set the bike on its centerstand. Grab the swingarm on each side, just ahead of the axle. Rock the swingarm from side to side - there should be no discernible movement at the rear. If there's a little movement or a slight clicking can be heard, make sure the pivot shaft nuts are tight. If the pivot nuts are tight but movement is still noticeable, the swingarm will have to be removed and the bearings replaced as described in Chapter 6.
7   Inspect the tightness of the rear suspension nuts and bolts.

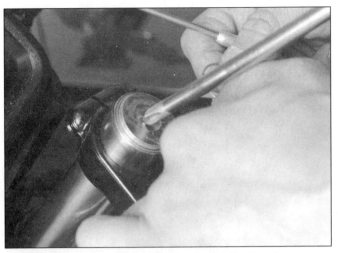

29.3b Release the spring tension on the top plug

29.4 Lift out the top plug and inspect its O-ring

29.5 Lift out the fork spring

29.6 There's a fork drain screw at the bottom of each fork leg

---

29 Fork oil - replacement

Refer to illustrations 29.3a, 29.3b, 29.4, 29.5, 29.6 and 29.10

1   Place the motorcycle on the centerstand. Remove the lower fairing (if equipped) and position a jack with a block of wood on the jack head under the engine to support the motorcycle when the fork cap bolts are removed.

2   Remove the handlebar from one side (see Chapter 6).

3   Loosen the upper pinch bolts **(see illustration)**. Push the top plug downward against spring pressure with a Phillips screwdriver or similar tool, remove the retaining ring and release the spring pressure **(see illustration)**.

4   Lift out the top plug and O-ring **(see illustration)**.

5   Lift out the fork spring **(see illustration)**.

6   Place a drain pan under the fork leg and remove the drain screw **(see illustration)**. **Warning:** *Do not allow the fork oil to contact the brake disc, pads or tire. If it does, clean the disc with brake system cleaner, wipe off the tire, and replace the pads with new ones before riding the motorcycle.*

7   After most of the oil has drained, slowly compress and release the forks to pump out the remaining oil. An assistant will most likely be required to do this procedure.

8   Check the drain screw gasket for damage and replace it if necessary. Clean the threads of the drain screw with solvent and let it dry, then install the screw and gasket, tightening it securely.

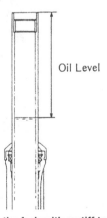

Oil Level

29.10 Measure oil level in the fork with a stiff tape measure; add or drain oil to correct the level

9   Pour the type and amount of fork oil, listed in this Chapter's Specifications, into the fork tube through the opening at the top. Remove the jack from under the engine and slowly pump the forks a few times to purge the air from the upper and lower chambers.

10   Fully compress the front forks (you may need an assistant to do this). Insert a stiff tape measure into the fork tube and measure the distance from the oil to the top of the fork tube **(see illustration)**.

Compare your measurement to the value listed in this Chapter's Specifications. Drain or add oil, as necessary, until the level is correct.

11   Check the O-ring on the top plug, then coat it with a thin layer of multi-purpose grease. Install the fork spring. Install the top plug, push it down against the spring pressure, install the retaining ring and release the top plug.

12   Tighten the fork tube pinch bolts to the torque listed in the Chapter 6 Specifications. Install the handlebar, tightening the bolts to the torque listed in the Chapter 6 Specifications.

13   Repeat the procedure to the other fork. Note that it is essential that the oil quantity and level is identical in each fork.

14   Install the lower fairing (if equipped).

Chapter 2 Engine, clutch and transmission

Contents

2

Specifications

General

Bore	2.913 inch (74.0 mm)
Stroke	2.283 inch (58.0 mm)
Displacement	498 cc
Compression ratio	10.8 : 1

Camshaft and rocker arms

Lobe height (intake and exhaust)	
Standard	1.403 to 1.408 inch (35.635 to 35.761 mm)
Minimum	1.40 inch (35.55 mm)
Bearing oil clearance	
Standard	0.001 to 0.003 inch (0.030 to 0.071 mm)
Maximum	0.006 inch (0.16 mm)
Journal diameter	
Standard	0.982 to 0.983 inch (24.950 to 24.970 mm)
Minimum	0.981 inch (24.92 mm)

Camshaft and rocker arms (continued)

Camshaft runout
 Standard... 0.001 inch (0.03 mm) or less
 Maximum.. 0.003 inch (0.1 mm)
Camshaft chain 20-link length (maximum) .... 5-5/64 inch (128.9 mm)
Rocker arm inside diameter
 Standard... 0.492 to 0.493 inch (12.50 to 12.518 mm)
 Maximum.. 0.494 inch (12.55 mm)
Rocker shaft diameter
 Standard... 0.490 to 0.491 inch (12.466 to 12.484 mm)
 Minimum... 0.489 inch (12.44 mm)

Cylinder head, valves and valve springs

Cylinder head warpage limit .... 0.002 inch (0.05 mm)
Valve stem bend limit .... 0.002 inch (0.05 mm)
Valve stem diameter
 Standard
  Intake .... 0.2155 to 0.216 inch (5.475 to 5.490 mm)
  Exhaust .... 0.2147 to 0.215 inch (5.455 to 5.470 mm)
 Minimum
  Intake .... 0.2149 inch (5.46 mm)
  Exhaust .... 0.2141 inch (5.44 mm)
Valve head thickness
 Standard
  Intake .... 0.020 inch (0.5 mm)
  Exhaust .... 0.039 inch (1.0 mm)
 Minimum
  Intake .... 0.010 inch (0.25 mm)
  Exhaust .... 0.027 inch (0.7 mm)
Valve guide inside diameter (intake and exhaust)
 Standard... 0.2165 to 0.2170 inch (5.50 to 5.512 mm)
 Maximum.. 0.2196 inch (5.58 mm)
Valve seat width (intake and exhaust) .... 0.020 to 0.040 in (0.5 to 1.0 mm)
Valve spring free length
 Standard
  Inner... 1.429 inch (36.3 mm)
  Outer.. 1.59 inch (40.4 mm)
 Minimum
  Inner... 1.378 inch (35 mm)
  Outer.. 1.535 inch (39 mm)

Cylinder block

Bore diameter
 Standard... 2.9133 to 2.9138 inch (74.0 to 74.012 mm)
 Maximum.. 2.9177 inch (74.11 mm)
Taper limit.. 0.002 inch (0.05 mm)
Out-of-round limit .... 0.002 inch (0.05 mm)

Pistons

Piston diameter
 Standard... 2.9111 to 2.9116 inch (73.942 to 73.957 mm)
 Minimum... 2.905 inch (73.79 mm)
Piston-to-cylinder clearance
 Standard... 0.0017 to 0.0027 inch (0.044 to 0.070 mm)
 Maximum.. 0.0066 inch (0.17 mm)
Oversize pistons and rings .... +0.020 inch (+ 0.5 mm) (one oversize only)
Ring side clearance
 Standard
  Top... 0.0017 to 0.0027 inch (0.03 to 0.07 mm)
  Second.. 0.0007 to 0.0023 inch (0.02 to 0.06 mm)
 Maximum
  Top... 0.0066 inch (0.17 mm)
  Second.. 0.0062 inch (0.16 mm)
Ring groove width
 Standard
  Top... 0.032 to 0.033 inch (0.82 to 0.84 mm)
  Second.. 0.039 to 0.040 inch (1.01 to 1.03 mm)
  Oil .... 0.079 to 0.080 inch (2.01 to 2.03 mm)

Maximum
    Top.. 0.036 inch (0.92 mm)
    Second.. 0.044 inch (1.12 mm)
    Oil.. 0.083 inch (2.11 mm)
Ring thickness (top and second)
    Standard.. 0.030 to 0.031 inch (0.77 to 0.79 mm)
    Minimum.. 0.027 inch (0.7 mm)
Ring end gap
    Standard
        Top and second..................................... 0.008 to 0.013 inch (0.2 to 0.35 mm)
        Oil .... 0.008 to 0.027 inch (0.2 to 0.7 mm)
    Maximum
        Top and second..................................... 0.027 inch (0.7 mm)
        Oil .... 0.039 inch (1.0 mm)

Crankshaft and bearings

Main bearing oil clearance
    Standard.. 0.0008 to 0.0017 inch (0.020 to 0.044 mm)
    Maximum.. 0.003 inch (0.08 mm)
Main bearing journal diameter
    No mark on crank throw.............................. 1.4166 to 1.4170 inch (35.984 to 35.992 mm)
    "1" mark on crank throw .... 1.4170 to 1.4173 inch (35.993 to 36.000 mm)
Main bearing bore diameter
    No mark on case.. 1.5357 to 1.5360 inch (39.009 to 30.016 mm)
    "0" mark on case.. 1.5354 to 1.5357 inch (39.000 to 39.008 mm)
Crankshaft endplay
    Standard.. 0.002 to 0.010 inch (0.05 to 0.25 mm)
    Maximum.. 0.016 inch (0.4 mm)
Crankshaft runout limit .... 0.002 inch (0.05 mm)
Connecting rod side clearance
    Standard.. 0.005 to 0.013 inch (0.13 to 0.33 mm)
    Maximum.. 0.019 inch (0.5 mm)
Connecting rod bearing oil clearance
    Standard.. 0.0016 to 0.0025 inch (0.036 to 0.066 mm)
    Maximum.. 0.004 inch (0.1 mm)
Connecting rod big-end bore diameter
    No mark on side of rod .... 1.6141 to 1.6144 inch (41.00 to 41.008 mm)
    "0" mark on side of rod .... 1.6145 to 1.6148 inch (41.009 to 41.016 mm)
Connecting rod journal (crank pin) diameter
    No mark on crank throw................................ 1.4954 to 1.4958 inch (37.984 to 37.994 mm)
    "0" mark on crank throw .... 1.4958 to 1.4960 inch (37.995 to 38.000 mm)
Connecting rod bend and twist, maximum .... 0.008 inch (0.2 mm) per 3.94 inch (100 mm)
Primary chain 20-link length (maximum) .... 7-39/64 in (193.4 mm)

Oil pump and relief valve

Oil pressure (warm)... 40 to 48 psi (2.8 to 3.3 Bars) @ 4000 rpm
Relief valve opening pressure........................... 63 to 85 psi (4.3 to 5.9 Bars)

Balancer shaft

Balancer shaft bearing oil clearance
    Standard.. 0.0008 to 0.0019 inch (0.02 to 0.05 mm)
    Maximum.. 0.0035 inch (0.09 mm)
Balancer shaft journal diameter
    No mark on balancer.................................... 1.1018 to 1.1020 inch (27.987 to 27.993 mm)
    "0" mark on balancer .... 1.1021 to 1.1023 inch (27.994 to 28.00 mm)
Balancer shaft bearing bore diameter
    No mark on case.. 1.2210 to 1.2214 inch (30.014 to 31.025 mm)
    "0" mark on case.. 1.2204 to 1.2210 inch (31.000 to 31.013 mm)

Clutch

Spring free length
    Standard.. 1.346 inch (34.2 mm)
    Minimum.. 1.303 inch (33.1 mm)
Friction plate thickness
    Standard.. 0.114 to 0.122 inch (2.9 to 3.1 mm)
    Minimum.. 0.108 inch (2.75 mm)
Friction and steel plate warpage
    Standard.. 0.008 inch (0.2 mm)
    Limit .... 0.012 inch (0.3 mm)

2

Transmission

Gear backlash
    Standard... 0.0008 to 0.0074 inch (0.02 to 0.19 mm)
    Maximum.. 0.009 inch (0.23 mm)
Shift fork groove width
    Standard... 0.199 to 0.202 inch (5.05 to 5.15 mm)
    Maximum.. 0.208 inch (5.3 mm)
Shift fork ear thickness
    Standard... 0.193 to 0.197 inch (4.9 to 5.0 mm)
    Minimum... 0.189 inch (4.8 mm)
Shift fork guide pin diameter
    Standard... 0.311 to 0.315 inch (7.9 to 8.0 mm)
    Minimum... 0.307 inch (7.8 mm)
Shift drum groove width
    Standard... 0.317 to 0.323 inch (8.05 to 8.2 mm)
    Maximum.. 0.326 inch (8.3 mm)

Torque specifications

Valve cover bolts .... 87 in-lbs (9.8 Nm)
Camshaft bearing cap bolts .... 78 in-lbs (8.8 Nm)
Camshaft sprocket bolts .... 11 ft-lbs (15 Nm)
Rocker arm shafts .... 29 ft-lbs (39 Nm)
Oil pipe bolts (on camshaft bearing caps).......................... not specified
Camshaft chain tensioner cap.. 43 in-lbs (4.9 Nm)
Camshaft chain tensioner mounting bolts........................... 78 in-lbs (8.8 Nm)
Cylinder head bolts
    6 mm bolts .... 87 in-lbs (9.8 Nm)
    8 mm bolts .... 38 ft-lbs (51 Nm)
Crankcase bolts
    6 mm bolts .... 104 in-lbs (12 Nm)
    8 mm bolts .... 20 ft-lbs (27 Nm)
Connecting rod nuts .... 27 ft-lbs (36 Nm)
Primary chain guide bolts .... 104 in-lbs (12 Nm)
Clutch cover bolts .... not specified
Clutch spring bolts .... 82 in-lbs (9.3 Nm)
Clutch hub nut .... 98 ft-lbs (130 Nm)
Oil pan bolts .... 104 in-lbs (12 Nm)
Oil pipe-to-cylinder head union bolts .... 174 in-lbs (20 Nm)
Oil pipe-to-crankcase union bolts
    Left front corner of case.. 104 in-lbs (12 Nm)
    Left side of case (upper bolt) .... 69 in-lbs (7.8 Nm)
    Left side of case (lower bolt) .... 104 in-lbs (12 Nm)
    Bottom of case (inside oil pan).. 104 in-lbs (12 Nm)
    Right rear corner of engine .... 69 in-lbs (7.8 Nm)
    Cylinder head "Y" line to case .... 174 in-lbs (20 Nm)
Relief valve-to-oil pan.. 11 ft-lbs (15 Nm)
Shift drum bearing retainer bolts .... not specified

---

1   General information

The engine/transmission unit is a water-cooled, in-line, parallel twin. The valves are operated by double overhead camshafts which are chain driven off the crankshaft. The engine/transmission assembly is constructed from aluminum alloy. The crankcase is divided horizontally.

The crankcase incorporates a wet sump, pressure-fed lubrication system which uses a gear-driven, dual-rotor oil pump, an oil filter and by-pass valve assembly, a relief valve and an oil pressure switch. Also contained in the crankcase is the balancer shaft and the starter motor clutch.

Power from the crankshaft is routed to the transmission via the clutch, which is of the wet, multi-plate type and is chain-driven off the crankshaft. The transmission is a six-speed, constant-mesh unit.

2   Operations possible with the engine in the frame

The components and assemblies listed below can be removed without having to remove the engine from the frame. If, however, a number of areas require attention at the same time, removal of the engine is recommended.

Gear selector mechanism external components
Water pump
Starter motor
Alternator
Clutch assembly (except housing)
Oil pan, oil pump and relief valve
Valve cover, camshafts and rocker arms
Cam chain tensioner
Cylinder head
Cylinder block and pistons

5.15a Remove the nut from the front mounting bolt. . .

5.15b . . .then pull out the bolt and spacer (engine removed for clarity)

3 Operations requiring engine removal

It is necessary to remove the engine/transmission assembly from the frame and separate the crankcase halves to gain access to the following components:

Clutch housing
Crankshaft, connecting rods and bearings
Transmission shafts
Shift drum and forks
Balancer shaft
Starter motor clutch
Camshaft chain
Primary chain

4 Major engine repair - general note

1   It is not always easy to determine when or if an engine should be completely overhauled, as a number of factors must be considered.
2   High mileage is not necessarily an indication that an overhaul is needed, while low mileage, on the other hand, does not preclude the need for an overhaul. Frequency of servicing is probably the single most important consideration. An engine that has regular and frequent oil and filter changes, as well as other required maintenance, will most likely give many miles of reliable service. Conversely, a neglected engine, or one which has not been broken in properly, may require an overhaul very early in its life.
3   Exhaust smoke and excessive oil consumption are both indications that piston rings and/or valve guides are in need of attention. Make sure oil leaks are not responsible before deciding that the rings and guides are bad. Refer to Chapter 1 and perform a cylinder compression check to determine for certain the nature and extent of the work required.
4   If the engine is making obvious knocking or rumbling noises, the connecting rod and/or main bearings are probably at fault.
5   Loss of power, rough running, excessive valve train noise and high fuel consumption rates may also point to the need for an overhaul, especially if they are all present at the same time. If a complete tune-up does not remedy the situation, major mechanical work is the only solution.
6   An engine overhaul generally involves restoring the internal parts to the specifications of a new engine. During an overhaul the piston rings are replaced and the cylinder walls are bored and/or honed. If a rebore is done, then new pistons are also required. The main and connecting rod bearings are generally replaced with new ones and, if necessary, the crankshaft is also replaced. Generally the valves are serviced as well, since they are usually in less than perfect condition at this point. While the engine is being overhauled, other components such as the carburetors and the starter motor can be rebuilt also. The end result should be a like-new engine that will give as many trouble free miles as the original.
7   Before beginning the engine overhaul, read through all of the re-

lated procedures to familiarize yourself with the scope and requirements of the job. Overhauling an engine is not all that difficult, but it is time consuming. Plan on the motorcycle being tied up for a minimum of two weeks. Check on the availability of parts and make sure that any necessary special tools, equipment and supplies are obtained in advance.
8   Most work can be done with typical shop hand tools, although a number of precision measuring tools are required for inspecting parts to determine if they must be replaced. Often a dealer service department or motorcycle repair shop will handle the inspection of parts and offer advice concerning reconditioning and replacement. As a general rule, time is the primary cost of an overhaul so it doesn't pay to install worn or substandard parts.
9   As a final note, to ensure maximum life and minimum trouble from a rebuilt engine, everything must be assembled with care in a spotlessly clean environment.

5 Engine - removal and installation

2

Note: *Engine removal and installation should be done with the aid of an assistant to avoid damage or injury that could occur if the engine is dropped. A hydraulic floor jack should be used to support and lower the engine if possible (they can be rented at low cost).*

Removal

Refer to illustrations 5.15a, 5.15b, 5.15c, 5.15d, 5.17 and 5.19
1   Set the bike on its centerstand.
2   Remove the seat and the fuel tank (see Chapter 4).
3   Remove the side covers, upper fairing and lower fairing (if equipped) (see Chapter 8).
4   Drain the coolant and the engine oil (see Chapter 1).
5   Remove the air cleaner housing (see Chapter 5).
6   Remove the air suction valve and the vacuum switching valve (see Chapter 1).
7   Remove the carburetors (see Chapter 4) and plug the intake openings with rags.
8   Remove the radiator, radiator hoses and coolant tubes (see Chapter 3).
9   Remove the ignition coils and brackets (see Chapter 5).
10   Remove the exhaust system (see Chapter 4).
11   Remove the shift pedal (see Section 21).
12   Remove the engine sprocket cover, unbolt the engine sprocket and detach the sprocket and chain from the engine (see Chapter 6).
13   Disconnect the lower end of the clutch cable from the lever and bracket (see Chapter 1).
14   Mark and disconnect the wires from the oil pressure switch, neutral switch and the starter motor. Unplug the alternator, sidestand and pickup coil electrical connectors (see Chapters 5 and 9).
15   Remove the engine front mounting bolt, nut and spacer and the bolts holding the downtube to the frame **(see illustrations)**.

5.15c Remove two lower bolts. . .

5.15d . . .and two upper bolts that secure the frame downtube

5.17 Remove the nuts from the rear engine mounting bolts (arrows)

16   Support the engine with a floor jack and a wood block.

17   Remove the nuts from the rear mounting bolts **(see illustration)**.

18   With the engine supported, pull the rear mounting bolts out. Make sure no wires or hoses are still attached to the engine assembly.

19   Slowly and carefully lower the engine assembly to the floor, then guide it out from under the bike **(see illustration)**.

Installation

20   Installation is the reverse of removal. Note the following points:
  a) Don't tighten any of the engine mounting bolts until they all have been installed.
  b) Use new gaskets at all exhaust pipe connections.
  c) Tighten the engine mounting bolts and frame downtube bolts securely.
  d) Adjust the drive chain, throttle cables, choke cable and clutch cable following the procedures in Chapter 1.

---

6   Engine disassembly and reassembly - general information

Refer to illustrations 6.2a, 6.2b and 6.3

1   Before disassembling the engine, clean the exterior with a degreaser and rinse it with water. A clean engine will make the job easier and prevent the possibility of getting dirt into the internal areas of the engine.

2   In addition to the precision measuring tools mentioned earlier, you will need a torque wrench, a valve spring compressor, oil gallery brushes, a piston ring removal and installation tool, a piston ring compressor, a pin-type spanner wrench and a clutch holder tool (which is described in Section 19). Some new, clean engine oil of the correct grade and type, some engine assembly lube (or moly-based grease), a tube of Kawasaki Bond liquid gasket (part no. 92104-1003) or equivalent, and a tube of RTV (silicone) sealant will also be required. Although it may not be considered a tool, some Plastigage (type HPG-1) should also be obtained to use for checking bearing oil clearances **(see illustrations)**.

3   An engine support stand made from short lengths of 2 x 4's bolted together will facilitate the disassembly and reassembly procedures **(see illustration)**. The perimeter of the mount should be just big enough to accommodate the engine oil pan. If you have an automotive-type enginestand, an adapter plate can be made from a piece of plate, some angle iron and some nuts and bolts.

4   When disassembling the engine, keep "mated" parts together (including gears, cylinders, pistons, etc. that have been in contact with each other during engine operation). These "mated" parts must be reused or replaced as an assembly.

5   Engine/transmission disassembly should be done in the following general order with reference to the appropriate Sections.
    Remove the cylinder head
    Remove the cylinder block

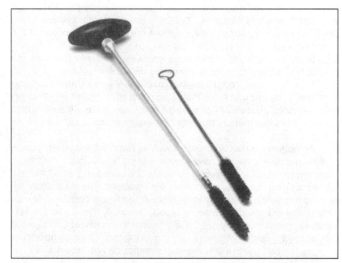

5.19 With the engine supported by a floor jack, have an assistant help you lower it and guide it out of the frame

6.2a A selection of brushes is required for cleaning holes and passages in the engine components

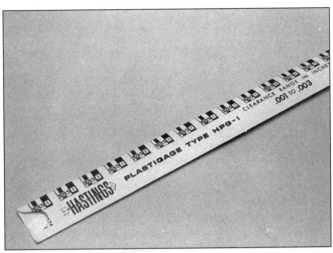

6.2b Type HPG-1 Plastigage is needed to check the crankshaft, connecting rod and camshaft oil clearances

6.3 An engine stand can be made from short lengths of 2 x 4 lumber and lag bolts or nails

Remove the pistons
Remove the clutch
Remove the oil pan
Remove the external shift mechanism
Remove the alternator rotor/stator coils and starter clutch
  (see Chapter 9)
Separate the crankcase halves
Remove the crankshaft and connecting rods
Remove the balancer shaft and gears
Remove the transmission shafts/gears
Remove the shift drum/forks

6   Reassembly is accomplished by reversing the general disassembly sequence.

7   Valve cover - removal and installation

Refer to illustrations 7.7, 7.8, 7.9, 7.11a and 7.11b
Note: *The valve cover can be removed with the engine in the frame. If the engine has been removed, ignore the steps which don't apply.*

Removal
1   Set the bike on its centerstand.
2   Drain the engine coolant (see Chapter 1).
3   Remove the fuel tank (see Chapter 4).

4   Remove the upper fairing (and lower fairing, if equipped) (see Chapter 8).
5   Remove the air suction valve and the vacuum switching valve (see Chapter 1).
6   If necessary for removal access, remove the ignition coils and their brackets, along with the spark plug wires (see Chapter 5).
7   Remove the valve cover bolts **(see illustration)**.
8   Lift the cover off the cylinder head **(see illustration)**. If it's stuck, don't attempt to pry it off - tap around the sides with a plastic hammer to dislodge it. **Note:** *Pay attention to the locating dowels as you remove the cover - if they fall into the engine, major disassembly may be required to get them out.*

Installation
9   Remove the locating dowels from the valve cover **(see illustration)**. Peel the rubber gasket from the cover. If it's cracked, hardened, has soft spots or shows signs of general deterioration, replace it with a new one.
10   Clean the mating surfaces of the cylinder head and the valve cover with lacquer thinner, acetone or brake system cleaner. Apply a thin film of RTV sealant to the half-circle cutouts on each side of the head.
11   Install the gasket to the cover. Make sure it fits completely into the cover groove **(see illustration)**. Apply a small amount of silicone

2

7.7 Remove the valve cover bolts (arrow)

7.8 Lift the cover off the engine - if it's stuck, tap gently on the side with a soft faced hammer; don't pry the cover loose

7.9 Be careful not to lose the locating dowels (arrows) or let them fall into the engine

7.11a Be sure the gasket seats securely in the groove (arrow)

7.11b Apply a small amount of silicone sealant to the corners of the half-circle portions of the gasket (arrows)

sealer to the corners of the half-circle portions of the gasket **(see illustration)**.

12   Position the cover on the cylinder head, making sure the gasket doesn't slip out of place.

13   Check the rubber seals on the valve cover bolts, replacing them if necessary. Install the bolts, tightening them evenly to the torque listed in this Chapter's Specifications.

14   The remainder of installation is the reverse of removal. Fill the cooling system with the recommended type and amount of coolant (see Chapter 1).

---

8   Camshaft chain tensioner - removal and installation

Refer to illustrations 8.1 and 8.9

Removal

Caution: *Once you start to remove the tensioner bolts, you must remove the tensioner all the way and reset it before tightening the bolts. The tensioner extends and locks in place, so if you loosen the bolts part way and then retighten them, the tensioner or cam chain will be damaged.*

1   Loosen the tensioner cap bolt while the tensioner is still installed **(see illustration)**.

2   Remove the tensioner mounting bolts and take it off the engine.

3   Remove the tensioner cap bolt and O-ring.

Installation

4   Check the O-ring on the tensioner body for cracks or hardening. It's a good idea to replace this O-ring whenever the tensioner cap is removed.

Original tensioner

5   Place the tensioner mounting bolts where you can reach them with one hand while the other hand holds the tensioner in position in Step 7.

6   Press the end of the rod that contacts the chain into the tensioner body. At the same time, turn the other end of the rod clockwise with a screwdriver until the rod protrudes about 3/8-inch (10 mm) from the tensioner body. **Caution:** *Don't turn the rod counterclockwise (anticlockwise) or it may separate from the tensioner. If this happens it can't be reassembled.*

7   Place the tensioner in position on the engine. Push it firmly against the engine, remove the screwdriver, and install the mounting bolts finger-tight. **Caution:** *If the tensioner moves away from the engine before you tighten the bolts, the rod will extend too far. If this happens (or you think it might have happened), remove the tensioner and repeat Step 6, then continue with Step 7.*

8   Tighten the mounting bolts to the torque listed in this Chapter's Specifications.

New tensioner

9   New tensioners come with a keeper that fits in the tensioner rod slot and holds the rod in the correct position for installation **(see illustration)**.

8.1 Loosen the tensioner cap bolt (A) while the tensioner is still on the engine, then remove the mounting bolts (B)

8.9 New tensioners come with a keeper (arrow) to hold the rod in position for installation; add the keeper to your tool collection for the next time you need to remove and install the tensioner

9.3a Position the EX mark on the exhaust camshaft even with the cylinder head surface and the sprocket punch mark up (arrows). . .

9.3b . . .the IN mark on the intake camshaft should also be even with the head surface and the sprocket punch mark should be up. . .

10   Place the tensioner on the engine. Install the mounting bolts and tighten them to the torque listed in this Chapter's Specifications.

11   Pull the keeper out with needle nosed pliers. **Note:** *Save the keeper and place it in your toolbox for future use. You can use it to hold the tensioner rod in position next time you install the tensioner, leaving both hands free.*

Original or new tensioner

12   Install the tensioner cap and O-ring. Tighten the cap to the torque listed in this Chapter's Specifications.

---

9   Camshafts, rocker arm shafts and rocker arms - removal, inspection and installation

---

Note: *This procedure can be performed with the engine in the frame.*

Camshafts

Removal

Refer to illustrations 9.3a, 9.3b, 9.3c, 9.4, 9.5, 9.6, 9.7a, 9.7b and 9.8

1   Remove the valve cover (see Section 7).

2   Remove the camshaft chain tensioner (see Section 8).

3   Turn the engine to position no. 2 cylinder at TDC compression (see Chapter 1 - Valve clearances - check and adjustment). When the engine is positioned correctly, the EX mark on the exhaust camshaft and the IN mark on the intake camshaft will align with the cylinder

9.3c . . .once the camshafts are positioned correctly, mark across the chain and sprocket with felt pen to ease reassembly

head top surface (see illustrations). To ease reassembly, mark the sprockets and chain with felt pen (see illustration).

4   Remove the upper chain guide (see illustration).

5   Remove the bolts and lift the oil pipes and O-rings from the cylinder head (see illustration).

6   Unscrew the bearing cap bolts for one of the camshafts, a little at a time, until they are all loose, then unscrew the bearing cap bolts for the other camshaft. **Caution:** *If the bearing cap bolts aren't loosened evenly, the camshaft may bind. Remove the bolts and lift off the*

9.4 The center four camshaft bearing cap bolts also secure the chain guide; its arrow points toward the front of the engine

9.5 Remove the oil line bolts (arrows) and lift the oil lines and O-rings out of the engine

9.6 The camshaft bearing caps have letter marks to indicate position; the caps must be reinstalled in the correct locations to prevent camshaft seizure

9.7a Lift the camshafts out of the head and disengage them from the chain

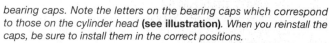

9.7b The camshafts are identified by punch marks

9.8 This protrusion in the bottom of the engine case is designed to prevent the cam chain from falling out of mesh with the crankshaft sprocket, but to be safe, tie the chain up so it can't drop down

bearing caps. Note the letters on the bearing caps which correspond to those on the cylinder head **(see illustration)**. *When you reinstall the caps, be sure to install them in the correct positions.*

7   Pull up on the camshaft chain and carefully guide the camshaft out **(see illustration)**. With the chain still held taut, remove the other camshaft. Look for marks on the camshafts **(see illustration)**. The in- take camshaft should have an IN mark and the exhaust camshaft should have an EX mark. If you can't find these marks, label the camshafts to ensure they are installed in their original locations. **Note:** *Don't remove the sprockets from the camshafts unless absolutely nec- essary.*

8   While the camshafts are out, don't allow the chain to go slack - there's a protrusion inside the crankcase that's designed to keep the chain from falling off the sprocket on the crankshaft **(see illustration)**, but if it's worn, the chain may fall off and bind between the crankshaft and case, which could damage these components. Wire the chain to another component to prevent it from dropping down. Also, cover the top of the cylinder head with a rag to prevent foreign objects from falling into the engine.

Inspection

Refer to illustrations 9.10a, 9.10b, 9.12, 9.13a, 9.13b, 9.15a, 9.15b and 9.18

Note: *Before replacing camshafts or the cylinder head and bearing caps because of damage, check with local machine shops specializing in motorcycle engine work. In the case of the camshafts, it may be possible for cam lobes to be welded, reground and hardened, at a cost far lower than that of a new camshaft. If the bearing surfaces in the cylinder head are damaged, it may be possible for them to be bored*

out to accept bearing inserts. Due to the cost of a new cylinder head it is recommended that all options be explored before condemning it as trash!

9   Inspect the cam bearing surfaces of the head and the bearing caps. Look for score marks, deep scratches and evidence of spalling (a pitted appearance).

10   Check the camshaft lobes for heat discoloration (blue appear- ance), score marks, chipped areas, flat spots and spalling **(see illus- tration)**. Measure the height of each lobe with a micrometer **(see illus- tration)** and compare the results to the minimum lobe height listed in this Chapter's Specifications. If damage is noted or wear is excessive, the camshaft must be replaced. Also, be sure to check the condition of the rocker arms, as described later in this Section.

11   Next, check the camshaft bearing oil clearances. Clean the camshafts, the bearing surfaces in the cylinder head and the bearing caps with a clean, lint-free cloth, then lay the cams in place in the cylinder head, with the IN and EX marks on the gears facing away from each other and level with the valve cover gasket surface of the cylinder head **(see illustrations 9.3a and 9.3b)**. Engage the cam chain with the cam gears, so the camshafts don't turn as the bearing caps are tight- ened.

12   Cut eight strips of Plastigage (type HPG-1) and lay one piece on each bearing journal, parallel with the camshaft centerline **(see illus- tration)**.

9.10a Check the lobes of the camshaft for wear - here's a good example of damage which will require replacement (or repair) of the camshaft

9.10b Measure the height of the camshaft lobes with a micrometer

9.12 Position a strip of Plastigage on each cam bearing journal, parallel with the centerline of the crankshaft

9.13a Make sure the bearing cap dowels are in position

2

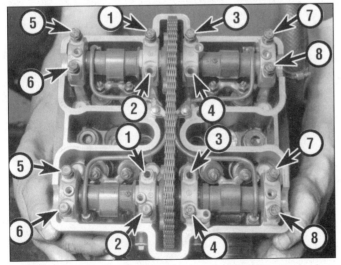

9.13b Camshaft bearing cap tightening sequence (the center four bolts also secure the chain guide) - tighten the no. 1 and no. 2 bolts evenly to specifications first, then tighten the others in numerical order

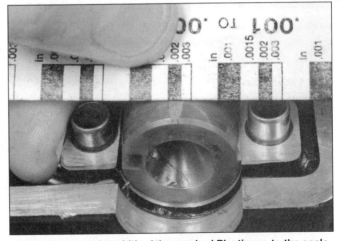

9.15a Compare the width of the crushed Plastigage to the scale on the Plastigage envelope to obtain the clearance

13   Make sure the bearing cap dowels are installed **(see illustration)**. Install the bearing caps in their proper positions (the arrows on the caps must face toward the front of the engine and the letters on the caps must correspond with those on the cylinder head) and install the

bolts. Tighten the bolts in three steps, following the recommended sequence **(see illustration)**, to the torque listed in this Chapter's Specifications. While doing this, DO NOT let the camshafts rotate!
14   Now unscrew the bolts, a little at a time, and carefully lift off the bearing caps.
15   To determine the oil clearance, compare the crushed Plastigage (at its widest point) on each journal to the scale printed on the Plastigage container **(see illustration)**. Compare the results to this Chap-

9.15b Measure the cam bearing journal with a micrometer

9.18 Each sprocket has two sets of bolt holes; those labeled EX are used for the exhaust camshaft, while those labeled IN are used for the intake camshaft

ter's Specifications. If the oil clearance is greater than specified, measure the diameter of the cam bearing journal with a micrometer **(see illustration)**. If the journal diameter is less than the specified limit, replace the camshaft with a new one and recheck the clearance. If the clearance is still too great, replace the cylinder head and bearing caps with new parts (see the Note that precedes Step 9).

16   Except in cases of oil starvation, the camshaft chain wears very little. If the chain has stretched excessively, which makes it difficult to maintain proper tension, replace it with a new one (see Section 28).

17   Check the sprockets for wear, cracks and other damage, replacing them if necessary. If the sprockets are worn, the chain is also worn, and also the sprocket on the crankshaft (which can only be remedied by replacing the crankshaft). If wear this severe is apparent, the entire engine should be disassembled for inspection.

18   If you remove the sprockets, be sure to install them correctly; they're identical, with each sprocket having bolt holes for the intake and exhaust camshafts. The intake camshaft sprocket uses the bolt holes labeled IN; the exhaust camshaft sprocket uses the bolt holes labeled EX **(see illustration)**.

19   Check the chain guide for wear or damage. If it is worn or damaged, the chain is worn out or improperly adjusted. Replacement of the guide requires removal of the cylinder head and cylinder block.

Installation

Refer to illustration 9.22

20   Make sure the bearing surfaces in the cylinder head and the bearing caps are clean, then apply a light coat of engine assembly lube or moly-based grease to each of them.

21   Apply a coat of moly-based grease to the camshaft lobes. Make sure the camshaft bearing journals are clean, then lay the camshafts in the cylinder head (do not mix them up), ensuring the marks on the cam sprockets are aligned properly **(see illustrations 9.3a, 9.3b and 9.3c)**.

22   Make sure the timing marks are aligned as described in Step 11, then mesh the chain with the camshaft sprockets. Count the number of chain link pins between the EX mark and the IN mark **(see illustration)**. There should be no slack in the chain between the two sprockets.

Camshaft Chain Timing (left side view)

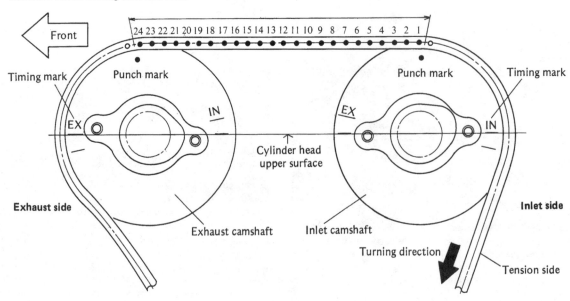

#2 Piston TDC

9.22 With no slack in the timing chain, there should be 24 link pins present between the punch marks on the cam sprockets

9.30a Insert an Allen wrench into the rocker shaft head (a bit like this one is necessary for tightening the plug to specifications). . .

9.30b . . .unscrew the shaft and pull it out

23   Carefully set the bearing caps in place (arrows pointing toward the front of the engine and in their proper positions) **(see illustration 9.6)** and install the bolts. Tighten them in the recommended sequence **(see illustration 9.13b)**, to the torque listed in this Chapter's Specifications.

24   Insert your finger or a wood dowel into the cam chain tensioner hole and apply pressure to the cam chain. Check the timing marks to make sure they are aligned (see Step 3) and there are still the correct number of link pins between the punch marks on the cam sprockets. If necessary, change the position of the sprocket(s) on the chain to bring all of the marks into alignment. **Caution:** *If the marks are not aligned exactly as described, the valve timing will be incorrect and the valves may contact the pistons, causing extensive damage to the engine.*

25   Install the tensioner as described in Section 8.

26   Adjust the valve clearances (see Chapter 1).

27   Turn the engine with a socket on the crankshaft rotationl bolt. If you feel a sudden increase in resistance, stop turning. The valves may be hitting the pistons due to incorrect assembly. Find the problem and fix it before turning the engine any further, or serious damage may occur.

28   The remainder of installation is the reverse of removal.

Rocker arm shafts and rocker arms

Removal

Refer to illustrations 9.30a, 9.30b and 9.31

29   Remove the camshafts following the procedure given above. Be sure to keep tension on the camshaft chain.

30   Unscrew one rocker shaft from the cylinder head and pull it out **(see illustrations)**.

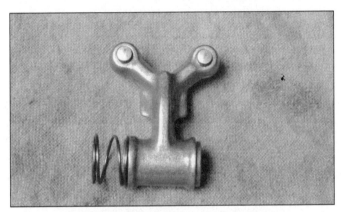

9.31 Remove the rocker arms and springs

31   Remove the rocker arms and springs **(see illustration)**.

32   Repeat the above Steps to remove the other rocker arm shafts and rocker arms. Keep all of the parts in order so they can be reinstalled in their original locations.

Inspection

Refer to illustrations 9.33, 9.34a, 9.34b and 9.34c

33   Clean all of the components with solvent and dry them off. Blow through the oil passages in the rocker arms with compressed air, if available. Inspect the rocker arm faces for pits, spalling, score marks and rough spots **(see illustration)**. Check the rocker arm-to-shaft contact areas and the adjusting screws, as well. Look for cracks in each rocker arm. If the faces of the rocker arms are damaged, the rocker arms and the camshafts should be replaced as a set.

34   Measure the diameter of the rocker arm shafts, in the area where the rocker arms ride, and compare the results with this Chapter's

2

9.33 Inspect the rocker arms, especially the faces that contact the cam lobes, for wear

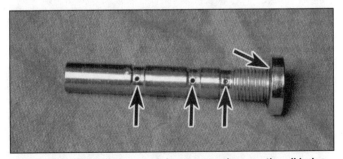

9.34a Check the rocker shaft for wear, make sure the oil holes (lower arrows) are clear and inspect the O-ring under the head (upper arrow); it's a good idea to replace the O-ring whenever the shaft is removed

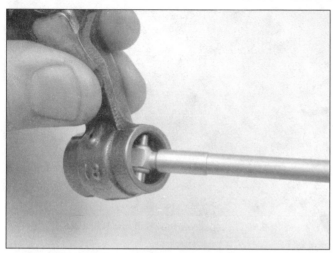

9.34b Measure the inside diameter of the rocker arm - in this case a telescoping gauge is expanded against the bore of the rocker arm, then locked. . .

9.34c . . .and a micrometer is used to measure the gauge

Specifications. Also measure the inside diameter of the rocker arms **(see illustrations)** and compare the results with this Chapter's Specifications. If either the shaft or the rocker arms are worn beyond the specified limits, replace them as a set.

35   Check the O-ring under the head of the rocker arm shaft, replacing it if necessary.

Installation

Refer to illustration 9.36

36   Position a rocker arm and spring in the cylinder head, with the spring toward the center of the cylinder head **(see illustration)**.

37   Lubricate the rocker arm shaft with engine oil and slide it into the cylinder head and through the rocker arm and spring. Tighten it to the torque listed in this Chapter's Specifications.

38   Repeat Steps 36 and 37 to install the remaining rocker arms and shafts.

39   Install the camshafts following the procedure described earlier in this Section.

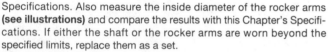

10   Cylinder head - removal and installation

Caution: *The engine must be completely cool before beginning this procedure, or the cylinder head may become warped.*

Note: *This procedure can be performed with the engine in the frame. If the engine has been removed, ignore the steps which don't apply.*

Removal

Refer to illustrations 10.6, 10.7a, 10.7b, 10.8a, 10.8b, 10.9 and 10.10

1   Set the bike on its centerstand.

2   Remove the valve cover (see Section 7).

3   Remove the exhaust system (see Chapter 4).

4   Remove the cam chain tensioner (see Section 8).

5   Remove the camshafts (see Section 9).

6   Remove the oil pipe banjo bolts and washers from the rear of the cylinder head **(see illustration)**.

7   Remove the small cylinder block-to-cylinder head bolts and the main oil pipe mounting bolt **(see illustrations)**.

8   Loosen the cylinder head bolts, a little at a time, using the reverse order of the tightening sequence **(see illustrations)**.

9   Pull the cylinder head off the cylinder block **(see illustration)**. If the head is stuck, tap upward against the rocker shaft heads with a rubber mallet to jar it loose, or use two wooden dowels inserted into the intake or exhaust ports to lever the head off. Don't attempt to pry the head off by inserting a screwdriver between the head and the cylinder block - you'll damage the sealing surfaces.

10   Lift the head gasket off the cylinder block **(see illustration)**.

11   Stuff a clean rag into the cam chain tunnel to prevent the entry of debris.

9.36 The rocker arm springs (arrow) go between the rocker arm and the center of the head

10.6 Remove the oil line banjo bolts

10.7a Remove one small head-to-block bolt (upper arrow), the oil line mounting bolt (lower arrow). . .

10.7b . . .and one small head-to-block bolt located inside the head

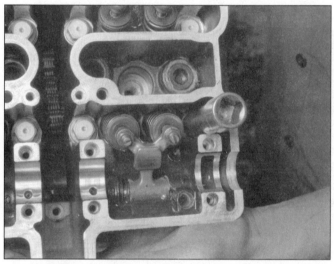

10.8a Use a deep socket to remove the head bolts

10.8b Head bolt TIGHTENING sequence - the arrow points to the front of the engine

2

10.9 Lift the head off the cylinder block

10.10 Remove the old gasket

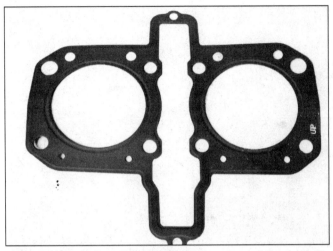

10.15 The UP mark on the head gasket goes toward the right side of the engine

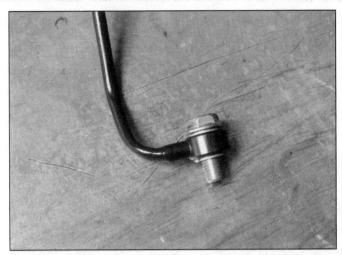

10.20 There's a washer on each side of the oil line banjo bolt fittings - replace them whenever the banjo bolts are removed

12   Locate the two dowel pins to make sure they haven't fallen into the engine. If they are in the head, put them in their holes in the cylinder block.
13   Check the cylinder head gasket and the mating surfaces on the cylinder head and block for leakage, which could indicate warpage. Refer to Section 12 and check the flatness of the cylinder head.
14   Clean all traces of old gasket material from the cylinder head and block. Be careful not to let any of the gasket material fall into the crankcase, the cylinder bores or the water passages.

Installation

Refer to illustrations 10.15 and 10.20
15   Lay the new gasket in place on the cylinder block. Make sure the UP mark on the gasket is positioned on the right-hand side of the engine **(see illustration)**. Never reuse the old gasket and don't use any type of gasket sealant.
16   Carefully lower the cylinder head over the studs. It is helpful to have an assistant support the camshaft chain with a piece of wire so it doesn't fall and become kinked or detached from the crankshaft. When the head is resting against the cylinder block, wire the cam chain to another component to keep tension on it.
17   Install the head bolts. Using the proper sequence **(see illustration 10.8b)**, tighten the bolts to approximately half of the torque listed in this Chapter's Specifications.
18   Using the same sequence, tighten the bolts to the full torque listed in this Chapter's Specifications.
19   Install the small cylinder block-to-cylinder head bolts, tightening them to the torque listed in this Chapter's Specifications.
20   Install the oil line mounting and banjo bolts. Use new washers on the banjo bolts **(see illustration)**.
21   Install the camshafts and the valve cover (see Sections 9 and 7).
22   Change the engine oil (see Chapter 1)

11   Valves/valve seats/valve guides - servicing

1   Because of the complex nature of this job and the special tools and equipment required, servicing of the valves, the valve seats and the valve guides (commonly known as a valve job) is best left to a professional.
2   The home mechanic can, however, remove and disassemble the head, do the initial cleaning and inspection, then reassemble and deliver the head to a dealer service department or properly equipped motorcycle repair shop for the actual valve servicing. Refer to Section 12 for those procedures.
3   The dealer service department will remove the valves and springs, recondition or replace the valves and valve seats, replace the valve guides, check and replace the valve springs, spring retainers and

keepers (as necessary), replace the valve seals with new ones and reassemble the valve components.
4   After the valve job has been performed, the head will be in likenew condition. When the head is returned, be sure to clean it again very thoroughly before installation on the engine to remove any metal particles or abrasive grit that may still be present from the valve service operations. Use compressed air, if available, to blow out all the holes and passages.

12   Cylinder head and valves - disassembly, inspection and reassembly

1   As mentioned in the previous Section, valve servicing and valve guide replacement should be left to a dealer service department or motorcycle repair shop. However, disassembly, cleaning and inspection of the valves and related components can be done (if the necessary special tools are available) by the home mechanic. This way no expense is incurred if the inspection reveals that service work is not required at this time.
2   To properly disassemble the valve components without the risk of damaging them, a valve spring compressor is absolutely necessary. This special tool can usually be rented, but if it's not available, have a dealer service department or motorcycle repair shop handle the entire process of disassembly, inspection, service or repair (if required) and reassembly of the valves.

Disassembly

Refer to illustrations 12.7a, 12.7b, 12.7c and 12.7d
3   Remove the rocker arm shafts and rocker arms (see Section 9). Store the components in such a way that they can be returned to their original locations without getting mixed up (labeled plastic bags work well).
4   Before the valves are removed, scrape away any traces of gasket material from the head gasket sealing surface. Work slowly and do not nick or gouge the soft aluminum of the head. Gasket removing solvents, which work very well, are available at most motorcycle shops and auto parts stores.
5   Carefully scrape all carbon deposits out of the combustion chamber area. A hand held wire brush or a piece of fine emery cloth can be used once the majority of deposits have been scraped away. Do not use a wire brush mounted in a drill motor, or one with extremely stiff bristles, as the head material is soft and may be eroded away or scratched by the wire brush.
6   Before proceeding, arrange to label and store the valves along with their related components so they can be kept separate and reinstalled in the same valve guides they are removed from (again, plastic bags work well for this).

12.7a Compressing the valve springs with a valve spring compressor

12.7b Remove the valve keepers/collets with needle-nose pliers or tweezers

7   Compress the valve spring on the first valve with a spring compressor, then remove the keepers/collets **(see illustrations)** and the retainer from the valve assembly. Do not compress the springs any more than is absolutely necessary. Carefully release the valve spring compressor and remove the springs and the valve from the head **(see illustration)**. If the valve binds in the guide (won't pull through), push it back into the head and deburr the area around the keeper/collet groove with a very fine file or whetstone **(see illustration)**.
8   Repeat the procedure for the remaining valves. Remember to keep the parts for each valve together so they can be reinstalled in the same location.

9   Once the valves have been removed and labeled, pull off the valve stem seals with pliers and discard them (the old seals should never be reused), then remove the spring seats.
10   Next, clean the cylinder head with solvent and dry it thoroughly. Compressed air will speed the drying process and ensure that all holes and recessed areas are clean.
11   Clean all of the valve springs, keepers/collets, retainers and spring seats with solvent and dry them thoroughly. Do the parts from one valve at a time so that no mixing of parts between valves occurs.
12   Scrape off any deposits that may have formed on the valve, then use a motorized wire brush to remove deposits from the valve heads and stems. Again, make sure the valves do not get mixed up.

Inspection
Refer to illustrations 12.14, 12.15, 12.16a, 12.16b, 12.17, 12.18a, 12.18b, 12.19a and 12.19b

13   Inspect the head very carefully for cracks and other damage. If cracks are found, a new head will be required. Check the cam bearing surfaces for wear and evidence of seizure. Check the camshafts and rocker arms for wear as well (see Section 9).
14   Using a precision straightedge and a feeler gauge, check the head gasket mating surface for warpage. Lay the straightedge lengthwise, across the head and diagonally (corner-to-corner), intersecting the head bolt holes, and try to slip a 0.002 in (0.05 mm) feeler gauge under it, on either side of each combustion chamber **(see illustration)**.

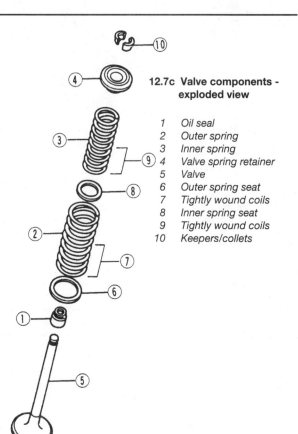

12.7c Valve components - exploded view

1   Oil seal
2   Outer spring
3   Inner spring
4   Valve spring retainer
5   Valve
6   Outer spring seat
7   Tightly wound coils
8   Inner spring seat
9   Tightly wound coils
10   Keepers/collets

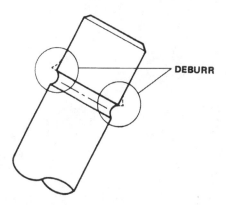

DEBURR

12.7d If the valve binds in the guide, deburr the area above the keeper/collet groove

2

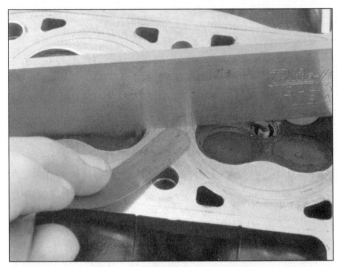

12.14 Lay a precision straightedge across the cylinder head and try to slide a feeler gauge of the specified thickness (equal to the maximum allowable warpage) under it

12.15 Measuring the valve seat width

12.16a Insert a small hole gauge into the valve guide and expand it so there's a slight drag when it's pulled out

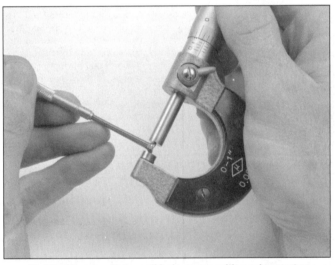

12.16b Measure the small hole gauge with a micrometer

12.17 Check the valve face, stem and keeper groove for signs of wear and damage

If the feeler gauge can be inserted between the head and the straightedge, the head is warped and must either be machined or, if warpage is excessive, replaced with a new one.

15   Examine the valve seats in each of the combustion chambers. If they are pitted, cracked or burned, the head will require valve service that is beyond the scope of the home mechanic. Measure the valve seat width **(see illustration)** and compare it to this Chapter's Specifications. If it is not within the specified range, or if it varies around its circumference, valve service work is required.

16   Clean the valve guides to remove any carbon buildup, then measure the inside diameters of the guides (at both ends and the center of the guide) with a small hole gauge and a 0-to-1-inch micrometer **(see illustrations)**. Record the measurements for future reference. These measurements, along with the valve stem diameter measurements, will enable you to compute the valve stem-to-guide clearance. This clearance, when compared to the Specifications, will be one factor that will determine the extent of the valve service work required. The guides are measured at the ends and at the center to determine if they are worn in a bell-mouth pattern (more wear at the ends). If they are, guide replacement is an absolute must.

17   Carefully inspect each valve face for cracks, pits and burned spots. Check the valve stem and the keeper/collet groove area for cracks **(see illustration)**. Rotate the valve and check for any obvious

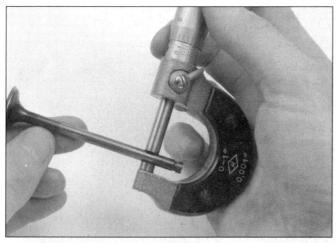

12.18a Measure the valve stem diameter with a micrometer

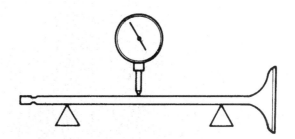

12.18b Check the valve stem for bends with a V-block (or blocks, as shown here) and a dial indicator

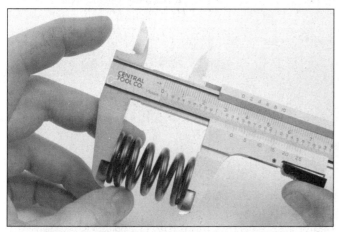

12.19a Measure the free length of the valve springs

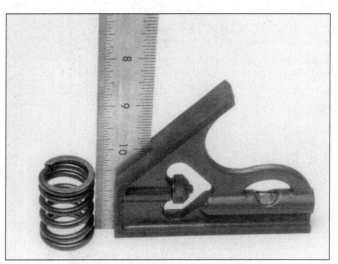

12.19b Check the valve springs for squareness

2

indication that it is bent. Check the end of the stem for pitting and excessive wear and make sure the bevel is the specified width. The presence of any of the above conditions indicates the need for valve servicing.

18   Measure the valve stem diameter **(see illustration)**. By subtracting the stem diameter from the valve guide diameter, the valve stem-to-guide clearance is obtained. If the stem-to-guide clearance is greater than listed in this Chapter's Specifications, the guides and valves will have to be replaced with new ones. Also check the valve stem for bending. Set the valve in a V-block with a dial indicator touching the middle of the stem **(see illustration)**. Rotate the valve and note the reading on the gauge. If the stem runout exceeds the value listed in this Chapter's Specifications, replace the valve.

19   Check the end of each valve spring for wear and pitting. Measure the free length **(see illustration)** and compare it to this Chapter's Specifications. Any springs that are shorter than specified have sagged and should not be reused. Stand the spring on a flat surface and check it for squareness **(see illustration)**.

20   Check the spring retainers and keepers/collets for obvious wear and cracks. Any questionable parts should not be reused, as extensive damage will occur in the event of failure during engine operation.

21   If the inspection indicates that no service work is required, the valve components can be reinstalled in the head.

Reassembly

Refer to illustrations 12.23, 12.24a, 12.24b, 12.24c and 12.27

22   Before installing the valves in the head, they should be lapped to ensure a positive seal between the valves and seats. This procedure requires fine valve lapping compound (available at auto parts stores)

and a valve lapping tool. If a lapping tool is not available, a piece of rubber or plastic hose can be slipped over the valve stem (after the valve has been installed in the guide) and used to turn the valve.

23   Apply a small amount of fine lapping compound to the valve face **(see illustration)**, then slip the valve into the guide. **Note:** *Make sure the valve is installed in the correct guide and be careful not to get any lapping compound on the valve stem.*

24   Attach the lapping tool (or hose) to the valve and rotate the tool between the palms of your hands. Use a back-and-forth motion rather

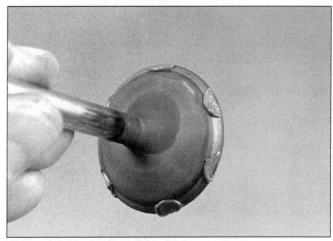

12.23 Apply the lapping compound very sparingly, in small dabs, to the valve face only

12.24a A hose, pushed over the end of the valve, can be used to turn the valve back and forth

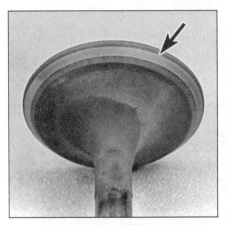

12.24b After lapping, the valve face should exhibit a uniform, unbroken contact pattern (arrow). . .

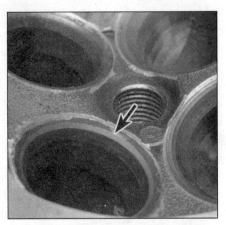

12.24c . . .and the seat should be the specified width (arrow) with a smooth, unbroken appearance

12.27 A small dab of grease will help hold the collets in place on the valve spring while the valve is released

than a circular motion **(see illustration)**. Lift the valve off the seat and turn it at regular intervals to distribute the lapping compound properly. Continue the lapping procedure until the valve face and seat contact area is of uniform width and unbroken around the entire circumference of the valve face and seat **(see illustrations)**.

25   Carefully remove the valve from the guide and wipe off all traces of lapping compound. Use solvent to clean the valve and wipe the seat area thoroughly with a solvent soaked cloth. Repeat the procedure for the remaining valves.

26   Lay the spring seats in place in the cylinder head, then install new valve stem seals on each of the guides. Use an appropriate size deep socket to push the seals into place until they are properly seated. Don't twist or cock them, or they will not seal properly against the valve stems. Also, don't remove them again or they will be damaged.

27   Coat the valve stems with assembly lube or moly-based grease, then install one of them into its guide. Next, install the springs and retainers, compress the springs and install the collets. **Note:** *Install the springs with the tightly wound coils at the bottom (next to the spring seat). When compressing the springs with the valve spring compressor, depress them only as far as is absolutely necessary to slip the collets into place. Apply a small amount of grease to the keepers* **(see illustration)** *to help hold them in place as the pressure is released from the springs. Make certain that the collets are securely locked in their retaining grooves.*

28   Support the cylinder head on blocks so the valves can't contact the workbench top, then very gently tap each of the valve stems with a soft-faced hammer. This will help seat the collets in their grooves.

29   Once all of the valves have been installed in the head, check for proper valve sealing by pouring a small amount of solvent into each of the valve ports. If the solvent leaks past the valve(s) into the combustion chamber area, disassemble the valve(s) and repeat the lapping procedure, then reinstall the valve(s) and repeat the check. Repeat the procedure until a satisfactory seal is obtained.

13.3 If you haven't already done so for cylinder head removal, remove the oil pipe mounting bolt

13   Cylinder block - removal, inspection and installation

Removal
Refer to illustrations 13.3, 13.4, 13.5 and 13.6

1   Following the procedure given in Section 10, remove the cylinder head. Make sure the crankshaft is positioned at Top Dead Center (TDC) for cylinder no. 2.

2   Remove the water pump together with the water pipe (see Chapter 3).

3   Remove the oil pipe mounting bolt **(see illustration)**.

4   Lift out the camshaft chain rear guide **(see illustration)**.

5   Lift the cylinder block straight up to remove it **(see illustration)**. If it's stuck, tap around its perimeter with a soft-faced hammer. Don't attempt to pry between the block and the crankcase, as you will ruin the sealing surfaces. As you lift, note the location of the dowel pins. Be careful not to let these drop into the engine.

6   Stuff clean shop towels around the pistons **(see illustration)** and remove the gasket and all traces of old gasket material from the surfaces of the cylinder block and the cylinder head.

Inspection
Refer to illustration 13.8

Caution: *Don't attempt to separate the liners from the cylinder block.*

7   Check the cylinder walls carefully for scratches and score marks.

13.4 Lift the rear cam chain guide out of the engine (cylinder block removed for clarity)

13.5 Lift the cylinder block up and off the crankcase and pistons

13.6 Place rags under the pistons to protect them and keep debris out of the crankcase

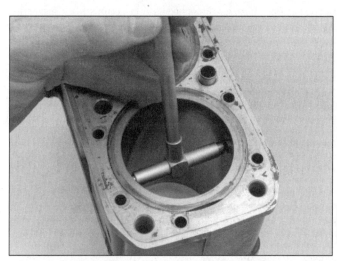

13.8 Measure the cylinder bore with a telescoping gauge (then measure the gauge with a micrometer)

2

8   Using the appropriate precision measuring tools, check each cylinder's diameter near the top, center and bottom of the cylinder bore, parallel to the crankshaft axis **(see illustration)**. Next, measure each cylinder's diameter at the same three locations across the crankshaft axis. Compare the results to this Chapter's Specifications. If the cylinder walls are tapered, out-of-round, worn beyond the specified limits, or badly scuffed or scored, have them rebored and honed by a dealer service department or a motorcycle repair shop. If a rebore is done, oversize pistons and rings will be required as well. **Note:** *Kawasaki supplies pistons in one oversize only - +0.020 in (+0.5 mm).*

9   As an alternative, if the precision measuring tools are not available, a dealer service department or motorcycle repair shop will make the measurements and offer advice concerning servicing of the cylinders.

10   If they are in reasonably good condition and not worn to the outside of the limits, and if the piston-to-cylinder clearances can be maintained properly (see Section 14), then the cylinders do not have to be rebored; honing is all that is necessary.

11   To perform the honing operation you will need the proper size flexible hone with fine stones, or a "bottle brush" type hone, plenty of light oil or honing oil, some shop towels and an electric drill motor. Hold the cylinder block in a vise (cushioned with soft jaws or wood blocks) when performing the honing operation. Mount the hone in the drill motor, compress the stones and slip the hone into the cylinder. Lubricate the cylinder thoroughly, turn on the drill and move the hone up and down in the cylinder at a pace which will produce a fine crosshatch pattern on the cylinder wall with the crosshatch lines intersecting at approximately a 60-degree angle. Be sure to use plenty of lubricant and do not take off any more material than is absolutely necessary to produce the desired effect. Do not withdraw the hone from the cylinder while it is running. Instead, shut off the drill and continue moving the hone up and down in the cylinder until it comes to a complete stop, then compress the stones and withdraw the hone. Wipe the oil out of the cylinder and repeat the procedure on the remaining cylinder. Remember, do not remove too much material from the cylinder wall. If you do not have the tools, or do not desire to perform the honing operation, a dealer service department or motorcycle repair shop will generally do it for a reasonable fee.

12   Next, the cylinders must be thoroughly washed with warm soapy water to remove all traces of the abrasive grit produced during the honing operation. Be sure to run a brush through the bolt holes and flush them with running water. After rinsing, dry the cylinders thoroughly and apply a coat of light, rust-preventative oil to all machined surfaces.

Installation

Refer to illustration 13.14

13   Lubricate the cylinder bores with plenty of clean engine oil. Apply a thin film of moly-based grease to the piston skirts.

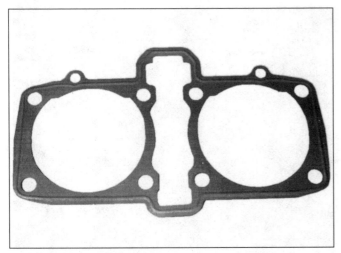

13.14 Install the base gasket with the ridge upward

14   Install the dowel pins, then place a new cylinder base gasket on the crankcase with the ripple in the gasket upward **(see illustration)**. Some gaskets also have an arrow, which must point to the front of the engine.

15   Slowly rotate the crankshaft until all of the pistons are at the same level. Slide lengths of welding rod or pieces of a straightened-out coat hanger under the pistons, on both sides of the connecting rods. This will help keep the pistons level as the cylinder block is lowered onto them.

16   Attach two piston ring compressors to the pistons and compress the piston rings. Large hose clamps can be used instead - just make sure they don't scratch the pistons, and don't tighten them too much.

17   Install the cylinder block over the pistons and carefully lower it down until the piston crowns fit into the cylinder liners. While doing this, pull the camshaft chain up, using a hooked tool or a piece of coat hanger. Push down on the cylinder block, making sure the pistons don't get cocked sideways, until the bottoms of the cylinder liners slide down past the piston rings. A wood or plastic hammer handle can be used to gently tap the block down, but don't use too much force or the pistons will be damaged.

18   Remove the piston ring compressors or hose clamps, being careful not to scratch the pistons. Remove the rods from under the pistons.

19   Install the cam chain rear guide **(see illustration 13.4)**.

20   The remainder of installation is the reverse of removal.

14   Pistons - removal, inspection and installation

1   The pistons are attached to the connecting rods with piston pins that are a slip fit in the pistons and rods.

2   Before removing the pistons from the rods, stuff a clean shop towel into each crankcase hole, around the connecting rods **(see illustration 13.6)**. This will prevent the circlips from falling into the crankcase if they are inadvertently dropped.

Removal

Refer to illustration 14.3

3   Using a sharp scribe, scratch the number of each piston into its crown. Each piston should also have an arrow pointing toward the front of the engine **(see illustration)**. If not, scribe an arrow into the piston crown before removal. Support the first piston, grasp the circlip with needle-nose pliers and remove it from the groove. If the pin won't come out, fabricate a piston pin removal tool from threaded stock (stud), nuts, washers and a piece of pipe.

4   Push the piston pin out from the opposite end to free the piston from the rod. You may have to deburr the area around the groove to enable the pin to slide out (use a triangular file for this procedure). Repeat the procedure for the other piston.

Inspection

Refer to illustrations 14.6, 14.11, 14.13, 14.14a, 14.14b and 14.15

5   Before the inspection process can be carried out, the pistons must be cleaned and the old piston rings removed.

6   Using a piston ring installation tool, carefully remove the rings from the pistons **(see illustration)**. Do not nick or gouge the pistons in the process.

7   Scrape all traces of carbon from the tops of the pistons. A hand-held wire brush or a piece of fine emery cloth can be used once most of the deposits have been scraped away. Do not, under any circumstances, use a wire brush mounted in a drill motor to remove deposits from the pistons; the piston material is soft and will be eroded away by the wire brush.

8   Use a piston ring groove cleaning tool to remove any carbon deposits from the ring grooves. If a tool is not available, a piece broken off the old ring will do the job. Be very careful to remove only the carbon deposits. Do not remove any metal and do not nick or gouge the sides of the ring grooves.

9   Once the deposits have been removed, clean the pistons with solvent and dry them thoroughly. Make sure the oil return holes below the oil ring grooves are clear.

10   If the pistons are not damaged or worn excessively and if the cylinders are not rebored, new pistons will not be necessary. Normal piston wear appears as even, vertical wear on the thrust surfaces of

14.3 Using a sharp scribe, scratch the cylinder numbers into the piston crowns - also note the arrow, which must point to the front

14.6 Remove the piston rings with a ring removal and installation tool

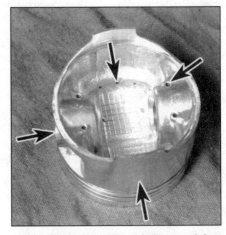

14.11 Check the piston pin bore and the piston skirt for wear, and make sure the internal holes are clear (arrows)

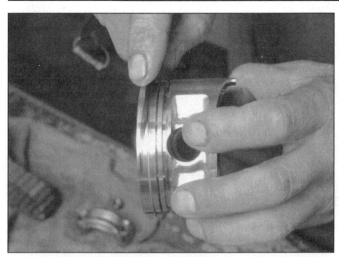

14.13 Measure the piston ring-to-groove clearance with a feeler gauge

14.14a Measure the piston diameter with a micrometer

the piston and slight looseness of the top ring in its groove. New piston rings, on the other hand, should always be used when an engine is rebuilt.

11   Carefully inspect each piston for cracks around the skirt, at the pin bosses and at the ring lands **(see illustration)**.

12   Look for scoring and scuffing on the thrust faces of the skirt, holes in the piston crown and burned areas at the edge of the crown. If the skirt is scored or scuffed, the engine may have been suffering from overheating and/or abnormal combustion, which caused excessively high operating temperatures. The oil pump and cooling system should be checked thoroughly. A hole in the piston crown, an extreme to be sure, is an indication that abnormal combustion (pre-ignition) was occurring. Burned areas at the edge of the piston crown are usually evidence of spark knock (detonation). If any of the above problems exist, the causes must be corrected or the damage will occur again.

13   Measure the piston ring-to-groove clearance by laying a new piston ring in the ring groove and slipping a feeler gauge in beside it **(see illustration)**. Check the clearance at three or four locations around the groove. Be sure to use the correct ring for each groove; they are different. If the clearance is greater than specified, new pistons will have to be used when the engine is reassembled.

14   Check the piston-to-bore clearance by measuring the bore (see Section 13) and the piston diameter. Make sure that the pistons and cylinders are correctly matched. Measure the piston across the skirt on the thrust faces at a 90-degree angle to the piston pin, about 1/2-inch (13 mm) up from the bottom of the skirt **(see illustration)**. Sub-

tract the piston diameter from the bore diameter to obtain the clearance. If it is greater than specified, the cylinders will have to be rebored and new oversized pistons and rings installed. If the appropriate precision measuring tools are not available, the piston-to-cylinder clearances can be obtained, though not quite as accurately, using feeler gauge stock. Feeler gauge stock comes in 12-inch lengths and various thicknesses and is generally available at auto parts stores. To check the clearance, select a 0.002 in (0.07 mm) feeler gauge and slip it into the cylinder along with the appropriate piston **(see illustration)**. The cylinder should be upside down and the piston must be positioned exactly as it normally would be. Place the feeler gauge between the piston and cylinder on one of the thrust faces (90-degrees to the piston pin bore). The piston should slip through the cylinder (with the feeler gauge in place) with moderate pressure. If it falls through, or slides through easily, the clearance is excessive and a new piston will be required. If the piston binds at the lower end of the cylinder and is loose toward the top, the cylinder is tapered, and if tight spots are encountered as the feeler gauge is placed at different points around the cylinder, the cylinder is out-of-round. Repeat the procedure for the remaining piston and cylinder. Be sure to have the cylinders and pistons checked by a dealer service department or a motorcycle repair shop to confirm your findings before purchasing new parts.

15   Apply clean engine oil to the pin, insert it into the piston and check for freeplay by rocking the pin back-and-forth **(see illustration)**. If the pin is loose, new pistons and pins must be installed.

16   Refer to Section 15 and install the rings on the pistons.

14.14b If you don't have a micrometer, piston clearance, out-of-round and cylinder taper can be measured with a piece of feeler gauge stock

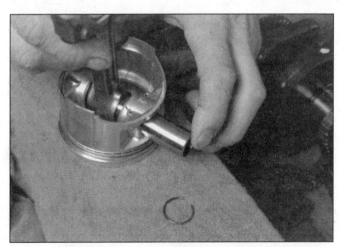

14.15 Slip the pin into the piston and try to wiggle it back-and-forth; if it's loose, replace the piston and pin

2

15.3a Square the ring in the bore by turning the piston upside down and tapping on the ring. . .

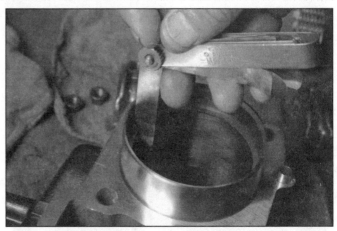

15.3b . . .then check the piston ring end gap with a feeler gauge

15.5 If the end gap is too small, clamp a file in a vise and file the ring ends (from the outside in only) to enlarge the gap slightly

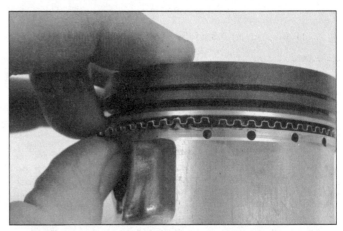

15.9a Installing the oil ring expander - make sure the ends don't overlap

Installation

17   Install the pistons in their original locations with the arrows pointing to the front of the engine. Lubricate the pins and the rod bores with clean engine oil. Install new circlips in the grooves in the inner sides of the pistons (don't reuse the old circlips). Push the pins into position from the opposite side and install new circlips. Compress the circlips only enough for them to fit in the piston. Make sure the clips are properly seated in the grooves.

---

15   Piston rings - installation

Refer to illustrations 15.3a, 15.3b, 15.5, 15.9a, 15.9b, 15.11, 15.12 and 15.15

1   Before installing the new piston rings, the ring end gaps must be checked.
2   Lay out the pistons and the new ring sets so the rings will be matched with the same piston and cylinder during the end gap measurement procedure and engine assembly.
3   Insert the top (No. 1) ring into the bottom of the first cylinder and square it up with the cylinder walls by pushing it in with the top of the piston **(see illustration)**. The ring should be about one inch above the bottom edge of the cylinder. To measure the end gap, slip a feeler gauge between the ends of the ring **(see illustration)** and compare the measurement to the Specifications.
4   If the gap is larger or smaller than specified, double check to make sure that you have the correct rings before proceeding.
5   If the gap is too small, it must be enlarged or the ring ends may come in contact with each other during engine operation, which can

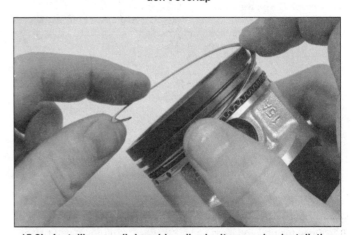

15.9b Installing an oil ring side rail - don't use a ring installation tool to do this

cause serious damage. The end gap can be increased by filing the ring ends very carefully with a fine file **(see illustration)**. When performing this operation, file only from the outside in.
6   Excess end gap is not critical unless it is greater than 0.040 in (1 mm). Again, double check to make sure you have the correct rings for your engine.
7   Repeat the procedure for each ring that will be installed in the first cylinder and for each ring in the remaining cylinder. Remember to keep the rings, pistons and cylinders matched up.

Cross Section of Piston Rings

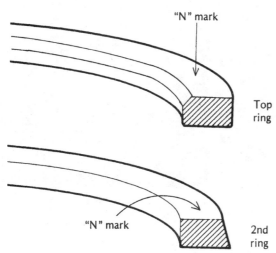

15.11 **Don't confuse the top ring with the second (middle) compression ring**

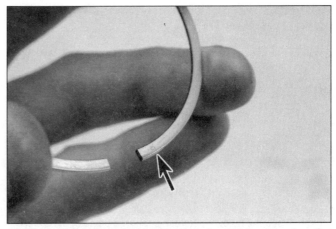

15.12 **Make sure the marks on the rings (arrow) face up when the rings are installed on the pistons**

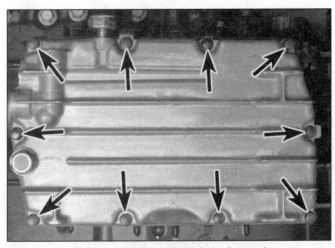

16.5a **Remove the oil pan bolts (arrows)**

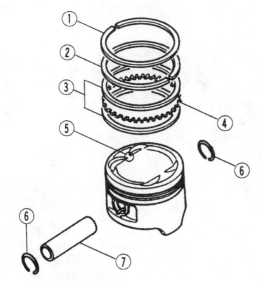

15.15 **Piston and piston ring details - when installing the oil ring side rails, stagger them approximately 30 to 40-degrees on either side of the top compression ring**

1	Top compression ring	4	Oil ring expander
2	Second compression ring	5	Arrow mark
3	Oil ring side rails	6	Circlip
		7	Piston pin

8   Once the ring end gaps have been checked/corrected, the rings can be installed on the pistons.

9   The oil control ring (lowest on the piston) is installed first. It is composed of three separate components. Slip the expander into the groove, then install the upper side rail **(see illustrations)**. Do not use a piston ring installation tool on the oil ring side rails as they may be damaged. Instead, place one end of the side rail into the groove between the spacer expander and the ring land. Hold it firmly in place and slide a finger around the piston while pushing the rail into the groove. Next, install the lower side rail in the same manner.

10   After the three oil ring components have been installed, check to make sure that both the upper and lower side rails can be turned smoothly in the ring groove.

11   Install the no. 2 (middle) ring next. It can be readily distinguished

from the top ring by its cross-section shape **(see illustration)**. Do not mix the top and middle rings.

12   To avoid breaking the ring, use a piston ring installation tool and make sure that the identification mark is facing up **(see illustration)**. Fit the ring into the middle groove on the piston. Do not expand the ring any more than is necessary to slide it into place.

13   Finally, install the no. 1 (top) ring in the same manner. Make sure the identifying mark is facing up.

14   Repeat the procedure for the remaining piston and rings. Be very careful not to confuse the no. 1 and no. 2 rings.

15   Once the rings have been properly installed, stagger the end gaps, including those of the oil ring side rails **(see illustration)**.

16 Oil pan - removal and installation

Refer to illustrations 16.5a and 16.5b
Note: *The oil pan can be removed with the engine in the frame.*

Removal

1   Set the bike on its centerstand.

2   Drain the engine oil and remove the oil filter (see Chapter 1).

3   Remove the exhaust system (see Chapter 4).

4   Remove the small screw and disconnect the wire from the oil pressure switch (see Chapter 9).

5   Remove the oil pan bolts and detach the pan from the crankcase **(see illustrations)**.

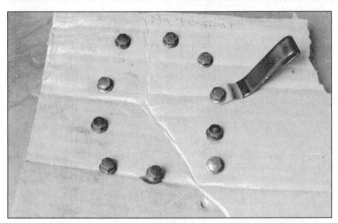

16.5b Place the bolts in a holder, such as a piece of cardboard with holes punched in it - the bolt that goes next to the oil pressure switch also secures a wiring harness retainer

16.7 Make sure the O-rings are in position (arrows); the three O-rings to the left have a flat side, which goes upward (against the crankcase and away from the oil pan)

6   Remove all traces of old gasket material from the mating surfaces of the oil pan and crankcase.

Installation

Refer to illustration 16.7

7   Check the small O-rings in the oil passages in the crankcase and the large O-ring around the oil filter hole (in the pan) for cracking and general deterioration **(see illustration)**. Replace them if necessary.

The flat side of the O-rings must face the crankcase.

8   Position a new gasket on the oil pan. A thin film of RTV sealant can be used to hold the gasket in place. Install the oil pan and bolts, tightening the bolts to the torque listed in this Chapter's Specifications, using a criss-cross pattern.

9   The remainder of installation is the reverse of removal. Install a new filter and fill the crankcase with oil (see Chapter 1), then run the engine and check for leaks.

17.2 To check the oil pressure, remove the plug (arrow) and connect an oil pressure gauge using the proper adapter

17.8 Unbolt the pickup from the pump so you can inspect the O-ring - use non-permanent thread locking agent on the bolt threads during assembly

17.9 Remove the snap-ring and the pump drive gear

17.10 Remove the pump mounting bolts

17.11 Lift out the pump and its oil pipe; if necessary, unbolt the pipe from the pump and remove them separately

17.16 The recessed side of the drive gear faces away from the oil pump - the snap-ring fits into the recess

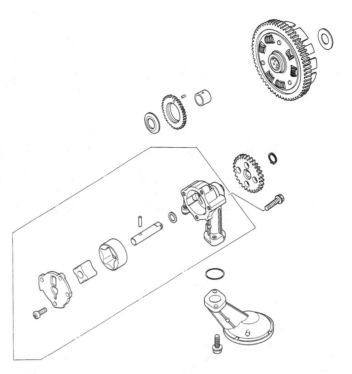

17.12 Oil pump - exploded view

again, at the specified engine rpm. Compare your findings with this Chapter's Specifications.

6　If the pressure is significantly lower than specified, check the relief valve and the oil pump.

Removal

Refer to illustrations 17.8, 17.9, 17.10 and 17.11

7　Remove the engine and disassemble the crankcase (see Sections 5 and 22).

8　Remove the oil pump pickup tube from the pump so you can inspect the O-ring **(see illustration)**.

9　Remove the snap-ring and detach the oil pump gear from the shaft **(see illustration)**.

10　Remove the pump mounting bolts **(see illustration)**.

11　Remove the pump and its oil pipe **(see illustration)**.

Inspection

Refer to illustration 17.12

12　Remove the oil pump cover screws and lift off the cover **(see illustration)**.

13　Remove the oil pump shaft, pin, inner rotor and outer rotor from the pump. Mark the rotors so they can be installed in the same relative positions.

14　Wash all the components in solvent, then dry them off. Check the pump body, the rotors and the cover for scoring and wear. Make sure the pick-up screen isn't clogged. Kawasaki doesn't publish clearance specifications, so if any damage or uneven or excessive wear is evident, replace the pump (individual parts aren't available). If you are rebuilding the engine, it's a good idea to install a new oil pump.

15　Reassemble the pump by reversing the disassembly steps, but before installing it, prime it by pouring oil into it while turning the shaft by hand - this will ensure that it begins to pump oil quickly.

Installation

Refer to illustration 17.16

16　Installation is the reverse of removal, with the following additions:

　a) Make sure the pickup O-ring is in place.

17 Oil pump - pressure check, removal, inspection and installation

Note: *Oil pump removal requires that the engine be removed and the crankcase disassembled.*

Check

Refer to illustration 17.2

Warning: *If the oil passage plug is removed when the engine is hot, hot oil will drain out - wait until the engine is cold before beginning this check (it must be cold to perform the relief valve opening pressure check, anyway).*

1　Remove the lower fairing (if equipped) (see Chapter 8).

2　Remove the plug at the bottom of the crankcase on the right-hand side and install an oil pressure gauge **(see illustration)**.

3　Start the engine and watch the gauge while varying the engine rpm. The pressure should stay within the relief valve opening pressure listed in this Chapter's Specifications. If the pressure is too high, the relief valve is stuck closed. To check it, see Section 18.

4　If the pressure is lower than the standard, either the relief valve is stuck open, the oil pump is faulty, or there is other engine damage. Begin diagnosis by checking the relief valve (see Section 18), then the oil pump. If those items check out okay, chances are the bearing oil clearances are excessive and the engine needs to be overhauled.

5　If the pressure reading is in the desired range, allow the engine to warm up to normal operating temperature and check the pressure

18.2 Location of the oil pressure relief valve (arrow)

19.3 Loosen the forward clutch cable nut to create slack

19.4 Disengage the end of the cable from the release lever

b) Use non-permanent thread locking agent on the pickup mounting screws and the oil pump mounting screws.
c) Install the drive gear with its recessed side away from the pump (see illustration).

---

18   Oil pressure relief valve - removal, inspection and installation

---

Refer to illustration 18.2

Removal

1   Remove the oil pan (see Section 16).
2   Unscrew the relief valve from the oil pan **(see illustration)**.

Inspection

3   Clean the valve with solvent and dry it, using compressed air if available.
4   Using a wood or plastic tool, depress the steel ball inside the valve and see if it moves smoothly. Make sure it returns to its seat completely. If it doesn't, replace it with a new one (don't attempt to disassemble and repair it).

Installation

5   Apply a non-permanent thread locking compound to the threads of the valve and install it into the oil pan, tightening it to the torque listed in this Chapter's Specifications.
6   The remainder of installation is the reverse of removal.

---

19   Clutch - removal, inspection and installation

Note: *The clutch (except the housing) can be removed with the engine in the frame. Removal of the housing requires that the engine be removed and the crankcase disassembled.*

Removal

Refer to illustrations 19.3, 19.4, 19.5a, 19.5b, 19.5c, 19.6a, 19.6b, 19.7, 19.8, 19.9a and 19.9b

1   Set the bike on its centerstand. Remove the lower fairing (if equipped) (see Chapter 8).
2   Drain the engine oil (see Chapter 1).
3   Completely loosen the forward adjustment nut on the clutch cable at its bracket on the clutch cover **(see illustration)**.
4   Pull the cable out of the bracket, then detach the cable end from the lever **(see illustration)**.
5   Remove the clutch cover bolts and take the cover off together with the release lever **(see illustrations)**. If the cover is stuck, tap around its perimeter with a soft-face hammer.
6   Loosen the clutch spring bolts in a criss-cross pattern **(see illustration)**. To prevent the assembly from turning, thread one of the cover mounting bolts into the case and wedge a screwdriver between the bolt and the clutch housing. Remove the clutch springs, spring plate and bearing **(see illustration)**.
7   Note the direction of the radial grooves in the friction plate, then remove the pushrod, friction plates and steel plates from the clutch housing **(see illustration)**.

19.5a Remove the clutch cover bolts (arrows). . .

19.5b . . .take the cover off (tap it gently with a soft-faced hammer if it's stuck). . .

19.5c . . .and note the location of the cover dowel

19.6a Loosen the spring bolts in a criss-cross pattern. . .

19.6b When spring tension is released, remove the springs and the spring plate

19.7 Remove the clutch pushrod from the hub, then remove the friction plates and metal plates - note the direction of the grooves in the friction plates; they must be reinstalled the same way

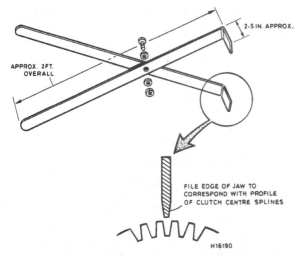

2.5 IN. APPROX.

APPROX. 2 FT. OVERALL

FILE EDGE OF JAW TO CORRESPOND WITH PROFILE OF CLUTCH CENTRE SPLINES

H16190

19.8 You can make your own clutch holding tool out of steel strap

8   Remove the clutch hub nut, using a special holding tool (Kawasaki tool no. 57001-305 or 1243) to prevent the clutch housing from turning. An alternative to this tool can be fabricated from some steel strap, bent at the ends and bolted together in the middle **(see illustration)**. The nut is self-locking, so discard it and replace it with a new one during installation.

9   Remove the washer, clutch hub and thrust washer **(see illustrations)**.

19.9a Remove the nut and washer, then remove the clutch hub and thrust washer

2

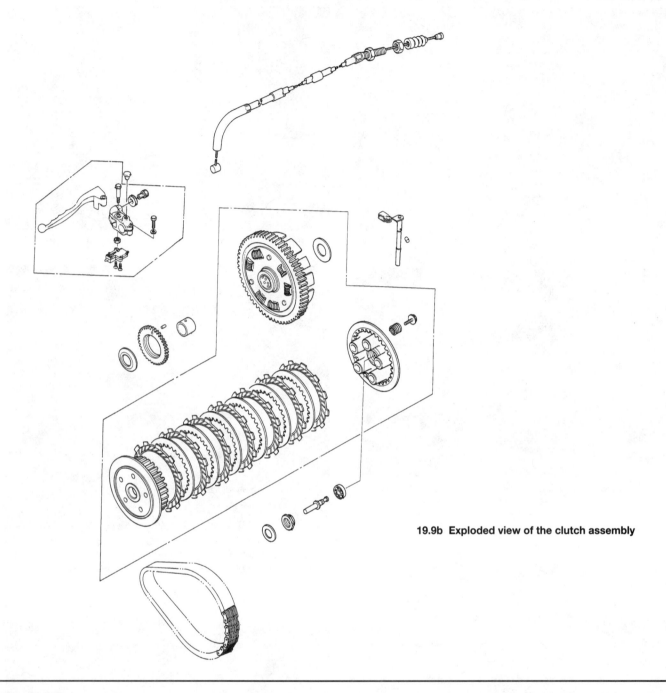

19.9b Exploded view of the clutch assembly

Inspection

Refer to illustrations 19.10, 19.11, 19.12, 19.13, 19.15 and 19.16

10   Examine the splines on both the inside and the outside of the clutch hub **(see illustration)**. If any wear is evident, replace the hub with a new one.

11   Measure the free length of the clutch springs **(see illustration)** and compare the results to this Chapter's Specifications. If the springs have sagged, or if cracks are noted, replace them with new ones as a set.

12   If the lining material of the friction plates smells burnt or if it is glazed, new parts are required. If the metal clutch plates are scored or discolored, they must be replaced with new ones. Measure the thickness of each friction plate **(see illustration)** and compare the results to this Chapter's Specifications. Replace with new parts any friction plates that are near the wear limit.

13   Lay the metal plates, one at a time, on a perfectly flat surface (such as a piece of plate glass) and check for warpage by trying to slip

a 0.012-inch (0.3 mm) feeler gauge between the flat surface and the plate **(see illustration)**. Do this at several places around the plate's circumference. If the feeler gauge can be slipped under the plate, it is warped and should be replaced with a new one.

14   Check the tabs on the friction plates for excessive wear and mushroomed edges. They can be cleaned up with a file if the deformation is not severe.

15   Check the edges of the slots in the clutch housing for indentations made by the friction plate tabs **(see illustration)**. If the indentations are deep they can prevent clutch release, so the housing should be replaced with a new one. If the indentations can be removed easily with a file, the life of the housing can be prolonged to an extent.

16   Check the clutch spring plate for wear and damage and make sure the pushrod is not bent (roll it on a perfectly flat surface or use V-blocks and a dial indicator). Check the fit of the pushrod in the spring plate bearing **(see illustration)**. Check the bearing for wear or damage. Replace the pushrod and bearing if they're worn.

**19.10 Check the clutch hub splines (arrows) for wear
and distortion**

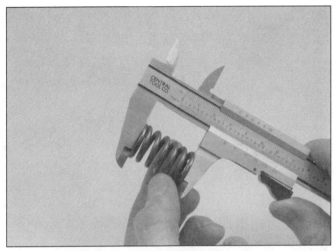

19.11 Measure the clutch spring free length

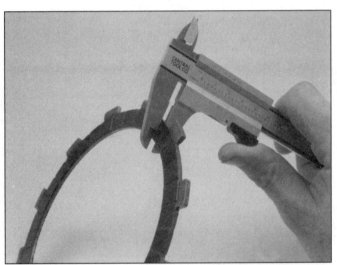

19.12 Measure the thickness of the friction plates

19.13 Check the metal plates for warpage

**19.15 Check the slots on the clutch hub for indentations - if
they're worn, the crankcase will have to be disassembled to
remove the clutch hub**

**19.16 Check the pushrod and the bearing in the spring plate for
wear and damage**

2

21.2 Remove the shift pedal Allen bolt

21.3 Remove the pinch bolt from the bottom of the shift lever

17   Clean all traces of old gasket material from the clutch cover. If the release shaft seal has been leaking, it can be replaced by removing the positioning bolt on the outside of the housing and pulling out the shaft. The seal can then be pried out and a new one driven in, using a hammer and a socket with an outside diameter slightly smaller than that of the seal.

Installation

18   Install the clutch housing thrust washer and the clutch hub. Install a new hub nut and tighten it to the torque listed in this Chapter's Specifications. Use the technique described in Step 8 to prevent the hub from turning.
19   Coat the clutch friction plates with engine oil. Install the clutch plates, starting with a friction plate and alternating them. There are seven friction plates and six steel plates. Be sure the radial grooves in the friction plates are pointed in the correct direction **(see illustration 19.7)**.
20   Lubricate the pushrod and install it through the spring plate. Mount the spring plate to the clutch assembly and install the springs and bolts, tightening them to the torque listed in this Chapter's Specifications in a criss-cross pattern.
21   Make sure the clutch cover dowel is in place **(see illustration 19.5c)**. Install the clutch cover and bolts, using a new gasket. Tighten the bolts, in a criss-cross pattern, to the torque listed in this Chapter's Specifications.
22   Connect the clutch cable to the release lever and adjust the freeplay (see Chapter 1).
23   Fill the crankcase with the recommended type and amount of engine oil (see Chapter 1).

20   Clutch cable - replacement

1   Disconnect the upper end of the clutch cable from the lever (see Chapter 1).
2   Disconnect the clutch cable from the release lever (see Section 19).
3   Before removing the cable from the bike, tape the lower end of the new cable to the upper end of the old cable. Slowly pull the lower end of the old cable out, guiding the new cable down into position. Using this method will ensure the cable is routed correctly.
4   Lubricate the cable (see Chapter 1). Reconnect the ends of the cable by reversing the removal procedure, then adjust the cable following the procedure given in Chapter 1.

21.4 Remove the retaining clip from the shift shaft

21   External shift mechanism - removal, inspection and installation

Shift lever and pedal

Refer to illustrations 21.2, 21.3, 21.4 and 21.5
1   Set the bike on its centerstand.
2   Remove the shift pedal bolt **(see illustration)**.
3   Remove the shift lever bolt **(see illustration)**.
4   To ease installation, make alignment marks on the shift lever shaft and the shift lever. Pry out the retaining clip and pull the shift lever off the shaft **(see illustration)**.
5   Installation is the reverse of removal. The shift linkage shaft should be at 90-degrees to the shift lever, as well as to the lever portion of the shift pedal. Adjust as needed with the nuts on the linkage shaft **(see illustration)**.

Shift mechanism

Refer to illustrations 21.9, 21.10, 21.11a and 21.11b
6   Remove the shift pedal and linkage (Steps 1 through 4).
7   Remove the drive chain, engine sprocket and chain guard (see Chapter 6).
8   Disconnect the electrical connector from the neutral switch (see Chapter 9).

21.5 Loosen the locknuts and turn the linkage rod so it's at 90-degrees to the shift lever and the lever portion of the shift pedal

21.9 Remove the cover bolts (A) - the larger bolt (B) secures the bottom end of the drive chain guard

21.10 Compress the shift arm (A) to disengage it from the shift cam, and slide the shift shaft (B) off the pin

21.11a Remove the nut (A) and detach the washer, gear positioning lever, spring and washer. Note return spring pin (B).

9   Remove the shift mechanism cover bolts and remove the cover **(see illustration)**.

10   Compress the shift mechanism arm against the spring tension to disengage it from the shift drum cam **(see illustration)**. Slide the shift mechanism off the shaft.

11   Remove the nut from the gear positioning lever **(see illustration)**. Remove the locating washer, lever, spring and washer **(see illustration)**.

Inspection

12   Check the shift shaft for bends and damage to the splines. If the shaft is bent, you can attempt to straighten it, but if the splines are damaged it will have to be replaced.

13   Check the condition of the gear positioning lever and spring, pin plate and shift drum cam. Replace them if they are cracked or distorted.

14   Check the shift mechanism arm for cracks, distortion and wear. If any of these conditions are found, replace the shift mechanism.

15   Make sure the return spring pin isn't loose. If it is, unscrew it, apply a non-permanent locking compound to the threads, then reinstall the pin and tighten it securely.

16   Check the condition of the seal in the cover. If it has been leaking, drive it out with a hammer and punch. Drive a new seal in with a socket.

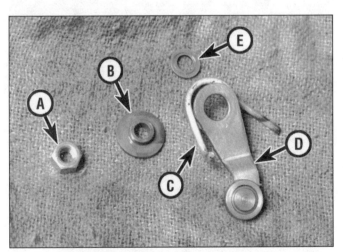

21.11b Details of the gear positioning lever

A) Nut
B) Washer (the collar fits inside the gear positioning lever hole)
C) Spring
D) Gear positioning lever
E) Washer

2

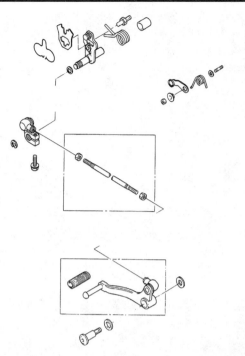

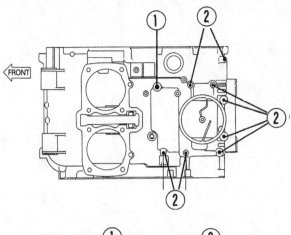

21.17 Shift pedal and external shift mechanism - exploded view

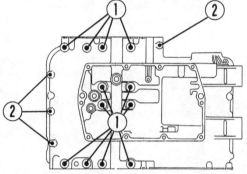

22.6a Loosen the small upper case bolts first, then the large bolt. . .

| 1) | Large bolts (8 mm) | 2) | Small bolts (6 mm) |

22.6b . . .and place them in order in a holder (a piece of cardboard with holes punched in it works well)

Installation

Refer to illustration 21.17

17   Slide the external shift mechanism into place, compressing the shift arm against the spring to clear the shift drum. Make sure the springs are positioned correctly **(see illustration)**.

18   Apply high-temperature grease to the lip of the seal. Wrap the splines of the shift shaft with electrical tape, so the splines won't damage the seal as the cover is installed.

19   Carefully guide the cover into place and install the screws, tightening them securely.

20   Install the engine sprocket, drive chain and engine sprocket cover (see Chapter 6).

21   Install and adjust the shift pedal and linkage (see Steps 1 through 5).

22   Check the engine oil level and add some, if necessary (see Chapter 1).

22   Crankcase - disassembly and reassembly

1   To examine and repair or replace the crankshaft, connecting rods, bearings, clutch housing, transmission components, balancer and starter motor clutch, the crankcase must be split into two parts.

2   Remove the clutch cover (see Section 19) and the external shift mechanism (see Section 21).

3   Remove the water pump and coolant pipe (on the cylinder block) (see Chapter 3).

4   Remove the alternator cover (see Chapter 9).

Disassembly

Refer to illustrations 22.6a, 22.6b, 22.9a, 22.9b, 22.9c, 22.10, 22.11a, 22.11b, 22.11c and 22.12

5   If the crankcase is being separated to remove the crankshaft, remove the alternator rotor and the stator (see Chapter 9), cylinder head, cylinder block and pistons (see Sections 10, 13 and 14).   Remove the clutch if you are separating the crankcase halves to disassemble the transmission main drive shaft (see Section 19).

6   Remove the small upper crankcase half bolts, then the single large bolt **(see illustrations)**.

7   Turn the engine upside-down and remove the oil filter (see Chapter 1, if necessary).

8   Remove the oil pan (see Section 16) and retrieve the O-rings from the oil passages.

9   Remove the oil pump outer pipe and main oil pipe connecting pipe **(see illustrations)**.

10   Remove the small lower crankcase half bolts, then the large bolts **(see illustration 22.6a and the accompanying illustration)**.

11   Carefully pry the crankcase apart. Pry ONLY in the areas indicated **(see illustrations)**.

12   Separate the crankcase halves **(see illustration)**.

22.9a Remove the mounting bolt and lift out the outer oil pipe

22.9b Remove the main oil pipe connecting bolt on the side of the case (arrow). . .

22.9c . . .and one in the oil pan (upper arrow), then disconnect the oil pipe from the engine (lower arrow)

22.10 The tightening sequence numbers for the large lower case bolts are cast into the case (arrows)

22.11a Pry only at the pry points; there's one on the end of the case (arrow). . .

22.11b . . .one on the clutch side (arrow). . .

22.11c . . .and one on the alternator side (arrow)

2

22.12 Lift the lower case half off the upper case half

22.15a Note the location of the case dowels (arrow). . .

22.15b . . .there's one in each end of the case

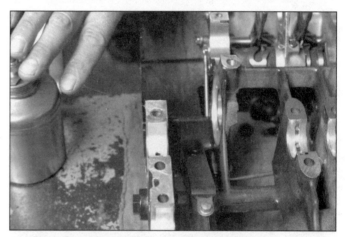

22.16 Spread a thin layer of gasket sealant on the mating surfaces, but don't place it too close to the bearings

22.17a When the shift drum is in neutral, the gear positioning lever fits into the slot in the shift cam (arrow)

22.17b The shift forks should be in the Neutral position. . .

13   Refer to Sections 23 through 31 for information on the internal components of the crankcase.

Reassembly

Refer to illustrations 22.15a, 22.15b, 22.16, 22.17a, 22.17b, 22.17c and 22.18

14   Remove all traces of sealant from the crankcase mating surfaces. Be careful not to let any fall into the case as this is done.

15   Check to make sure the two dowel pins are in place in their holes in the mating surface of the upper crankcase half **(see illustrations)**. Pour some engine oil over the transmission gears, the crankshaft main bearings and the shift drum. Don't get any oil on the crankcase mating surface.

16   Apply a thin, even bead of Kawasaki Bond sealant (part no. 56019-120) to the indicated areas of the crankcase mating surfaces **(see illustration)**. **Caution:** *Don't apply an excessive amount of*

22.17c ...and so should the fork slots in the gears (arrows) - while you're checking the gears, take a good look to make sure nothing is in the case that doesn't belong there

22.18 Be sure both ends of the breather tube fit into their holes when the cases are assembled (transmission output shaft removed for clarity)

sealant, and don't apply it next to the bearing inserts, as it will ooze out when the case halves are assembled and may obstruct oil passages and prevent the bearings from seating.

17   Check the position of the shift drum, shift forks and transmission shafts - make sure they're in the neutral position **(see illustrations)**.

18   Carefully assemble the crankcase halves. While doing this, make sure the shift forks fit into their gear grooves, and guide the breather tube into its hole in the lower crankcase half **(see illustration)**.

19   Install the lower crankcase half bolts and tighten them so they are just snug.

20   In two steps, tighten the larger bolts (8 mm), in the indicated sequence, to the torque listed in this Chapter's Specifications **(see illustration 22.6a)**.

21   Install the smaller (6 mm) bolts in the lower crankcase half, tightening them to the torque listed in this Chapter's Specifications.

22   Install the main oil connecting pipe **(see illustration 22.9b)**. Use new O-rings coated lightly with engine oil.

23   Apply engine oil to both ends of the oil pump outer pipe, then install the ends in their holes **(see illustration 22.9a)**. Apply non-permanent thread locking compound to the bolt that secures the outer pipe.

24   Install the oil pan (see Section 16).

25   Turn the case over and install the upper crankcase half bolts. Tighten the large (8 mm bolt) first, then tighten the others in the indicated sequence to the torque listed in this Chapter's Specifications **(see illustration 22.6a)**.

26   Turn the main drive shaft and the output shaft to make sure they turn freely. Also make sure the crankshaft turns freely.

27   The remainder of installation is the reverse of removal, with the following additions:

a) Once the external shift linkage is installed, shift the transmission through all the gear positions and back to Neutral. Because the positive neutral finder locks out second gear when the output shaft isn't spinning, you'll have to spin the output shaft to shift into second through sixth gears.

b) Be sure to refill the engine oil and coolant.

23   Crankcase components - inspection and servicing

Refer to illustrations 23.2a, 23.2b, 23.2c, 23.3, 23.4, 23.5, 23.6a and 23.6b

1   After the crankcases have been separated and the crankshaft, shift drum and forks and transmission components removed, the crankcases should be cleaned thoroughly with new solvent and dried with compressed air.

2   Remove any oil pipes that haven't already been removed. All oil passages and pipes should be blown out with compressed air **(see illustrations)**.

3   Remove the breather body **(see illustration)**. Inspect its O-ring; it's a good idea to install a new one.

2

23.2a Remove the oil line from the left front corner of the case...

23.2b ...the line farther back along the left side...

23.2c . . .and the oil passage plug so all the lines and passages can be cleaned

23.3 The breather body is secured by the center bolt (arrow)

23.4 Small burrs can be removed from the gasket surfaces with a fine sharpening stone

23.5 Check both primary chain guides for wear (the lower one is shown here) and replace them if necessary

23.6a Remove this lock-pin if you plan to remove the cam chain guide - DO NOT forget to reinstall it, or the chain guide retaining pin could slide out and damage the crankshaft while it's spinning. . .

23.6b . . .after removing the crankshaft, pull out the retaining pin and remove the cam chain guide

4   All traces of old gasket sealant should be removed from the mating surfaces. Minor damage to the surfaces can be cleaned up with a fine sharpening stone **(see illustration)**. **Caution:** *Be very careful not to nick or gouge the crankcase mating surfaces or leaks will result. Check both crankcase sections very carefully for cracks and other damage.*

5   Check the primary chain guides for wear - one is in the upper

case half and the other is in the lower case half **(see illustration)**. If they appear to be worn excessively, replace them.

6   Check the front cam chain guide for wear. If it's worn, remove the lock-pin **(see illustration)**. The retaining pin **(see illustration)** and chain guide can be removed after the crankshaft has been removed (see Section 25).

7   If any damage is found that can't be repaired, replace the crankcase halves as a set.

25.2 Slip the clutch housing back-and-forth to expose the inner bearing sleeve (arrow), then pull it out

25.3a Lift the clutch housing and transmission main drive shaft. . .

24 Main and connecting rod bearings - general note

1   Even though main and connecting rod bearings are generally replaced with new ones during the engine overhaul, the old bearings should be retained for close examination as they may reveal valuable information about the condition of the engine.

2   Bearing failure occurs mainly because of lack of lubrication, the presence of dirt or other foreign particles, overloading the engine and/or corrosion. Regardless of the cause of bearing failure, it must be corrected before the engine is reassembled to prevent it from happening again.

3   When examining the bearings, remove the main bearings from the case halves and the rod bearings from the connecting rods and caps and lay them out on a clean surface in the same general position as their location on the crankshaft journals. This will enable you to match any noted bearing problems with the corresponding side of the crankshaft journal.

4   Dirt and other foreign particles get into the engine in a variety of ways. It may be left in the engine during assembly or it may pass through filters or breathers. It may get into the oil and from there into the bearings. Metal chips from machining operations and normal engine wear are often present. Abrasives are sometimes left in engine components after reconditioning operations such as cylinder honing, especially when parts are not thoroughly cleaned using the proper cleaning methods. Whatever the source, these foreign objects often end up imbedded in the soft bearing material and are easily recognized. Large particles will not imbed in the bearing and will score or gouge the bearing and journal. The best prevention for this cause of bearing failure is to clean all parts thoroughly and keep everything spotlessly clean during engine reassembly. Frequent and regular oil and filter changes are also recommended.

5   Lack of lubrication or lubrication breakdown has a number of interrelated causes. Excessive heat (which thins the oil), overloading (which squeezes the oil from the bearing face) and oil leakage or throw off (from excessive bearing clearances, worn oil pump or high engine speeds) all contribute to lubrication breakdown. Blocked oil passages will also starve a bearing and destroy it. When lack of lubrication is the cause of bearing failure, the bearing material is wiped or extruded from the steel backing of the bearing. Temperatures may increase to the point where the steel backing and the journal turn blue from overheating.

6   Riding habits can have a definite effect on bearing life. Full throttle low speed operation, or lugging (labouring) the engine, puts very high loads on bearings, which tend to squeeze out the oil film. These loads cause the bearings to flex, which produces fine cracks in the bearing face (fatigue failure). Eventually the bearing material will loosen in pieces and tear away from the steel backing. Short trip riding leads to corrosion of bearings, as insufficient engine heat is produced to drive off the condensed water and corrosive gases produced. These

25.3b . . .and disengage the housing from the primary chain

products collect in the engine oil, forming acid and sludge. As the oil is carried to the engine bearings, the acid attacks and corrodes the bearing material.

7   Incorrect bearing installation during engine assembly will lead to bearing failure as well. Tight fitting bearings which leave insufficient bearing oil clearances result in oil starvation. Dirt or foreign particles trapped behind a bearing insert result in high spots on the bearing which lead to failure.

8   To avoid bearing problems, clean all parts thoroughly before reassembly, double check all bearing clearance measurements and lubricate the new bearings with engine assembly lube or moly-based grease during installation.

25 Clutch hub, crankshaft and main bearings - removal, inspection, main bearing selection and installation

Clutch housing removal
Refer to illustrations 25.2, 25.3a and 25.3b

1   If you haven't already done so, remove all clutch components except the housing (see Section 19).

2   Slide the clutch housing back and forth on the shaft within the limits allowed by the primary chain to expose the inner bearing **(see illustration)**. Pull the bearing out.

3   Lift the transmission main drive shaft and clutch hub from the case **(see illustration)**. Slip the transmission shaft out of the clutch housing and disengage the housing from the primary chain **(see illustration)**.

25.5 Measure the endplay with a feeler gauge inserted between the no. 2 crank journal and the case web - if the endplay isn't as listed in this Chapter's Specifications, the case halves must be replaced

25.6 The crankshaft, primary chain and cam chain

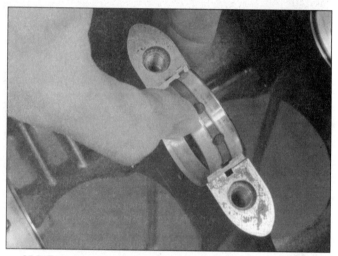

25.7 To remove a main bearing insert, push it sideways and lift it out

25.8 Inspect the bearing in the center of the clutch housing - replace the clutch housing if it's worn or damaged

Crankshaft removal

Refer to illustrations 25.5, 25.6 and 25.7

4   If you haven't already done so, remove the connecting rod caps (see Section 26).

5   Before removing the crankshaft check the endplay. This can be done with a dial indicator mounted in-line with the crankshaft, or feeler gauges inserted between the crankshaft and no. 2 crankcase main journal **(see illustration)**. Compare your findings with this Chapter's Specifications. If the endplay is excessive, the case halves must be replaced.

6   Lift the crankshaft out, together with the cam chain and primary chain and set them on a clean surface **(see illustration)**.

7   The main bearing inserts can be removed from their saddles by pushing their centers to the side, then lifting them out **(see illustration)**. Keep the bearing inserts in order. The main bearing oil clearance should be checked, however, before removing the inserts (see Step 13).

Inspection

Refer to illustrations 25.8 and 25.10

8   Check the clutch hub bearing for wear or damage **(see illustration)**. Replace the clutch hub if necessary. Also inspect the slots in the hub (see Section 19).

9   If you haven't already done so, mark and remove the connecting

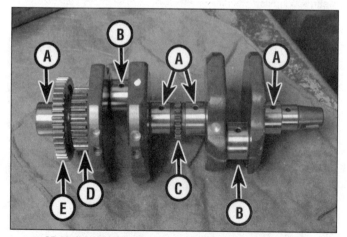

25.10 Inspect the crankshaft at the following points:

A) *Main bearing journals*
B) *Connecting rod journals*
C) *Cam chain gear*
D) *Primary chain gear*
E) *Balancer gear*

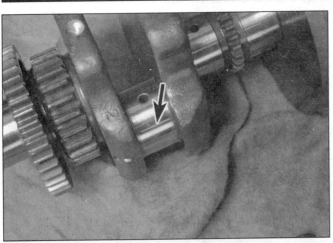

25.13 Lay the Plastigage strips (arrow) on the journals, parallel to the crankshaft centerline

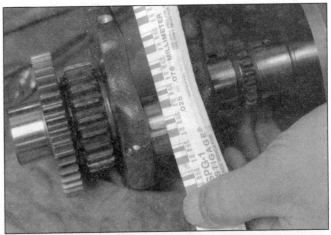

25.15 Measuring the width of the crushed Plastigage (be sure to use the correct scale - standard and metric are included)

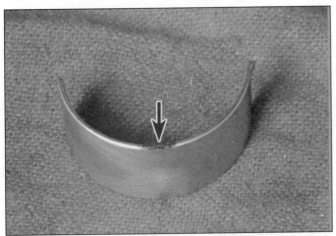

25.16 Bearing thicknesses are identified by color codes on the sides of the bearings

25.18 Measure the diameter of each crankshaft journal at several points to detect taper and out-of-round conditions

rods from the crankshaft (see Section 26).

10   Clean the crankshaft with solvent, using a rifle-cleaning brush to scrub out the oil passages. If available, blow the crank dry with compressed air. Check the main and connecting rod journals for uneven wear, scoring and pits **(see illustration)**. Rub a copper coin across the journal several times - if a journal picks up copper from the coin, it's too rough. Replace the crankshaft.

11   Check the balancer gear, camshaft chain gear and primary chain gear on the crankshaft for chipped teeth and other wear. If any undesirable conditions are found, replace the crankshaft. Check the chains as described in Section 28. Check the rest of the crankshaft for cracks and other damage. It should be magnafluxed to reveal hidden cracks - a dealer service department or motorcycle machine shop will handle the procedure.

12   Set the crankshaft on V-blocks and check the runout with a dial indicator touching one of the center main journals, comparing your findings with this Chapter's Specifications. If the runout exceeds the limit, replace the crank.

Main bearing selection

Refer to illustrations 25.13, 25.15, 25.16, 25.18, 25.20, 25.21 and 25.22

13   To check the main bearing oil clearance, clean off the bearing inserts (and reinstall them, if they've been removed from the case) and lower the crankshaft into the upper half of the case. Cut four pieces of Plastigage (type HPG-1) and lay them on the crankshaft main journals, parallel with the journal axis **(see illustration)**.

14   Very carefully, guide the lower case half down onto the upper case half. Install the large (8 mm) bolts and tighten them, using the recommended sequence, to the torque listed in this Chapter's Specifications (see Section 22). Don't rotate the crankshaft!

15   Now, remove the bolts and carefully lift the lower case half off. Compare the width of the crushed Plastigage on each journal to the scale printed on the Plastigage envelope to obtain the main bearing oil clearance **(see illustration)**. Write down your findings, then remove all traces of Plastigage from the journals, using your fingernail or the edge of a credit card.

16   If the oil clearance falls into the specified range, no bearing replacement is required (provided they are in good shape). If the clearance is more than the standard range, but within the service limit, replace the bearing inserts with inserts that have blue paint marks **(see illustration)**, then check the oil clearance once again (these are the thickest bearing inserts, and may be thick enough to bring bearing clearance within the specified range). Always replace all of the inserts at the same time.

17   The clearance might be slightly greater than the standard clearance, but that doesn't matter, as long as it isn't greater than the maximum clearance or less than the minimum clearance.

18   If the clearance is greater than the service limit listed in this Chapter's Specifications, measure the diameter of the crankshaft journals with a micrometer **(see illustration)** and compare your findings with this Chapter's Specifications. Also, by measuring the diameter at a number of points around each journal's circumference, you'll be able to determine whether or not the journal is out-of-round. Take the

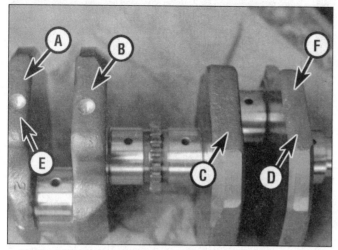

25.20 Use the marks (or absence of marks) on the crankshaft (this crankshaft has no marks). . .

A) No. 1 main bearing journal mark
B) No. 2 main bearing journal mark
C) No. 3 main bearing journal mark
D) No. 4 main bearing journal mark
E) No. 1 connecting rod journal mark
F) No. 2 connecting rod journal mark

25.21 . . .in conjunction with the marks (or absence of marks) on the case (this case has no marks)

A) No. 1 main bearing bore mark
B) No. 2 main bearing bore mark
C) No. 3 main bearing bore mark
D) No. 4 main bearing bore mark

Crankshaft Main Bearing Insert Selection

Crankcase Main Bearing Bore Diameter Mark	Crankshaft Main Journal Diameter Mark	Bearing Insert*		
		Size Color	Part Number	Journal Nos.
○	1	Brown	92028-1102	2, 3
			92028-1274	1, 4
None	None	Blue	92028-1100	3
			92028-1272	1, 4
○	None	Black	92028-1101	2, 3
None	1		92028-1273	1, 4

*The bearing inserts for Nos. 2 and 3 journals have oil grooves.

25.22 . . .to determine the proper main bearing sizes

measurement at each end of the journal, near the crank throws, to determine if the journal is tapered.

19   If any crank journal has worn down past the service limit, replace the crankshaft.

20   If the diameters of the journals aren't less than the service limit but differ from the original markings on the crankshaft **(see illustration)**, apply new marks with a hammer and punch.

   If the journal measures within the "no mark" range listed in the Specifications, don't make any marks on the crank (there shouldn't be any marks there, anyway).

   If the journal measures within the "1" mark range listed in the Specifications, make a "1" mark on the crank in the area indicated (if it's not already there).

21   Remove the main bearing inserts and assemble the case halves (see Section 22). Using a telescoping gauge and a micrometer, measure the diameters of the main bearing bores, then compare the measurements with the marks on the upper case half **(see illustration)**. Compare the bore measurements with those listed in this Chapter's Specifications. Also compare the bore measurements to the marks on the crankcase to find out whether the marks are accurate.

22   Using the marks on the crank and the marks on the case, determine the bearing sizes required by referring to the accompanying bearing selection chart **(see illustration)**.

25.23 Make sure the tabs in the bearing inserts (arrows) fit into the notches in the web; the center two main bearings have oil grooves

Installation

Refer to illustrations 25.23, 25.27, 25.30a and 25.30b

23   Separate the case halves once again. Clean the bearing saddles in the case halves, then install the bearing inserts in their webs in the case **(see illustration)**. The center two bearing inserts have oil grooves. When installing the bearings, use your hands only - don't tap them into place with a hammer.

24   Lubricate the bearing inserts with engine assembly lube or moly-based grease.

25   You can install the connecting rods on the crankshaft at this point if the top end was removed from the engine (see Section 26).

26   Loop the camshaft chain and the primary chain over the crankshaft and lay them onto their gears.

27   Check to make sure the cam chain guide retaining pin and lock-pin are in position. If the connecting rods are in the engine, place pieces of hose over the studs to protect the crankshaft **(see illustration)**.

28   Carefully lower the crankshaft into place. If the connecting rods are in the engine, guide them onto the crankshaft journals.

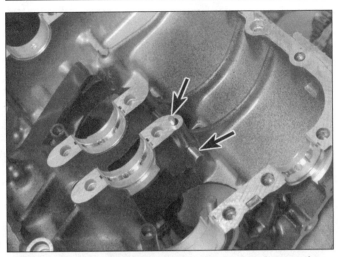

25.27 Before you install the crankshaft, check to be sure the
cam chain guide retainer pin (lower arrow) is pushed all the
way in and its lock-pin (upper arrow) is in place - if the connecting
rods are installed, put pieces of hose on the studs to protect
the crankshaft

25.30a The pin in the oil pump drive gear must engage the notch
in the clutch housing (arrows). . .

25.30b . . .and the beveled side of the clutch housing thrust
washer must face toward the ball bearing on the
transmission shaft

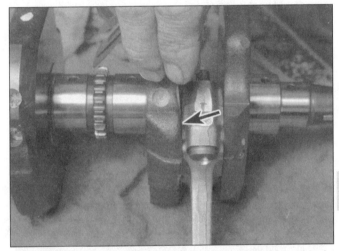

26.1 Slip a feeler gauge blade between the connecting rod and
crankshaft throw (arrow) to check connecting rod side clearance

29   Assemble the case halves (see Section 22) and check to make
sure the crankshaft and the transmission shafts turn freely.
30   Install the oil pump drive gear and clutch housing. The pin in the
gear must engage the notch in the housing (see illustration). The
beveled side of the clutch housing thrust washer faces the ball bearing
on the transmission main drive shaft (see illustration).

**26   Connecting rods and bearings - removal, inspection, bearing
selection and installation**

Removal

Refer to illustrations 26.1, 26.2, 26.3a and 26.3b

1   Before removing the connecting rods from the crankshaft, measure the side clearance of each rod with a feeler gauge (see illustration). If the clearance on any rod is greater than that listed in this
Chapter's Specifications, that rod will have to be replaced with a new
one.
2   Using a center punch, mark the position of each rod and cap, relative to its position on the crankshaft (see illustration).

26.2 Make number marks (arrows) on the connecting rod and cap
so they can be reassembled in their original positions, and note
the relationship of the connecting rod to the crankshaft - the
letter mark across the rod and cap indicates the connecting rod
weight grade

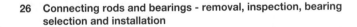

26.3a Remove the connecting rod nuts (arrows). . .

26.3b . . .and take the cap off the studs

3   Unscrew the bearing cap nuts, separate the cap from the rod, then detach the rod from the crankshaft **(see illustrations)**. If the cap is stuck, tap on the ends of the rod bolts with a soft face hammer to free them.
4   Separate the bearing inserts from the rods and caps, keeping them in order so they can be reinstalled in their original locations. Wash the parts in solvent and dry them with compressed air, if available.

Inspection

Refer to illustration 26.5
5   Check the connecting rods for cracks and other obvious damage. Lubricate the piston pin for each rod, install it in the proper rod and check for play **(see illustration)**. If it is loose, replace the connecting rod and/or the pin.
6   Refer to Section 24 and examine the connecting rod bearing inserts. If they are scored, badly scuffed or appear to have been seized, new bearings must be installed. Always replace the bearings in the connecting rods as a set. If they are badly damaged, check the corresponding crankshaft journal. Evidence of extreme heat, such as discoloration, indicates that lubrication failure has occurred. Be sure to thoroughly check the oil pump and pressure relief valve as well as all oil holes and passages before reassembling the engine.
7   Have the rods checked for twist and bending at a dealer service department or other motorcycle repair shop.

Bearing selection

Refer to illustrations 26.20a, 26.20b and 26.21
8   If the bearings and journals appear to be in good condition, check the oil clearances as follows:
9   Start with the rod for the number one cylinder. Wipe the bearing inserts and the connecting rod and cap clean, using a lint-free cloth.
10   Install the bearing inserts in the connecting rod and cap. Make sure the tab on the bearing engages with the notch in the rod or cap.
11   Wipe off the connecting rod journal with a lint-free cloth. Lay a strip of Plastigage (type HPG-1) across the top of the journal, parallel with the journal axis **(see illustration 25.13)**.
12   Position the connecting rod on the bottom of the journal, then install the rod cap and nuts. Tighten the nuts to the torque listed in this Chapter's Specifications, but don't allow the connecting rod to rotate at all.
13   Unscrew the nuts and remove the connecting rod and cap from the journal, being very careful not to disturb the Plastigage. Compare the width of the crushed Plastigage to the scale printed in the Plastigage envelope **(see illustration 25.15)** to determine the bearing oil clearance.
14   If the clearance is within the range listed in this Chapter's Specifications and the bearings are in perfect condition, they can be reused.

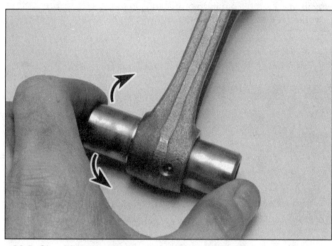

26.5 Checking the piston pin and connecting rod bore for wear

If the clearance is beyond the standard range, but within the service limit, replace the bearing inserts with inserts that have blue paint marks, then check the oil clearance once again (these are the thickest bearing inserts, and may be thick enough to bring bearing clearance with the specified range). Always replace all of the inserts at the same time.
15   The clearance might be slightly greater than the standard clearance, but that doesn't matter, as long as it isn't greater than the maximum clearance or less than the minimum clearance.
16   If the clearance is greater than the service limit listed in this Chapter's Specifications, measure the diameter of the connecting rod journal with a micrometer and compare your findings with this Chapter's Specifications. Also, by measuring the diameter at a number of points around the journal's circumference, you'll be able to determine whether or not the journal is out-of-round. Take the measurement at each end of the journal to determine if the journal is tapered.
17   If any journal has worn down past the service limit, replace the crankshaft.
18   If the diameter of the journal isn't less than the service limit but differs from the original markings on the crankshaft **(see illustration 25.20)**, apply new marks with a hammer and punch.
      If the journal measures within the *"no mark"* range listed in this Chapter's Specifications, don't make any marks on the crank (there shouldn't be one there anyway).
      If the journal measures within the "0" mark range listed in this Chapter's Specifications, make a "0" mark on the crank in the area indicated (if not already there).

00

0

0

0

0

0

0

0

0

0

0

0

0

0

0

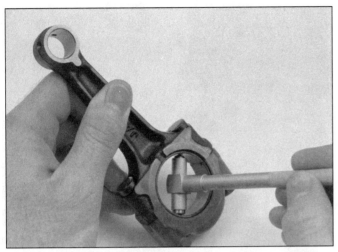

26.20a Assemble the connecting rod and measure the diameter of the bore with a telescoping gauge - then measure the gauge with a micrometer

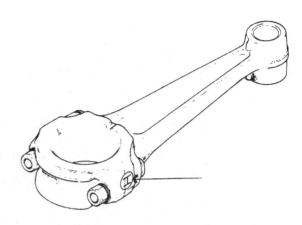

26.20b There's a letter that indicates weight grade on each connecting rod; a "0" or the absence of a "0" around the letter. . .

Connecting Rod Big End Bearing Insert Selection

Con-rod Big End Bore Diameter Mark	Crankpin Diameter Mark	Bearing Insert	
		Size Color	Part Number
O	O	Black	92028-1349
None	None	Black	92028-1349
O	None	Blue	92028-1348
None	O	Brown	92028-1350

26.21 . . .can be used, in conjunction with this chart, to determine the correct bearing inserts to install

19 Remove the bearing inserts from the connecting rod and cap, then assemble the cap to the rod. Tighten the nuts to the torque listed in this Chapter's Specifications.
20 Using a telescoping gauge and a micrometer, measure the inside diameter of the connecting rod (see illustration). The mark on the connecting rod (if any) should coincide with the measurement, but if it doesn't, make a new mark (see illustration).

If the inside diameter measures within the "no mark" range listed in this Chapter's Specifications, don't make any mark on the rod (there shouldn't be one there anyway).

If the inside diameter measures within the "0" mark range, make a 0 mark on the rod (it should already be there).
21 By referring to the accompanying chart (see illustration), select the correct connecting rod bearing inserts.
22 Repeat the bearing selection procedure for the remaining connecting rod.

Installation
23 Wipe off the bearing inserts, connecting rods and caps. Install the inserts into the rods and caps, using your hands only, making sure the tabs on the inserts engage with the notches in the rods and caps. When all the inserts are installed, lubricate them with engine assembly lube or moly-based grease. Don't get any lubricant on the mating surfaces of the rod or cap.
24 Assemble each connecting rod to its proper journal, making sure the previously applied matchmarks correspond to each other and the arrow casting on the piston points to the front of the engine (see illustration 14.3a). Also, the letter present at the rod/cap seam on one side

27.2 Correct alignment of the marks on the balancer gear and crankshaft gear is essential to prevent severe engine vibration

of the connecting rod is a weight mark. If new rods are being installed, they should both have the same letter on them to minimize vibration.
25 When you're sure the rods are positioned correctly, tighten the nuts to the torque listed in this Chapter's Specifications.
26 Turn the rods on the crankshaft. If any of them feel tight, tap on the bottom of the connecting rod caps with a hammer - this should relieve stress and free them up. If it doesn't, recheck the bearing clearance.
27 As a final step, recheck the connecting rod side clearances (see Step 1). If the clearances aren't correct, find out why before proceeding with engine assembly.

27 Balancer shaft - removal, inspection, bearing selection and installation

Removal
Refer to illustration 27.2
1 Split the crankcase (see Section 22).
2 If you're only planning to remove the balancer (not the crankshaft), turn the crankshaft until the marks on the balancer and crankshaft gears are aligned (see illustration).
3 Lift the balancer shaft and gear out of the crankcase.

2

27.5a The balancer bearing inserts near the external oil line have oil grooves. . .

27.5b . . .while the inserts at the opposite end of the balancer are smooth

Inspection

Refer to illustrations 27.5a and 27.5b

4   Check the shaft and gear for wear and damage. Make sure the springs inside the gear are not broken. Replace the balancer shaft if you find any undesirable conditions.

5   Check the bearings for wear and for damage such as grooves, nicks or small bits of foreign material stuck in their surfaces **(see illustrations)**. Replace them if they aren't in perfect condition.

Bearing selection

Refer to illustrations 27.13 and 27.15

6   To check the balancer bearing oil clearance, clean off the bearing inserts (and reinstall them, if they've been removed from the case) and lower the balancer shaft into the upper half of the case. Cut two pieces of Plastigage (type HPG-1) and lay them on the balancer journals, parallel with the journal axis.

7   Very carefully, guide the lower case half down onto the upper case half. Install the large (8 mm) bolts and tighten them, using the recommended sequence, to the torque listed in this Chapter's Specifications (see Section 22). Don't rotate the balancer!

8   Now, remove the bolts and carefully lift the lower case half off. Compare the width of the crushed Plastigage on each journal to the scale printed on the Plastigage envelope to obtain the balancer bearing oil clearance. Write down your findings, then remove all traces of Plastigage from the journals, using your fingernail or the edge of a credit card.

9   If the oil clearance falls into the specified range, no bearing replacement is required (provided they are in good shape). If the clearance is more than the standard range, but within the service limit, replace the bearing inserts with inserts that have blue paint marks **(see illustration 25.15)**, then check the oil clearance once again (these are the thickest bearing inserts, and may be thick enough to bring bearing clearance within the specified range). Always replace all of the inserts at the same time.

10   The clearance might be slightly greater than the standard clearance, but that doesn't matter, as long as it isn't greater than the maximum clearance or less than the minimum clearance.

11   If the clearance is greater than the service limit listed in this Chapter's Specifications, measure the diameter of the balancer journals with a micrometer and compare your findings with this Chapter's Specifications. Also, by measuring the diameter at a number of points around each journal's circumference, you'll be able to determine whether or not the journal is out-of-round. Take the measurement at each end of the journal to determine if the journal is tapered.

12   If either balancer journal has worn down past the service limit, replace the balancer shaft.

27.13 There's a journal diameter mark (or no mark, as on this balancer) on each balancer weight; there's also a size mark for each bearing bore on the case. . .

A)   Left bearing bore size mark
B)   Right bearing bore size mark

13   If the diameters of the journals aren't less than the service limit but differ from the original markings on the balancer shaft **(see illustration)**, apply new marks with a hammer and punch.

If the journal measures within the "no mark" range listed in the Specifications, don't make any marks on the balancer (there shouldn't be any marks there, anyway).

If the journal measures within the "0" mark range listed in the Specifications, make a "0" mark on the balancer in the area indicated (if it's not already there).

14   Remove the balancer bearing inserts and assemble the case halves (see Section 22). Using a telescoping gauge and a micrometer, measure the diameters of the balancer bearing bores, then compare the measurements with the marks on the upper case half **(see illustration 27.13)**. Compare the bore measurements with those listed in this Chapter's Specifications. Also compare the bore measurements to the marks on the crankcase to find out whether the marks are accurate.

15   Using the marks on the crank and the marks on the case, determine the bearing sizes required by referring to the accompanying bearing selection chart **(see illustration)**.

Installation

16   Separate the case halves once again. Clean the bearing saddles in the case halves, then install the bearing inserts in their webs in the

Bearing Insert Selection

Crankcase Bearing Inside Diameter Mark	Balancer Shaft Journal Diameter Mark	Bearing Insert	
		Size Color	Part Number
○	○	Brown	92028-1497
None	None	Blue	92028-1495
○	None	Black	92028-1496
None	○		

27.15 . . .use them in conjunction with this table to select the correct bearing size

case **(see illustrations 27.5a and 27.5b)**. The bearing insert next to the oil line has an oil groove. When installing the bearings, use your hands only - don't tap them into place with a hammer.

17   Lubricate the bearing inserts with engine assembly lube or moly-based grease.

18   Carefully lay the balancer in the bearings. Be sure the " - " mark on the balancer gear aligns with the "0" mark on the crankshaft gear **(see illustration 27.2)**. Incorrect alignment will cause severe engine vibration.

19   The remainder of installation is the reverse of the removal steps.

28   Primary chain, camshaft chain and guides - removal, inspection and installation

Removal

Primary chain and camshaft chain

1   Remove the engine (see Section 5).
2   Separate the crankcase halves (see Section 22).
3   Remove the crankshaft (see Section 25).
4   Remove the chains from the crankshaft.

Chain guides

5   The cam chain front guide can be lifted from the cylinder block after the head has been removed (see Section 13).
6   The cam chain rear guide is fastened to the crankcase with a retaining pin and lock-pin **(see illustrations 23.6a and 23.6b)**. Pull out the lock-pin and push the retaining pin out, then lift out the chain guide.
7   The primary chain guide in the lower case half is secured by a bolt **(see illustration 23.5)**.
8   The primary chain guide in the upper case half is secured by two bolts.

Inspection

Primary chain and camshaft chain

Refer to illustration 28.9

9   The primary chain and camshaft chains are checked in a similar manner. Pull the chain tight to eliminate all slack and measure the length of twenty links, pin-to-pin **(see illustration)**. Compare your findings to this Chapter's Specifications.

10   Also check the chains for binding and obvious damage.

11   If the twenty-link length is not as specified, or there is visible damage, replace the chain.

Chain guides

12   Check the guides for deep grooves, cracking and other obvious damage, replacing them if necessary.

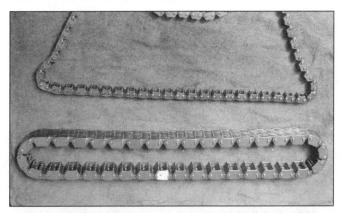

28.9 When checking the camshaft chain or the primary chain, measure the length of twenty links and compare to the length listed in this Chapter's Specifications

Installation

13   Installation of these components is the reverse of the removal procedure. When installing the primary chain guides, apply a non-hardening thread locking compound to the threads of the bolts. Tighten the bolts to the torque listed in this Chapter's Specifications. Apply engine oil to the faces of the guides and to the chains.

29   Transmission shafts - removal and installation

Refer to illustrations 29.3a and 29.3b

Removal

1   Remove the engine and clutch, then separate the case halves (see Sections 5, 19 and 22).

2   Before removing either shaft, check the backlash of each set of gears. To do this, mount a dial indicator with the plunger of the indicator touching a tooth on one of the gears, then move the gear back and forth within its freeplay, holding its companion gear stationary. Check each set of gears, recording the measurements, and compare the results to this Chapter's Specifications. If the backlash between any pair of gears exceeds the limit, replace both gears (see Section 30).

3   The output shaft can simply be lifted out of the upper half of the case **(see illustration)**. The main drive shaft **(see illustration)** is removed together with the clutch housing (see Section 25). If they are stuck, use a soft-face hammer and gently tap on the bearings on the ends of the shafts to free them.

29.3a The output shaft (arrow) can simply be lifted out. . .

2

29.3b ...the main drive shaft is removed together with the clutch housing

29.5 At each end of the shafts there's a set pin for the small bearing and a set ring for the large bearing

29.6a The hole in the small bearing (arrow)...

29.6b ...must fit over the set pin (lower arrow) - the groove in the large bearing must fit over the set ring (upper arrow)...

29.6c ...if the bearings are correctly installed, they will fit into their saddles with no gap between the bearing and case

4   Refer to Section 30 for information pertaining to transmission shaft service and Section 31 for information pertaining to the shift drum and forks.

Installation

Refer to illustration 29.5, 29.6a, 29.6b and 29.6c

5   Check to make sure the set pins and rings are present in the upper case half, where the shaft bearings seat **(see illustration)**.

6   Carefully lower each shaft into place. The holes in the needle bearing outer races must engage with the set pins, and the grooves in the ball bearing outer races must engage with the set rings **(see illustrations)**.

7   The remainder of installation is the reverse of removal.

---

30 Transmission shafts - disassembly, inspection and reassembly

---

Note: *When disassembling the transmission shafts, place the parts on a long rod or thread a wire through them to keep them in order and facing the proper direction.*

1   Remove the shafts from the case (see Section 29).

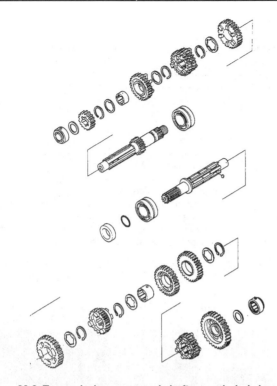

30.2 Transmission gears and shafts - exploded view

30.4a Remove the bearing plug. . .

30.4b . . .the outer bearing, inner bearing and spacer (arrow). . .

30.4c . . .slide off second gear. . .

Main drive shaft

Disassembly

Refer to illustrations 30.2 and 30.4a through 30.4j

2   All of the main drive shaft parts slide off the shaft except first gear, which is integral with the shaft, and the ball bearing, which is a press fit **(see illustration)**.

3   Each freewheeling gear is secured with a toothed washer and snap-ring. Use snap-ring pliers to remove the snap-rings. **Caution:** *There are two sizes of snap-ring, with only a small difference between them. Be sure to keep the snap rings in their original locations and to replace them with ones of the same size.*

4   To disassemble the main drive shaft, refer to the accompanying photographs **(see illustrations)**.

30.4d . . .remove the snap-ring and toothed washer, then slide off sixth gear. . .

30.4e . . .slide off the sixth gear bushing and toothed washer. . .

30.4f . . .then remove the snap-ring. . .

30.4g . . .slide the third-fourth gear cluster off the shaft. . .

Inspection

Refer to illustration 30.8

5   Wash all of the components in clean solvent and dry them off. Rotate the ball bearing on the shaft, feeling for tightness, rough spots and excessive looseness and listening for noises. If any of these conditions are found, replace the bearing. This will require the use of a hydraulic press or a bearing puller setup. If you don't have access to these tools, take the shaft and bearing to a Kawasaki dealer or other motorcycle repair shop and have them press the old bearing off the shaft and install the new one.

6   Measure the shift fork groove between third and fourth gears. If the groove width exceeds the figure listed in this Chapter's Specifications, replace the third/fourth gear assembly, and also check the third/fourth gear shift fork (see Section 31).

7   Check the gear teeth for cracking and other obvious damage. Check the sixth gear bushing and the surface in the inner diameter of sixth gear (and the fifth gear bushing, if equipped) for scoring or heat discoloration. If the gear or bushing is damaged, replace it.

8   Inspect the dogs and the dog holes in the gears for excessive wear **(see illustration)**. Replace the paired gears as a set if necessary.

9   Check the needle bearing and outer race for wear or heat discoloration and replace them if necessary.

30.4h . . .remove the snap-ring and toothed washer. . .

30.4i . . .slide off fifth gear. . .

30.4j . . .and the fifth gear bushing (if equipped)

30.8 If the gear dogs and dog holes (arrows) show signs of excessive wear, replace the gears as a set

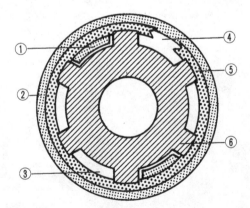

30.10 The teeth of the toothed washers should not be aligned with the gap in the snap-ring; the gap in the snap-ring should be centered within a shaft groove

1) Teeth of toothed washer	4) Gap in snap-ring
2) Toothed washer	5) Snap-ring
3) Shaft groove	6) Shaft

Reassembly

Refer to illustrations 30.10, 30.11a through 30.11m and 30.12

10   During reassembly, always use new snap-rings and align the opening of the ring with a spline groove **(see illustration)**.

11   To reassemble the main drive shaft, refer to the accompanying illustrations. Lubricate the components with engine oil before assembling them **(see illustrations)**.

12   Check the assembled main drive shaft to make sure all parts are installed correctly **(see illustration)**.

Output shaft

Disassembly

Refer to illustrations 30.15a through 30.15p

13   All of the output shaft parts slide off the shaft except the ball bearing, which is a press fit. Fifth gear is secured to the shaft by three steel balls, installed in channels in the gear, which must be spun outward by centrifugal force. To do this, spin the shaft with one hand, and at the same time, lift the gear with the other hand. This may take several tries.

30.11a If the main drive shaft fifth gear has a separate bushing, install it so its oil hole lines up with the hole in the shaft

30.11b Install fifth gear with its dogs facing away from first gear; install a toothed washer and secure it with a snap-ring

30.11c Install the third-fourth gear cluster with third gear (the smaller gear) toward fifth gear

30.11d Install a snap-ring in the next shaft groove. . .

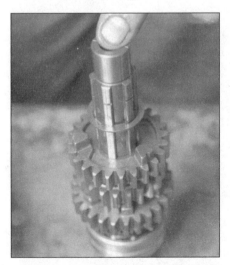

30.11e . . .and place a toothed washer against it

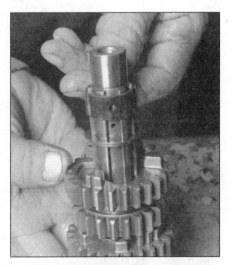

30.11f . . .Align the oil hole in the sixth gear bushing with the oil hole in the shaft, then slide the bushing down against the toothed washer

30.11g Install sixth gear with its flat side away from fourth gear and place a toothed washer next to it. . .

2

30.11h ...then secure the gear and
washer with a snap-ring

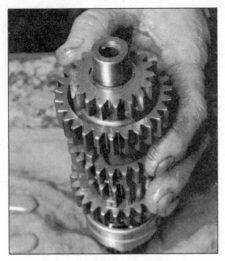

30.11i Install second gear...

30.11j ...its spacer...

30.11k ...the bearing...

30.11l ...the bearing outer race...

30.11m ...and the plug

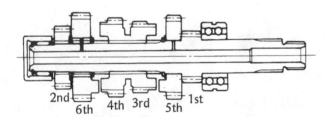

30.12 Main drive shaft components - assembled view

30.15a Pull off the bearing outer race...

14   Each freewheeling gear is secured with a toothed washer and
snap-ring. Use snap-ring pliers to remove the snap-rings.
15   To disassemble the output shaft, refer to the accompanying illustrations.

Inspection

16   Refer to Steps 5 through 9 for the inspection procedures. They
are the same, except that when checking the shift fork groove width
you'll be checking it on fifth gear and sixth gear.

Reassembly

Refer to illustrations 30.17a through 30.17p

17   Reassembly is basically the reverse of the disassembly procedure **(see illustrations)**, but take note of the following points:
   a) Always use new snap-rings and align the opening of the ring with

30.15b ...the bearing and spacer (arrows)

30.15c Slide first gear off the shaft

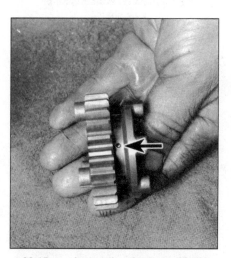

30.15d The next gear on the output shaft is fifth gear...

30.15e ...it contains three steel balls (arrow) that will prevent the gear from being removed unless they're flung outward by centrifugal force...

30.15f ...to disengage them from these slots (arrow) - to do so, spin the shaft rapidly with one hand while trying to slide the gear off with the other; it may take several tries, but the gear will come off with light hand pressure once the balls are spun outward

2

30.15g Remove the snap-ring and toothed washer, then slide third gear off the shaft...

30.15h ...this will expose the bushing shared by third and fourth gears...

30.15i ...slide off the bushing and fourth gear

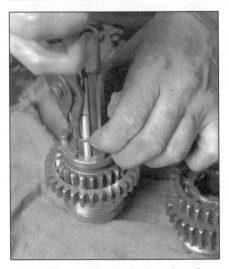

30.15j Remove the toothed washer, then the snap-ring. . .

30.15k . . .and slide sixth gear off the shaft

30.15l Remove the snap-ring. . .

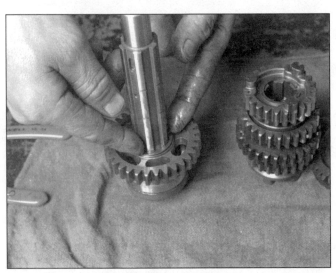

30.15m . . .and the toothed washer. . .

30.15n . . .and slide second gear off the shaft

30.15o Pull the oil seal off the bearing collar

30.15p If the bearing is worn or damaged, place it in a bearing splitter, press it off the shaft and press a new one on (or have the job done by a motorcycle dealer)

30.17a Stand the shaft on its ball bearing end. . .

30.17b . . .and install second gear (flat side toward bearing), then secure it with a toothed washer and snap-ring

30.17c Install sixth gear with its fork groove away from second gear

30.17d Install a snap-ring in the groove farthest down the shaft. . .

30.17e . . .place a toothed washer next to it. . .

30.17f . . .install fourth gear. . .

30.17g . . .and its bushing (align BOTH oil holes in the bushing with those in the shaft)

a spline groove (see illustration 30.10).

b) When installing the bushing for third and fourth gear, align the oil hole in the bushing with the hole in the shaft.

c) When installing fifth gear, don't use grease to hold the balls in place - to do so would impair the positive neutral finder mechanism. Just set the balls in their holes (the holes that they can't

pass through), keep the gear in a vertical position and carefully set it on the shaft (engine oil will help keep them in place). The spline grooves that contain the holes with the balls must be aligned with the slots in the shaft spline grooves.

d) Lubricate the components with engine oil before assembling them.

2

30.17h Install third gear. . .

30.17i . . .install a toothed washer next to it. . .

30.17j . . .and secure them with a snap-ring; the slots in the shaft (arrow). . .

30.17k . . .must align with the balls in fifth gear (arrow) when it's installed

30.17l Install first gear and its spacer. . .

30.17m . . .the bearing. . .

30.17n . . .and the bearing outer race - the assembled output shaft should look like this. . .

30.17o . . .don't forget the seal on the other end of the shaft

---

31 Shift drum and forks - removal, inspection and installation

Removal

Refer to illustrations 31.2a, 31.2b, 31.2c, 31.3, 31.4, 31.5a and 31.5b

1   Remove the engine and separate the crankcase halves (see Sec-

tions 5 and 22).

2   Support the shift forks and pull the shift rod out **(see illustrations)**.

3   Remove the shift drum bearing retaining bolts **(see illustration)**.

4   Remove the cotter pin (split pin) and pull out the guide pin **(see illustration)**.

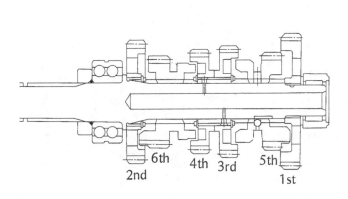

30.17p Output shaft details

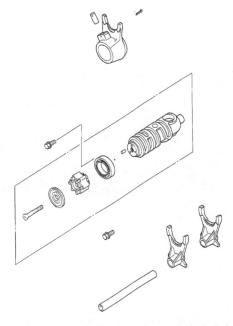

31.2a Internal shift mechanism - exploded view

31.2b Note the positions of the shift forks on the shaft, then slide out the shaft and remove the forks

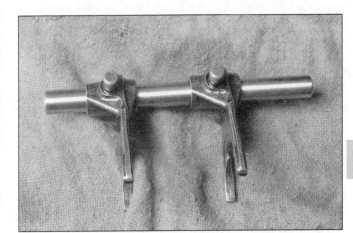

31.2c It's a good idea to reassemble the forks to the shaft temporarily so you don't forget how they go

31.3 Remove the shift drum bearing retainer bolts (arrows)

31.4 Remove the cotter pin (split pin) and guide pin (arrows)...

2

31.5a . . .and slide the shift drum out of the fork and case

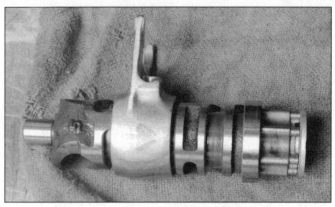

31.5b Reassemble the shift fork to the drum

5   Pull the shift drum out of the case far enough to remove the third/fourth shift fork **(see illustration)**, then slide the shift drum out of the case **(see illustration)**.

Inspection

Refer to illustration 31.7
6   Check the edges of the grooves in the drum for signs of excessive wear. Measure the widths of the grooves and compare your findings to this Chapter's Specifications. Check the holder and bearing on the end of the shift drum for wear and damage. If undesirable conditions are found, remove the holder screw and replace the holder and bearing.
7   Check the shift forks for distortion and wear, especially at the fork ears. Measure the thickness of the fork ears and compare your findings with this Chapter's Specifications **(see illustration)**. If they are discolored or severely worn they are probably bent. If damage or wear is evident, check the shift fork groove in the corresponding gear as well. Inspect the guide pins and the shaft bore for excessive wear and distortion and replace any defective parts with new ones.
8   Check the shift fork shafts for evidence of wear, galling and other damage. Make sure the shift forks move smoothly on the shafts. If the shafts are worn or bent, replace them with new ones.
Installation
9   Installation is the reverse of removal, noting the following points:
  a) Install the shift drum part-way into the case and install the third/fourth shift fork (the long end goes onto the drum first).
  b) Be sure to use a new cotter pin (split pin) and install it correctly **(see illustration 31.4)**.
  c) Lubricate all parts with engine oil before installing them.
  d) Apply a non-permanent locking agent to the threads of the bearing retainer bolts and tighten them securely.

32 Initial start-up after overhaul

Note: *Make sure the cooling system is checked carefully (especially the coolant level) before starting and running the engine.*
1   Make sure the engine oil level is correct, then remove the spark plugs from the engine. Place the engine STOP switch in the Off position and unplug the primary (low tension) wires from the coil.
2   Turn on the key switch and crank the engine over with the starter until the oil pressure indicator light goes off (which indicates that oil pressure exists). Reinstall the spark plugs, connect the wires and turn the switch to On. **Note:** *If the oil pressure light won't go out, remove the oil filter (see Chapter 1). Hold the filter with the open end upright and pour oil into the center hole until the filter is full. Let the oil settle, then top it off again (you may need to do this twice). Reinstall the filter (a small amount of oil may leak out when you install it).*
3   Make sure there is fuel in the tank, then turn the fuel tap to the On position and operate the choke.
4   Start the engine and allow it to run at a moderately fast idle until it reaches operating temperature. **Warning:** *If the oil pressure indicator*

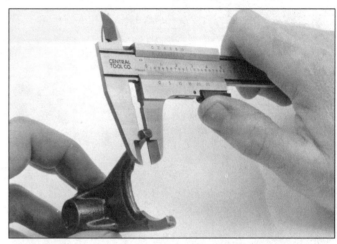

31.7 Measure the thickness of the shift fork ears

light doesn't go off, or it comes on while the engine is running, stop the engine immediately.
5   Check carefully for oil leaks and make sure the transmission and controls, especially the brakes, function properly before road testing the machine. Refer to Section 33 for the recommended break-in procedure.
6   Upon completion of the road test, and after the engine has cooled down completely, recheck the valve clearances (see Chapter 1).

33 Recommended break-in procedure

1   Any rebuilt engine needs time to break-in, even if parts have been installed in their original locations. For this reason, treat the machine gently for the first few miles to make sure oil has circulated throughout the engine and any new parts installed have started to seat.
2   Even greater care is necessary if the engine has been rebored or a new crankshaft has been installed. In the case of a rebore, the engine will have to be broken in as if the machine were new. This means greater use of the transmission and a restraining hand on the throttle until at least 500 miles (800 km) have been covered. There's no point in keeping to any set speed limit - the main idea is to keep from lugging (labouring) the engine and to gradually increase performance until the 500 mile (800 km) mark is reached. These recommendations can be lessened to an extent when only a new crankshaft is installed. Experience is the best guide, since it's easy to tell when an engine is running freely.
3   If a lubrication failure is suspected, stop the engine immediately and try to find the cause. If an engine is run without oil, even for a short period of time, severe damage will occur.

Chapter 3 Cooling system

Contents

Specifications

General

Coolant type	See Chapter 1
Mixture ratio...	See Chapter 1
Radiator cap pressure rating	14 to 18 psi (1.0 to 1.2 Bars)
Thermostat rating	
Opening temperature	157 to 163-degrees F (69.5 to 72.5-degrees C)
Valve travel (when fully open)	Not less than 5/16-in (8 mm)

Torque specifications

Thermostatic fan switch-to-radiator	
1987 through 1989 models	65 in-lbs (7.4 Nm)
1990 and later models..	13 ft-lbs (18 Nm)
Coolant temperature sender unit-to-thermostat housing................	69 in-lbs (7.8 Nm)

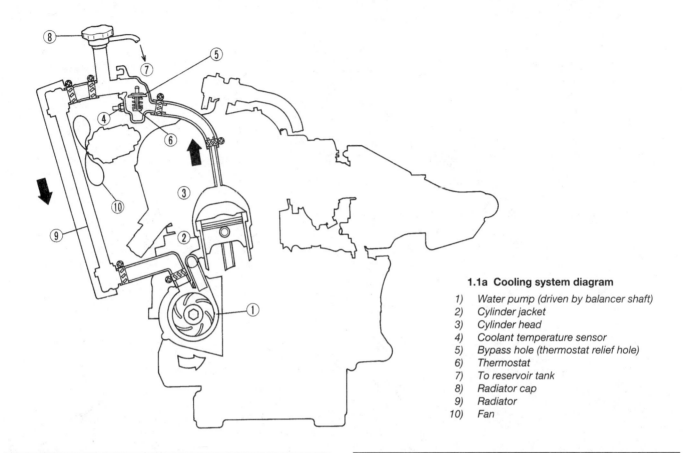

1.1a Cooling system diagram

1)   *Water pump (driven by balancer shaft)*
2)   *Cylinder jacket*
3)   *Cylinder head*
4)   *Coolant temperature sensor*
5)   *Bypass hole (thermostat relief hole)*
6)   *Thermostat*
7)   *To reservoir tank*
8)   *Radiator cap*
9)   *Radiator*
10) *Fan*

1   General information

Refer to illustration 1.1

The models covered by this manual are equipped with a liquid cooling system which utilizes a water/antifreeze mixture to carry away excess heat produced during the combustion process **(see illustrations)**. The cylinders are surrounded by water jackets, through which the coolant is circulated by the water pump. The pump is mounted to the right side of the crankcase and is driven by the balancer shaft. The coolant passes up through a flexible hose and a coolant pipe, which distributes water around the cylinders. It flows through the water passages in the cylinder head, through a pair of tubes and hoses and into the thermostat housing. The hot coolant then flows down into the radiator (which is mounted on the frame downtubes to take advantage of maximum air flow), where it is cooled by the passing air, through another hose and back to the water pump, where the cycle is repeated.

An electric fan, mounted behind the radiator and automatically controlled by a thermostatic switch, provides a flow of cooling air through the radiator when the motorcycle is not moving. Under certain conditions, the fan may come on even after the engine is stopped, and the ignition switch is off, and may run for several minutes.

The coolant temperature sending unit, threaded into the radiator, senses the temperature of the coolant and controls the coolant temperature gauge on the instrument cluster.

The entire system is sealed and pressurized. The pressure is controlled by a valve which is part of the radiator cap. By pressurizing the coolant, the boiling point is raised, which prevents premature boiling of the coolant. An overflow hose, connected between the radiator and reservoir tank, directs coolant to the tank when the radiator cap valve is opened by excessive pressure. The coolant is automatically siphoned back to the radiator as the engine cools.

Many cooling system inspection and service procedures are considered part of routine maintenance and are included in Chapter 1.

Warning: *Do not allow antifreeze to come in contact with your skin or painted surfaces of the motorcycle. Rinse off spills immediately with plenty of water. Antifreeze is highly toxic if ingested. Never leave antifreeze lying around in an open container or in puddles on the floor; children and pets are attracted by its sweet smell and may drink it. Check with local authorities about disposing of used antifreeze. Many communities have collection centers which will see that antifreeze is disposed of safely.*

Caution: *Do not remove the pressure cap from the thermostat housing when the engine and radiator are hot. Scalding hot coolant and steam may be blown out under pressure, which could cause serious injury. To open the pressure cap, remove the left side panel on the inside of the fairing. When the engine has cooled, lift up the panel and place a thick rag, like a towel, over the radiator cap; slowly rotate the cap counterclockwise (anticlockwise) to the first stop. This procedure allows any residual pressure to escape. When the steam has stopped escaping, press down on the cap while turning counterclockwise (anticlockwise) and remove it.*

2   Radiator cap - check

If problems such as overheating and loss of coolant occur, check the entire system as described in Chapter 1. The radiator cap opening pressure should be checked by a dealer service department or service station equipped with the special tester required to do the job. If the cap is defective, replace it with a new one.

3   Coolant reservoir - removal and installation

1   Remove the fairing (see Chapter 8).
2   Disconnect the coolant hoses from the reservoir.
3   Unbolt the reservoir from the bracket and take it out.
4   Installation is the reverse of the removal steps.

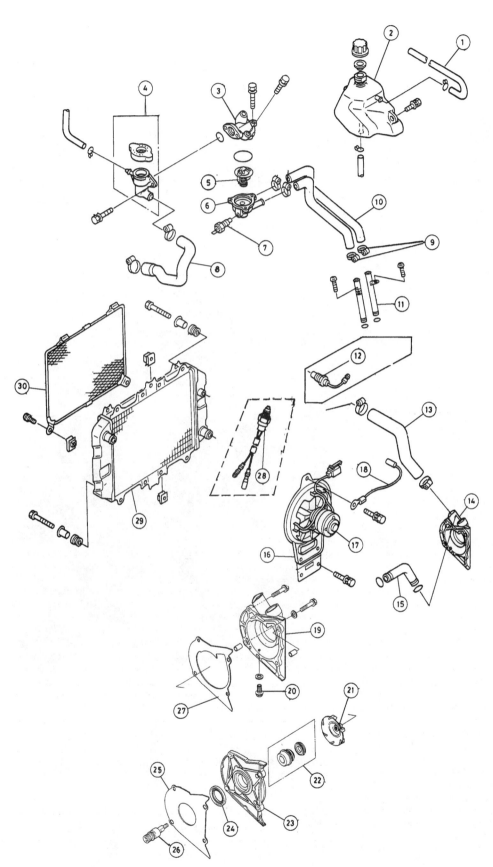

1.1b Exploded view of cooling system

1 Reservoir tank hose
2 Reservoir tank
3 Thermostat housing cover
4 Pressure cap and filler neck
5 Thermostat and O-ring
6 Thermostat housing
7 Coolant temperature sender
8 Hose
9 Hose clamps
10 Hoses
11 Coolant tubes
12 Thermostat fan switch (early models)
13 Ground/earth wire
14 Water pump cover
15 Coolant pipe and O-rings
16 Fan motor bracket
17 Fan motor
18 Ground wire
19 Water pump cover
20 Drain plug
21 Impeller
22 Mechanical seal
23 Water pump housing
24 Oil seal
25 Gasket
26 Water pump shaft
27 Gasket
28 Thermostatic fan switch (later models)
29 Radiator
30 Stone guard

3

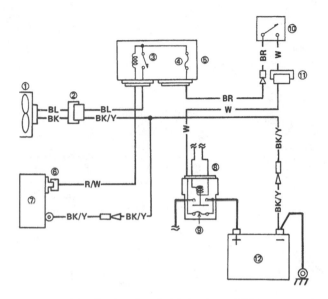

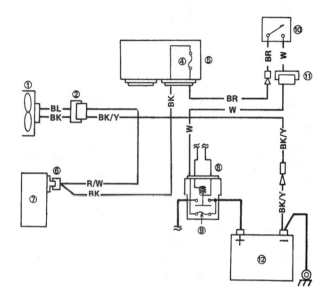

4.1a Cooling fan circuit (early models)

1)	Cooling fan	5)	Junction box	10)	Ignition
2)	Two-pin	6)	Fan switch		switch
	connector	7)	Radiator	11)	Six-pin
3)	Fan relay	8)	Starter relay		connector
4)	Fan fuse	9)	Main fuse	12)	Battery

4.1b Cooling fan circuit (later models)

1)	Cooling fan	5)	Junction box	10)	Ignition
2)	Two-pin	6)	Fan switch		switch
	connector	7)	Radiator	11)	Six-pin
3)	Not used	8)	Starter relay		connector
4)	Fan fuse	9)	Main fuse	12)	Battery

4   Cooling fan and thermostatic switch - check and replacement

Check

Refer to illustrations 4.1a and 4.1b

1   If the engine is overheating and the cooling fan isn't coming on, first remove the seat and check the fuses. If the fuse is blown, check the fan circuit for a short to ground/earth (see the Wiring diagrams at the end of this book). If the fuses are all good, unplug the fan electrical connector **(see illustrations)**. Using two jumper wires, apply battery voltage to the terminals in the fan motor side of the electrical connector. If the fan doesn't work, replace the motor.

2   If the fan does come on, the problem lies in the thermostatic fan switch, the junction block, or the wiring that connects the components. Remove the jumper wires and reconnect the electrical connector to the fan.

  a) If you're working on an early model (with a single-wire fan switch harness), unplug the electrical connector to the fan switch, attach a jumper wire to the harness side of the connector and ground/earth the other end of the jumper wire. If the fan comes on, the circuit to the motor is good, and the thermostatic fan switch is defective (see Step 10).

  b) If you're working on a later model (with a double-wire fan switch connector), unplug the connector. Connect the terminals in the harness side of the connector together with a jumper wire. If the fan comes on, the circuit to the motor is good and the switch is defective.

3   If you're working on an early model and the fan still doesn't work, place your hand on the junction block. Repeatedly touch the jumper wire to ground/earth - if you feel a clicking inside the junction block, the relay is probably good. If it's not clicking, check the wiring from the thermostatic fan switch to the junction block. If it is clicking, check the wiring from the junction block to the fan motor. If the wiring checks out okay, the fan relay is likely the problem, in which case the junction block must be replaced (the relays aren't replaceable individually). Complete junction block testing, including the fan relay, is included in Chapter 9.

4   If you're working on a later model and the fan still doesn't work,

4.6 Remove the fan bracket-to-radiator bolts and separate the fan from the radiator

check the wiring to the junction block. If the wiring is okay, test the junction block as described in Chapter 9.

Replacement

Fan motor

Refer to illustrations 4.6, 4.7 and 4.8

Warning: The engine must be completely cool before beginning this procedure.

5   Disconnect the cable from the negative terminal of the battery and remove the radiator (see Section 7).

6   Remove the three bolts securing the fan bracket to the radiator **(see illustration)**. On early models, note which bolt secures the fan motor ground/earth wire. Separate the fan and bracket from the radiator.

4.7 The fan blade assembly is retained to the motor shaft by a single nut

4.8 Remove the three screws that secure the motor to the bracket, then detach the motor

7   Remove the nut that retains the blades to the fan motor shaft **(see illustration)** and remove the fan blade assembly from the motor.
8   Remove the screws that attach the fan motor to the bracket **(see illustration)** and detach the motor from the bracket.
9   Installation is the reverse of the removal steps.

Thermostatic fan switch

Refer to illustration 4.11
Warning: *The engine must be completely cool before beginning this procedure.*
10   If you're working on an early model with a single-wire fan switch harness, don't place Teflon tape or silicone sealer on the switch threads. If not, prepare the new switch by wrapping the new threads with Teflon tape or by coating the threads with RTV sealant.
11   Unscrew the switch from the right-hand side of the radiator (early models) or from the left-hand side (later models) **(see illustration)**.
12   Quickly install the new switch, tightening it to the torque listed in this Chapter's Specifications.
13   Connect the electrical connector to the switch. Check, and if necessary, add coolant to the system (see Chapter 1).

5   Coolant temperature gauge and sender unit - check and replacement

Refer to illustration 5.4
Check

1   If the engine has been overheating but the coolant temperature gauge hasn't been indicating a hotter than normal condition, begin with a check of the coolant level (see Chapter 1). If it's low, add the recommended type of coolant and be sure to locate the source of the leak.
2   Remove the seat and the fuel tank (see Chapter 4).
3   Remove the fairing (see Chapter 8).
4   Locate the coolant temperature sender unit, which is screwed into the thermostat housing **(see illustration)**. Disconnect the electrical connector from the sender unit, turn the ignition key to the Run position (don't crank the engine over) and note the temperature gauge - it should read Cold.
5   With the ignition key still in the Run position, connect one end of a jumper wire to the sender unit wire and ground/earth the other end. The needle on the temperature gauge should swing over to the Hot mark. **Caution:** *Don't ground/earth the wire any longer than necessary or the gauge may be damaged.*
6   If the gauge passes both of these tests, but doesn't operate correctly under normal riding conditions, the temperature sender unit is

4.11 Disconnect the electrical connector and unscrew the switch from the radiator (later model shown; the switch on earlier models is on the other side of the radiator)

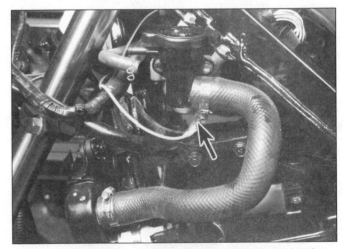

5.4 The coolant temperature sender (arrow) is located at the bottom of the thermostat housing

defective and must be replaced.
7   If the gauge didn't respond to the tests properly, either the wire to the gauge is bad or the gauge itself is defective.

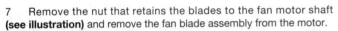

6.6 Remove the thermostat housing bolts (arrows); the forward bolt secures a ground/earth wire

7.4 The stone shield is secured by screws at the bottom and clips at the top (arrows)

Replacement

Sender unit

Warning: *The engine must be completely cool before beginning this procedure.*

8   Prepare the new sender unit by wrapping the threads with Teflon tape or coating them with silicone sealant.

9   Unscrew the sender unit from the thermostat housing and quickly install the new unit, tightening to the torque listed in this Chapter's Specifications.

10   Connect the electrical connector to the sender unit. Check, and if necessary, add coolant to the system (see Chapter 1).

Coolant temperature gauge

11   Refer to Chapter 9 for the coolant temperature gauge replacement procedure.

---

6   Thermostat - removal, check and installation

Refer to illustration 6.6,
Warning: *The engine must be completely cool before beginning this procedure.*

Removal

1   If the thermostat is functioning properly, the coolant temperature gauge should rise to the normal operating temperature quickly and then stay there, only rising above the normal position occasionally when the engine gets abnormally hot. If the engine does not reach normal operating temperature quickly, or if it overheats, the thermostat should be removed and checked, or replaced with a new one.

2   Refer to Chapter 1 and drain the cooling system.

3   Remove the seat and the fuel tank (see Chapter 4).

4   Remove the fairing (see Chapter 8).

5   Disconnect the hoses from the thermostat housing **(see illustration 5.4)**.

6   Unbolt the thermostat housing from the frame **(see illustration)**. The forward bolt also secures a ground/earth wire.

7   Remove the thermostat housing cover **(see illustration 1.1b)**.

8   Note the position of the relief hole, then lift out the thermostat .

9   Check the cover O-ring and replace it if its condition is in doubt. It's a good idea to replace the O-ring as a matter of course.

Check

10   Remove any coolant deposits, then visually check the thermostat for corrosion, cracks and other damage. If it was open when it was removed, the thermostat is defective.

11   To check the thermostat operation, submerge it in a container of water along with a thermometer. The thermostat should be suspended so it does not touch the sides of the container. **Warning**: *Antifreeze is poisonous. Do not use a cooking pan to test the thermostat.*

12   Gradually heat the water in the container with a hot plate or stove and check the temperature when the thermostat first starts to open.

13   Compare the opening temperature to the values listed in this Chapter's Specifications.

14   Continue heating the water until the valve is fully open.

15   Measure how far the thermostat valve has opened and compare to the value listed in this Chapter's Specifications.

16   If these specifications are not met, or if the thermostat doesn't open while the water is heated, replace it with a new one.

Installation

17   Install the thermostat into the housing with the relief hole positioned outward, away from the bike.

18   Install a new O-ring in the groove in the thermostat cover.

19   Place the cover on the housing and install the bolts, tightening them securely.

20   The remainder of installation is the reverse of the removal steps. Fill the cooling system with the recommended coolant (see Chapter 1).

---

7   Radiator - removal and installation

Refer to illustrations 7.4 and 7.5
Warning: *The engine must be completely cool before beginning this procedure.*

1   Set the bike on its centerstand. Remove the upper fairing (and lower fairing, if equipped) (see Chapter 8). Drain the cooling system (see Chapter 1).

2   Disconnect the fan motor connector. Disconnect the ground/earth wire for the fan switch (if equipped).

3   Loosen the radiator hose clamps. Work the hoses free from the fittings, taking care not to damage the fittings in the process.

4   Remove the stone shield from the radiator **(see illustration)**.

5   Remove the radiator mounting bolts **(see illustration)**. Take the radiator out.

6   Inspect the mounting bushings. Replace them if they're cracked or deteriorated.

7   Installation is the reverse of the removal steps, with the following additions:

   a) Don't forget to connect the fan switch ground/earth wire (if equipped).

   b) On all models, fill the cooling system with the recommended coolant (see Chapter 1).

7.5 Remove the radiator mounting bolts

8.5a Remove the cover bolts (arrows). . .

8.5b ..and lift the cover from the engine

8.6 If you can wiggle the impeller or pull it in-and-out, the pump is defective

8.12 Turn the impeller clockwise to remove it from the shaft

8 Water pump - check, removal and installation

Warning: *The engine must be completely cool before beginning this procedure.*

Check

Refer to illustrations 8.5a, 8.5b and 8.6

1   Visually check the area around the water pump for coolant leaks. Try to determine if the leak is simply the result of a loose hose clamp or deteriorated hose.

2   Set the bike on its centerstand.
3   Remove the lower fairing (if equipped). See Chapter 8.
4   Drain the engine coolant following the procedure in Chapter 1.
5   Loosen the hose clamp on the water pump cover fitting and remove the water pump cover bolts **(see illustration)**. Pull the cover away from the engine, separating the coolant pipe from the cylinder block as you do so **(see illustration)**.
6   Try to wiggle the pump impeller back-and-forth and in-and-out **(see illustration)**. If you can feel movement, the water pump must be replaced.
7   Check the impeller blades for corrosion. If they are heavily corroded, replace the water pump and flush the system thoroughly (it would also be a good idea to check the internal condition of the radiator).
8   If the cause of the leak was just a defective cover gasket, remove the old gasket and install a new one.

Removal

Refer to illustrations 8.12 and 8.15

9   Drain the coolant and remove the cover (if it hasn't already been removed).
10   Drain the engine oil (see Chapter 1).
11   Shift the transmission into first gear and press the rear brake pedal to keep the engine form turning.
12   Unscrew the impeller in a clockwise direction and take it off the shaft **(see illustration)**.
13   Take the water pump housing and gasket off the engine.
14   Turn the water pump shaft clockwise to remove it (if necessary).

3

8.15 Pry the oil seal out of the housing

8.18 Install a new oil seal and gasket

8.19 Position the housing on the engine, install a new gasket and
the dowels (arrows); turn the impeller counterclockwise to install
it on the shaft

8.20 The lower right cover bolt (arrow) is the only one with
a washer

15   Remove the gasket from the water pump housing and pry out the
oil seal **(see illustration)**.

Inspection

16   Check all parts for wear and damage and replace as necessary.
17   If the mechanical seal needs to be replaced, have it pressed out
and a new one pressed in by a Kawasaki dealer.

Installation

Refer to illustrations 8.18, 8.19 and 8.20

18   Install a new oil seal and gasket on the back side of the pump
housing **(see illustration)**.

19   Install the pump housing on the engine. Install the dowels (if they
were removed), the shaft (if removed), a new cover gasket and the impeller **(see illustration)**. Turn the impeller counterclockwise (anticlock-

9.2 Remove the Phillips screws that secure the tubes (it's a good
idea to replace them with Allen screws)

9.3 Pull the tubes out

9.4 Remove the O-rings with a pointed tool

9.5 Suspending the tubes from the handlebars will keep coolant from leaking out

wise) to tighten it.

20   Install the pump cover bolts. The lower right bolt is the only one with a washer **(see illustration)**.

---

9   Coolant tubes - removal and installation

Refer to illustrations 9.2, 9.3, 9.4 and 9.5

Warning: *The engine must be completely cool for this procedure.*

1   Remove the seat and fuel tank (see Chapter 4).

2   Remove the screws that secure the tubes to the engine **(see il-**

lustration). Note: *These Phillips screws may be very tight. Be sure to use the correct size screwdriver bit. It's a good idea to replace them with Allen screws that can be removed more easily in the future.*

3   Pull the tubes out of the engine **(see illustration)**.

4   Remove the O-ring from each tube with a pointed tool **(see illustration)**. Lightly coat new O-rings with high-temperature grease and install them on the tubes.

5   If the tubes are being removed to provide access for other work, suspend them from the handlebars with their ends up **(see illustration)**.

6   Installation is the reverse of the removal steps.

3

NOTES:

Chapter 4 Fuel and exhaust systems

Contents

4

Specifications

General

Carburetor type	Keihin CVK34 (two)
Fuel tank overall capacity..	18 liters (4.8 US gal, 4.0 Imp gal)
Fuel tank reserve capacity..	2.2 liters (0.6 US gal, 0.5 Imp gal)
Fuel grade...	Unleaded or low-lead (subject to local regulations), minimum octane rating 91 RON

Jet sizes

Main jet...	130
Main air jet..	100
Jet needle...	N36N
Pilot jet	35
Pilot air jet	130
Pilot screw setting...	2 turns out
Starter jet...	50
Carburetor adjustments	
Float height	0.669 inch (17 mm)
Fuel level	-0.2 inch (-0.5 mm)
Air switching valve closing vacuum...	17 to 19 inches Hg (430 to 490 mm Hg)

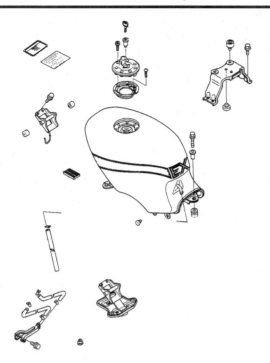

2.4 Fuel tank details

2.5 Push the liners off the fittings with a screwdriver; if you pull on them, they'll tighten on the fittings and be hard to remove

2.7 Inspect the lines under the tank

1   General information

The fuel system consists of the fuel tank, the fuel tap and filter, the carburetors and the connecting lines, hoses and control cables.

The carburetors used on these motorcycles are two constant vacuum Keihins with butterfly-type throttle valves. For cold starting, an enrichment circuit is actuated by a cable and the choke lever mounted on the left handlebar.

The exhaust system is a twin pipe design with a crossover pipe.

Many of the fuel system service procedures are considered routine maintenance items and for that reason are included in Chapter 1.

2   Fuel tank - removal and installation

Refer to illustrations 2.4, 2.5 and 2.7
Warning: *Gasoline (petrol) is extremely flammable, so take extra precautions when you work on any part of the fuel system. Don't smoke or allow open flames or bare light bulbs near the work area, and don't work in a garage where a natural gas-type appliance (such as a water heater or clothes dryer) is present. If you spill any fuel on your skin, rinse it off immediately with soap and water. When you perform any kind of work on the fuel system, wear safety glasses and have a fire extinguisher suitable for a Class B type fire (flammable liquids) on hand.*
1   The fuel tank is held in place at the forward end by two cups, one on each side of the tank, which slide over two rubber dampers on the frame. The rear of the tank is fastened to a bracket by a bolt and rubber insulator, which fit through a flange projecting from the tank.
2   Remove the seat and disconnect the cable from the negative terminal of the battery. Detach the fairing at the rear, then prop it out of the way with blocks of wood (see Chapter 8).
3   Mark and disconnect the breather hose and, on California models, the evaporative emission control system hoses from the tank.
4   Remove the bolt securing the rear of the tank to the bracket **(see illustration)**. **Note**: *If you're going to remove the tank bracket for access to other parts, leave it attached to the tank. Remove the four bracket bolts instead.*
5   Turn the fuel tap to the On or Reserve position, lift the rear of the tank up, slide back the hose clamps and push the fuel and vacuum lines **(see illustration)** off the fuel tap.
6   Slide the tank to the rear to disengage the front of the tank from

the rubber dampers, then carefully lift the tank away from the machine.
7   Before installing the tank, check the condition of the rubber mounting dampers and the hoses on the underside of the tank - if they're hardened, cracked, or show any other signs of deterioration, replace them **(see illustration)**.
8   When replacing the tank, reverse the above procedure. Make sure the tank seats properly and does not pinch any control cables or wires. If difficulty is encountered when trying to slide the tank cups onto the dampers, a small amount of light oil should be used to lubricate them.

3   Fuel tank - cleaning and repair

1   All repairs to the fuel tank should be carried out by a professional who has experience in this critical and potentially dangerous work. Even after cleaning and flushing of the fuel system, explosive fumes can remain and ignite during repair of the tank.
2   If the fuel tank is removed from the vehicle, it should not be placed in an area where sparks or open flames could ignite the fumes coming out of the tank. Be especially careful inside garages where a natural gas-type appliance is located, because the pilot light could cause an explosion.

4   Idle fuel/air mixture adjustment - general information

1   Due to the increased emphasis on controlling motorcycle exhaust emissions, certain governmental regulations have been formulated which directly affect the carburetion of this machine. In order to comply with the regulations, the carburetors on some models have a metal sealing plug pressed into the hole over the pilot screw (which controls

6.5 Loosen the clamps on the intake manifold tubes

6.7 Pull the spring bands back, toward the air cleaner housing

the idle fuel/air mixture) on each carburetor, so they can't be tampered with. These should only be removed in the event of a complete carburetor overhaul, and even then the screws should be returned to their original settings. The pilot screws on other models are accessible, but the use of an exhaust gas analyzer is the only accurate way to adjust the idle fuel/air mixture and be sure the machine doesn't exceed the emissions regulations.

2   If the engine runs extremely rough at idle or continually stalls, and if a carburetor overhaul does not cure the problem, take the motorcycle to a Kawasaki dealer service department or other repair shop equipped with an exhaust gas analyzer. They will be able to properly adjust the idle fuel/air mixture to achieve a smooth idle and restore low speed performance.

5   Carburetor overhaul - general information

1   Poor engine performance, hesitation, hard starting, stalling, flooding and backfiring are all signs that major carburetor maintenance may be required.

2   Keep in mind that many so-called carburetor problems are really not carburetor problems at all, but mechanical problems within the engine or malfunctions within the ignition system. Try to establish for certain that the carburetors are in need of a major overhaul before beginning.

3   Check the fuel tap filter, the fuel lines, the tank cap vent, the intake manifold hose clamps, the vacuum hoses, the air filter element, the cylinder compression, the spark plugs, the air suction system (US models only) and the carburetor synchronization before assuming that a carburetor overhaul is required. Also make sure that the end of the carburetor vent tube is not placed near the air intake. This will cause fuel starvation, resulting in poor performance above 3,500 rpm and a maximum engine speed of 5,000 rpm.

4   Most carburetor problems are caused by dirt particles, varnish and other deposits which build up in and block the fuel and air passages. Also, in time, gaskets and O-rings shrink or deteriorate and cause fuel and air leaks which lead to poor performance.

5   When the carburetor is overhauled, it is generally disassembled completely and the parts are cleaned thoroughly with a carburetor cleaning solvent and dried with filtered, unlubricated compressed air. The fuel and air passages are also blown through with compressed air to force out any dirt that may have been loosened but not removed by the solvent. Once the cleaning process is complete, the carburetor is reassembled using new gaskets, O-rings and, generally, a new inlet needle valve and seat.

6   Before disassembling the carburetors, make sure you have a carburetor rebuild kit (which will include all necessary O-rings and other parts), some carburetor cleaner, a supply of rags, some means of blowing out the carburetor passages and a clean place to work. It is recommended that only one carburetor be overhauled at a time to avoid mixing up parts.

6.8 Gently work the air inlet tubes on the air box free of the carburetors, then detach the carburetors from the intake manifold tubes

6   Carburetors - removal and installation

Warning: Gasoline (petrol) is extremely flammable, so take extra precautions when you work on any part of the fuel system. Don't smoke or allow open flames or bare light bulbs near the work area, and don't work in a garage where an appliance fueled by natural gas is present (such as a water heater or clothes dryer). If you spill any fuel on your skin, rinse it off immediately with soap and water. When you perform any kind of work on the fuel system, wear safety glasses and have a fire extinguisher suitable for a class B type fire (flammable liquids) on hand.

Removal

Refer to illustrations 6.5, 6.7 and 6.8

1   Remove the fuel tank (see Section 2).

2   If you're working on a US model, remove the vacuum switching valve for the air suction system (see Chapter 1).

3   Disconnect the choke cable from the carburetor assembly (see Section 10).

4   Loosen the lockwheel on the throttle cable adjuster at the handlebar and turn the adjuster in all the way.

5   Loosen the clamp screws on the intake manifolds (the rubber tubes that connect the carburetors to the engine) **(see illustration)**.

6   Mark and disconnect the vacuum hoses from the carburetors (see Chapter 1).

7   Slide the spring bands on the air inlet ducts away from the carburetors **(see illustration)**.

8   Pull the carburetor assembly clear of the air box tubes **(see illustration)**. Raise the assembly up far enough to disconnect the throttle cables from the throttle pulley, then remove the carburetors from the machine.

4

6.14a Route the carburetor vent tube (arrow) so it won't be pinched when the tank is installed . . .

6.14b . . .and be careful not to place its end near the air intake (arrow); this will cause fuel starvation

9   After the carburetors have been removed, stuff clean rags into the intake manifold tubes to prevent the entry of dirt or other objects.

Installation

Refer to illustrations 6.14a and 6.14b

10   Position the assembly over the intake manifold tubes. Lightly lubricate the ends of the throttle cables with multi-purpose grease and attach them to the throttle pulley. Make sure the accelerator and decelerator cables are in their proper positions.

11   Tilt the front of the assembly down and insert the fronts of the carburetors into the intake manifold tubes. Push the assembly forward and tighten the clamps.

12   Make sure the ducts from the air cleaner housing are seated properly, then slide the spring bands into position.

13   Connect the choke cable to the assembly and adjust it (see Section 10).

14   The remainder of installation is the reverse of the removal steps, with the following additions:

  a) Be sure the vent tube is routed next to the wiring harness so it isn't pinched **(see illustration)**. Don't place the end of the vent tube near the air intake **(see illustration)** or fuel starvation will occur, resulting in poor performance above 3,500 rpm and failure to rev past 5,000 rpm.

  b) Adjust the throttle grip freeplay (see Chapter 1).

  c) Check for fuel leaks.

  d) Check and, if necessary, adjust the idle speed and carburetor synchronization (see Chapter 1).

---

7   Carburetors - disassembly, cleaning and inspection

Warning: *Gasoline (petrol) is extremely flammable, so take extra precautions when you work on any part of the fuel system. Don't smoke or allow open flames or bare light bulbs near the work area, and don't work in a garage where an appliance fueled by natural gas is present (such as a water heater or clothes dryer). If you spill any fuel on your skin, rinse it off immediately with soap and water. When you perform any kind of work on the fuel system, wear safety glasses and have a fire extinguisher suitable for a class B type fire (flammable liquids) on hand.*

Disassembly

Refer to illustrations 7.2a, 7.2b, 7.2c, 7.3a, 7.3b, 7.4, 7.5a, 7.5b, 7.7, 7.8, 7.9, 7.10, 7.11, 7.12a and 7.12b

1   Remove the carburetors from the machine as described in Section 6. Set the assembly on a clean working surface. **Note**: *Unless the O-rings on the fuel and vent fittings between the carburetors are leaking, don't detach the carburetors from their mounting brackets. Also, work on one carburetor at a time to avoid getting parts mixed up.*

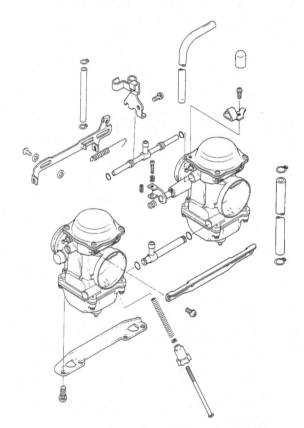

7.2a Carburetor mounting details

2   If the carburetors must be separated from each other (during a complete overhaul, for example) remove the idle adjusting screw assembly **(see illustration)**, being careful not to lose the spring and washer on the end of the screw. Disconnect the fuel hoses. Remove the choke lever spring and choke lever by removing the screw and plastic washers (two washers, one on each side of the lever) then remove the screws securing the upper and lower mounting plates to the carburetors **(see illustrations)**. Mark the position of each carburetor and gently separate them, noting how the throttle linkage is connected, and being careful not to lose any springs or fuel and vent fittings that are present between the carburetors.

3   Remove the four screws securing the top cover to the carburetor

7.2b On the back side of the carburetor assembly, remove the screws (lower arrows) that secure the lower mounting bracket and detach the upper bracket (upper arrow)

7.2c On the front side of the carburetor assembly, remove two screws (arrows) from each carburetor and detach the bracket

7.3a Each carburetor top cover is secured by four screws (arrows); one screw also secures the choke cable bracket

7.4 Remove the diaphragm/piston assembly from the carburetor body

body **(see illustration)**. Lift the cover off and remove the piston spring **(see illustration)**.

4   Peel the diaphragm away from its groove in the carburetor body, being careful not to tear it. Lift out the diaphragm/piston assembly **(see illustration)**.

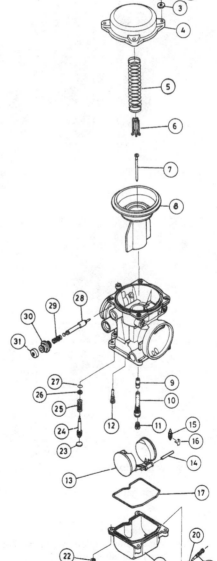

7.3b Carburetor - exploded view

1   Screw
2   Spring washer
3   Washer
4   Top cover
5   Piston spring
6   Spring seat
7   Jet needle
8   Diaphragm/ vacuum piston assembly
9   Needle jet
10   Needle jet holder/air bleed pipe
11   Main jet
12   Pilot jet
13   Float assembly
14   Pivot pin
15   Fuel inlet valve needle
16   Clip
17   O-ring
18   Float bowl
19   Drain screw
20   O-ring
21   Screw
22   Spring washer
23   Sealing plug (US models only)
24   Pilot screw
25   Spring
26   Washer
27   O-ring
28   Choke plunger
29   Spring
30   Nut
31   Cap

4

7.5a   Remove the vacuum piston spring seat from the piston

7.5b   Remove the needle from the piston

7.7   Push the float pivot pin out, then remove the float and valve needle assembly

7.8   Unscrew the main jet from the needle jet holder

7.9   Unscrew the needle jet holder/air bleed pipe

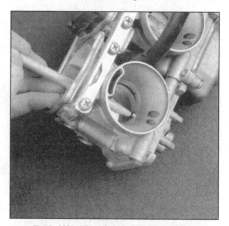

7.10   Working from the top of the carburetor, push the needle jet out with a wood or plastic tool

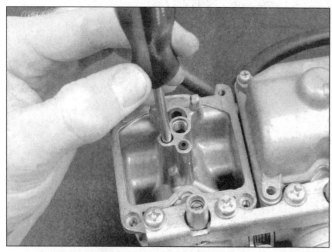

7.11   Unscrew the pilot jet

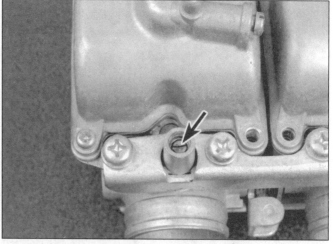

7.12a   Location of the pilot screw (arrow)

5   Remove the piston spring seat and separate the needle from the piston **(see illustrations)**.

6   Remove the four screws retaining the float bowl to the carburetor body, then detach the bowl **(see illustration 7.3b)**.

7   Push the float pivot pin out and detach the float (and fuel inlet valve needle) from the carburetor body **(see illustration)**. Detach the valve needle from the float.

8   Unscrew the main jet from the needle jet holder **(see illustration)**.

9   Unscrew the needle jet holder/air bleed pipe **(see illustration)**.

10   Using a wood or plastic tool, push the needle jet out of the carburetor body **(see illustration)**.

11   Using a small, flat-bladed screwdriver, remove the pilot jet **(see illustration)**.

12   The pilot (idle mixture) screw is located in the bottom of the carburetor body **(see illustration)**. On US models, this screw is hidden behind a plug which will have to be removed if the screw is to be taken out. The usual way to do this is to drill a hole in the plug, then pry it out. To avoid the risk of drilling into the screw, you can also drill a very

7.12b One way to remove the sealing plug is to drill a very small hole above it (left arrow), then reach into the hole with a hooked tool and push out the plug (right arrow)

small hole above the plug, then insert a hooked tool into the hole and push the plug out **(see illustration)**. On all models, turn the pilot screw in, counting the number of turns until it bottoms lightly. Record that number for use when installing the screw. Now remove the pilot screw along with its spring, washer and O-ring.

13   The choke plunger can be removed by unscrewing the nut that retains it to the carburetor body **(see illustration 7.3b)**, if the carburetors have been separated from each other (see Step 2).

Cleaning

Caution: *Use only a carburetor cleaning solution that is safe for use with plastic parts (be sure to read the label on the container).*

14   Submerge the metal components in the carburetor cleaner for approximately thirty minutes (or longer, if the directions recommend it).

15   After the carburetor has soaked long enough for the cleaner to loosen and dissolve most of the varnish and other deposits, use a brush to remove the stubborn deposits. Rinse it again, then dry it with compressed air. Blow out all of the fuel and air passages in the main and upper body. **Caution**: *Never clean the jets or passages with a piece of wire or a drill bit, as they will be enlarged, causing the fuel and air metering rates to be upset.*

Inspection

Refer to illustrations 7.17 and 7.22

16   Check the operation of the choke plunger. If it doesn't move smoothly, replace it, along with the return spring.

17   Check the tapered portion of the pilot screw for wear or damage **(see illustration)**. Replace the pilot screw if necessary.

18   Check the carburetor body, float bowl and top cover for cracks, distorted sealing surfaces and other damage. If any defects are found, replace the faulty component, although replacement of the entire carburetor will probably be necessary (check with your parts supplier for the availability of separate components).

19   Check the diaphragm for splits, holes and general deterioration. Holding it up to a light will help to reveal problems of this nature.

20   Insert the vacuum piston in the carburetor body and see that it moves up-and-down smoothly. Check the surface of the piston for wear. If it's worn excessively or doesn't move smoothly in the bore, replace the carburetor.

21   Check the jet needle for straightness by rolling it on a flat surface (such as a piece of glass). Replace it if it's bent or if the tip is worn.

22   Check the tip of the fuel inlet valve needle. If it has grooves or scratches in it, it must be replaced. Push in on the rod in the other end of the needle, then release it - if it doesn't spring back, replace the valve needle **(see illustration)**.

23   Check the O-rings on the float bowl and the drain plug (in the

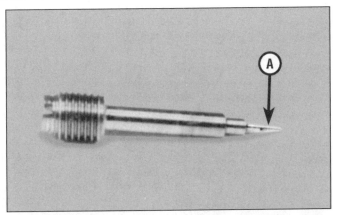

7.17 Check the tapered portion of the pilot screw (A) for wear or damage

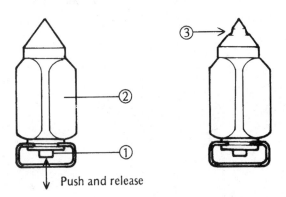

Push and release

7.22 Check the tip of the fuel inlet valve needle for grooves or scratches - also make sure the rod in the end of the needle pops back out quickly after it's pushed in

| 1 | Rod | 3 | Groove in tip |
| 2 | Valve needle | | |

float bowl). Replace them if they're damaged.

24   Operate the throttle shaft to make sure the throttle butterfly valve opens and closes smoothly. If it doesn't, replace the carburetor.

25   Check the floats for damage. This will usually be apparent by the presence of fuel inside one of the floats. If the floats are damaged, they must be replaced.

---

8   Carburetors - reassembly and fuel level adjustment

Caution: *When installing the jets, be careful not to over-tighten them - they're made of soft material and can strip or shear easily.*

Note: *When reassembling the carburetors, be sure to use the new O-rings, gaskets and other parts supplied in the rebuild kit.*

Reassembly

Refer to illustrations 8.4, 8.8, 8.10, 8.15 and 8.16

1   If the choke plunger was removed, install it in its bore, followed by its spring and nut. Tighten the nut securely and install the cap.

2   Install the pilot screw (if removed) along with its spring, washer and O-ring, turning it in until it seats lightly. Now, turn the screw out the number of turns that was previously recorded. If you're working on a US model, install a new metal plug in the hole over the screw. Apply a little bonding agent around the circumference of the plug after it has been seated.

3   Install the pilot jet, tightening it securely.

4

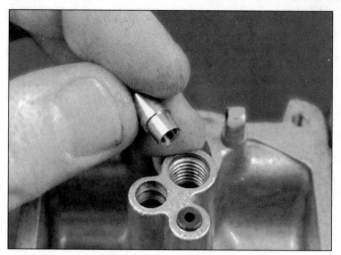

8.4 Install the needle jet, small diameter end first

8.8 Make sure the bead of the vacuum diaphragm seats in its groove, and that the diaphragm isn't distorted

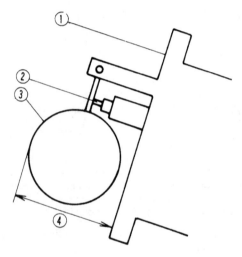

8.10 Float height adjustment details

1	Carburetor body	3	Float
2	Float valve needle rod	4	Float height

8.15 Make sure to install a plastic washer on each side of the choke lever when installing the screws

4   Turn the carburetor body upside-down and install the needle jet into its hole, small diameter first **(see illustration)**.

5   Install the needle jet holder/air bleed pipe, tightening it securely.

6   Install the main jet into the needle jet holder/air bleed pipe, tightening it securely.

7   Drop the jet needle down into its hole in the vacuum piston and install the spring seat over the needle. Make sure the spring seat doesn't cover the hole at the bottom of the vacuum piston - reposition it if necessary.

8   Install the diaphragm/vacuum piston assembly into the carburetor body. Lower the spring into the piston. Seat the bead of the diaphragm into the groove in the top of the carburetor body, making sure the diaphragm isn't distorted or kinked **(see illustration)**. This isn't always an easy task. If the diaphragm seems too large in diameter and doesn't want to seat in the groove, place the top cover over the carburetor diaphragm, insert your finger into the throat of the carburetor and push up on the vacuum piston. Push down gently on the top cover - it should drop into place, indicating the diaphragm has seated in its groove.

9   Install the top cover, tightening the screws securely. If you're working on the right-hand carburetor, don't forget to install the choke cable bracket on the corner.

10   Invert the carburetor. Attach the fuel inlet valve needle to the

float. Set the float into position in the carburetor, making sure the valve needle seats correctly. Install the float pivot pin. To check the float height, hold the carburetor so the float hangs down, then tilt it back until the valve needle is just seated (the rod in the end of the valve shouldn't be compressed). Measure the distance from the carburetor body to the top of the float **(see illustration)** and compare your measurement to the float height listed in this Chapter's Specifications. If it isn't as specified, carefully bend the tang that contacts the valve needle up or down until the float height is correct.

11   Install the O-ring into the groove in the float bowl. Place the float bowl on the carburetor and install the screws, tightening them securely.

12   If the carburetors were separated, install new O-rings on the fuel and vent fittings. Lubricate the O-rings on the fittings with a light film of oil and install them into their respective holes, making sure they seat completely **(see illustration 7.2a)**.

13   Position the coil springs between the carburetors, gently push the carburetors together, then make sure the throttle linkages are correctly engaged. Check the fuel and vent fittings to make sure they engage properly also.

14   Install the upper and lower mounting plates and install the screws, but don't tighten them completely yet. Set the carburetors on a sheet of glass, then align them with a straightedge placed along the edges of the bores. When the centerlines of the carburetors are both in horizontal and vertical alignment, tighten the mounting plate screws securely.

8.16 Install the throttle linkage springs

9.2 Cut the tie wrap that secures the cables to the wiring harness

15   Install the choke lever, making sure it engages correctly with both choke plungers. Position a plastic washer on each side of the choke lever **(see illustration)** and install the screws, tightening them securely. Install the lever return spring, then make sure the choke mechanism operates smoothly.

16   Install the throttle linkage springs **(see illustration)**. Visually synchronize the throttle butterfly valves, turning the adjusting screws on the throttle linkage, if necessary, to equalize the clearance between the butterfly valve and throttle bore of each carburetor. Check to ensure the throttle operates smoothly.

Fuel level adjustment

Refer to illustration 8.18

Warning: *Gasoline (petrol) is extremely flammable, so take extra precautions when you work on any part of the fuel system. Don't smoke or allow open flames or bare light bulbs near the work area, and don't work in a garage where an appliance fueled by natural gas is present (such as a water heater or clothes dryer). If you spill any fuel on your skin, rinse it off immediately with soap and water. When you perform any kind of work on the fuel system, wear safety glasses and have a fire extinguisher suitable for a class B type fire (flammable liquids) on hand.*

17   Lightly clamp the carburetor assembly in the jaws of a vise. Make sure the vise jaws are lined with wood. Set an auxiliary fuel tank next to the vise, but at an elevation that is higher than the carburetors (resting on a box, for example). Connect a hose from the fuel tank to the

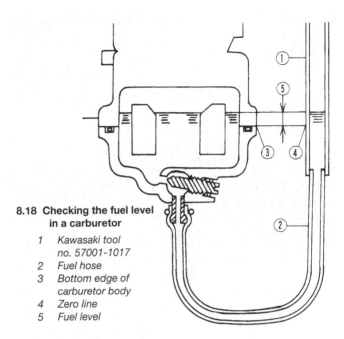

8.18 Checking the fuel level in a carburetor

1   *Kawasaki tool no. 57001-1017*
2   *Fuel hose*
3   *Bottom edge of carburetor body*
4   *Zero line*
5   *Fuel level*

fuel inlet fitting on the carburetor assembly.

18   Attach Kawasaki service tool no. 57001-1017 to the drain fitting on the bottom of one of the carburetor float bowls (both will be checked) **(see illustration)**. This is a clear plastic tube graduated in millimeters. An alternative is to use a length of clear plastic tubing and an accurate ruler. Hold the graduated tube (or the free end of the clear plastic tube) against the carburetor body, as shown in the accompanying illustration. If the Kawasaki tool is being used, raise the zero mark to a point several millimeters above the bottom edge of the carburetor main body. If a piece of clear plastic tubing is being used, make a mark on the tubing at a point several millimeters above the bottom edge of the carburetor main body.

19   Unscrew the drain screw at the bottom of the float bowl a couple of turns, then let fuel flow into the tube. Wait for the fuel level to stabilize, then slowly lower the tube until the zero mark is level with the bottom edge of the carburetor body. **Note**: *Don't lower the zero mark below the bottom edge of the carburetor then bring it back up - the reading won't be accurate.*

20   Measure the distance between the mark and top of the fuel level in the tube or gauge. This distance is the fuel level - write it down on a piece of paper, screw in the drain screw, close off the fuel supply, then move on to the next carburetor and check it the same way.

21   Compare your fuel level readings to the value listed in this Chapter's Specifications. If the fuel level in either carburetor is not correct, remove the float bowl and bend the tang up or down (see Step 10), as necessary, then recheck the fuel level. **Note**: *Bending the tang up increases the float height and lowers the fuel level - bending it down decreases the float height and raises the fuel level.*

22   After the fuel level for each carburetor has been adjusted, install the carburetor assembly (see Section 6).

---

9   Throttle cables - removal, installation and adjustment

Removal

Refer to illustrations 9.2, 9.4 and 9.5

1   Remove the fuel tank (see Section 2).

2   Cut the tie wrap that secures the cables to the wiring harness **(see illustration)**.

3   Loosen the accelerator cable lockwheel and screw the cable adjuster in.

4   Remove the cable/switch housing screws and detach the hous-

4

9.4 Detach the cable/switch housing from the handlebar

9.5 Lift the inner cables out of their grooves, align them with the slots in the throttle pulley and slip the cable ends out of the pulley

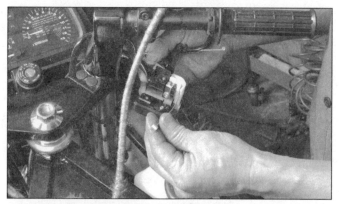

9.11 Route the decelerator cable through the guide in the cable/switch housing

9.12 Hold the rear half of the housing in place and install the accelerator cable

ing from the handlebar **(see illustration)**.

5   Detach the cables from the cable/switch housing, then lift them out of their grooves in the throttle pulley, align the cables with the pulley slots and slip the cable ends out of the throttle pulley **(see illustration)**.

6   Detach the decelerator and accelerator cables from the throttle pulley at the carburetor assembly (see Chapter 1).

7   Remove the cables, noting how they are routed.

Installation

Refer to illustrations 9.11 and 9.12

8   Route the cables into place. Make sure they don't interfere with any other components and aren't kinked or bent sharply.

9   Lubricate the end of the accelerator cable with multi-purpose grease and connect it to the throttle pulley at the carburetor. Pass the inner cable through the slot in the bracket, then seat the cable housing in the bracket.

10   Repeat the previous step to connect the decelerator cable.

11   Attach the rear half of the cable/switch housing to the handlebar, seating the decelerator cable in the groove in the housing as it's installed **(see illustration)**. Hook the decelerator cable to the throttle pulley.

12   Hold the rear half of the cable/switch housing to the handlebar and hook the accelerator cable to the throttle pulley, then push the accelerator cable guide into place, making sure it's correctly engaged with the housing **(see illustration)**.

13   Install the front half of the cable/switch housing, making sure the housing halves mate together and align correctly with the handlebar. Install the screws and tighten them securely.

14   Install a new tie wrap to secure the cables to the wiring harness.

Adjustment

15   Follow the procedure outlined in Chapter 1, Throttle operation/grip freeplay - check and adjustment, to adjust the cables.

16   Turn the handlebars back and forth to make sure the cables don't cause the steering to bind.

17   Operate the throttle and check the cable action. The cables should move freely and the throttle pulley at the carburetor should move back and forth in response to both acceleration and deceleration. If the cables don't operate properly, find and fix the problem before you put the fuel tank back on.

18   Install the fuel tank.

19   Start the engine. With the engine idling, turn the handlebars all the way to left and right while listening and watching the tachometer for changes in idle speed. If idle speed increases as the handlebars turn, the cables are improperly routed. This is dangerous. Find the problem and fix it before riding the bike.

---

10   Choke cable - removal, installation and adjustment

Removal

Refer to illustrations 10.2 and 10.3

1   Remove the seat and fuel tank (see Section 2). Cut the tie wrap that secures the choke and throttle cables to the wiring harness **(see illustration 9.2)**.

2   Pull the choke cable casing away from its mounting bracket at the carburetor and pass the inner cable through the opening in the bracket **(see illustration)**. Detach the cable end from the choke lever by the right-hand carburetor.

3   Remove the two screws securing the choke cable/switch housing halves to the left handlebar **(see illustration)**. Pull the front half of the housing off and separate the choke cable from the lever.

4   Remove the cable, noting how it's routed.

Installation

Refer to illustration 10.6

5   Route the cable into position. Connect the upper end of the cable

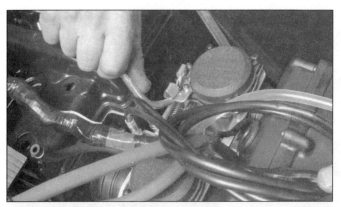

10.2 Separate the choke cable housing from the bracket at the carburetor

10.3 The choke cable/switch housing is held together by screws (arrows)

10.6 The cable housing should be securely seated in the bracket

11.4 The housing side covers are secured by screws

2   Remove the side covers (see Chapter 8 if necessary).
3   Remove the junction box bracket (see Chapter 9).
4   Remove the side covers from the air cleaner housing **(see illustration)**.
5   Disconnect the cables from the battery (negative cable first), then remove the battery.
6   If you're working on a US model, disconnect the large air suction hose from the front of the air filter housing.
7   Slide the spring bands that attach the ducts to the carburetors toward the air filter housing.
8   Disconnect the crankcase breather hose from the engine.
9   Lift the air filter housing up and out of the frame.
10 Installation is the reverse of removal.

---

12   Exhaust system - removal and installation

Refer to illustrations 12.4, 12.5, 12.6, 12.7, 12.9 and 12.10
1   Remove the lower fairing (if equipped) (see Chapter 8).
2   Drain the coolant (see Chapter 1).
3   Remove the radiator (see Chapter 3).
4   Remove the nuts that secure the exhaust pipe holders to the cylinder head, then remove the holders **(see illustration)**.
5   Loosen the clamp that secures the crossover pipe **(see illustration)**.
6   If you plan to separate the mufflers from the pipes, loosen the clamps **(see illustration)**.
7   Remove the muffler mounting bolts at the footpeg brackets **(see illustration)**.
8   Pull the exhaust system forward, separate the right side pipe from the left side pipe and remove the system from the machine.
9   Remove the gaskets from the cylinder head **(see illustration)**.
10 Installation is the reverse of removal, with the following additions:
  a) Install new gaskets at the cylinder head.
  b) Be sure the holders overlap correctly **(see illustration)**.

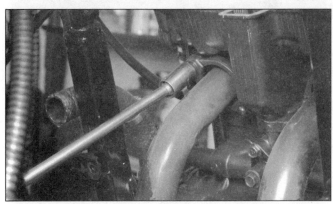

12.4 Remove the nuts and holders from the cylinder head studs

to the choke lever. Place the housing up against the handlebar, making sure the housing halves align correctly with each other and the handlebar. Install the screws, tightening them securely.
6   Connect the lower end of the cable to the choke lever. Pull back on the cable casing and connect it to the bracket on the right-hand carburetor **(see illustration)**.

Adjustment

7   Refer to Chapter 1, Section 11 for cable adjustment procedures.
8   Install the fuel tank and all of the other components that were previously removed. Replace the cut tie wrap with a new one.

---

11   Air filter housing - removal and installation

Refer to illustration 11.4
1   Remove the seat and fuel tank.

4

12.5 Loosen the crossover clamp

12.6 Loosen the muffler clamps if you
plan to separate the mufflers
from the pipes

12.7 Remove the muffler mounting bolts
at the rear footpegs

12.9 The gaskets at the cylinder head should be replaced
whenever the pipes are removed

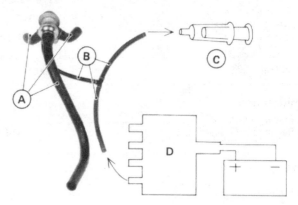

12.10 The holder halves are notched so they form a flush surface
when assembled correctly

13   Air switching valve - operational test

Refer to illustration 13.3

1   The air switching valve is part of the air suction system used on
US models. Routine checking procedures are described in Chapter 1.
If you suspect the valve has failed (for example, if the bike runs poorly
at low speed or backfires during deceleration), test it as follows:

2   Remove the valve and its hoses from the motorcycle (see Chapter 1).

3   Connect a vacuum gauge to one end of the vacuum line that
branches out from the T-fitting. Connect a vacuum pump to the other
end **(see illustration)**.

4   Try to blow air into the large air hose. It should flow easily when
there's no vacuum applied to the vacuum line.

5   Operate the vacuum pump and raise vacuum to the value listed in
this Chapter's Specifications. The valve should close, making it impos-
sible to blow air into the hose.

6   If the valve doesn't perform as described, replace it.

A. Air Hose   C. Syringe
B. Vacuum Hose   D. Vacuum Gauge Set:
                        57001-1198

13.3 Vacuum switching valve test setup

a   *Air hose*
b   *Vacuum line*
c   *Syringe (part of Kawasaki
      special tool) or hand
      vacuum pump*

d   *Vacuum gauge set (part
      of Kawasaki special tool
      57001-1198) or standard
      vacuum gauge*

Chapter 5 Ignition system

Contents

Specifications

Ignition coil

Primary resistance..	2.2 to 3.9 ohms
Secondary resistance..	10,000 to 16,000 ohms
Arcing distance	1/4 in (7 mm) or more

Pickup coil resistance...

360 to 440 ohms

Ignition timing ....

10-degrees BTDC @ idle (not adjustable)

5

---

1   General information

This motorcycle is equipped with a battery operated, fully transistorized, breakerless ignition system. The system consists of the following components:

Pickup coils
IC igniter unit
Battery and fuse
Ignition coils
Spark plugs
Stop and main (key) switches
Primary and secondary circuit wiring

The transistorized ignition system functions on the same principle as a conventional DC ignition system with the pickup unit and igniter performing the tasks previously associated with the breaker points and mechanical advance system. As a result, adjustment and maintenance of ignition components is eliminated (with the exception of spark plug replacement).

Because of their nature, the individual ignition system components can be checked but not repaired. If ignition system troubles occur, and the faulty component can be isolated, the only cure for the problem is to replace the part with a new one. Keep in mind that most electrical parts, once purchased, can't be returned. To avoid unnecessary expense, make very sure the faulty component has been positively identified before buying a replacement part.

2.3 With the wire attached, ground a spark plug to the engine and operate the starter - bright blue sparks should be visible

2.5 Unscrew the spark plug caps from the plug wires and measure their resistance with an ohmmeter

2.13 A simple spark gap testing fixture can be made from a block of wood, a large alligator clip, two nails, a screw and a piece of wire

2.14 Connect the tester to a good ground and attach one of the spark plug wires - when the engine is cranked, sparks should jump the gap between the nails

---

2   Ignition system - check

Refer to illustrations 2.3, 2.5, 2.13 and 2.14

Warning: *Because of the very high voltage generated by the ignition system, extreme care should be taken to avoid electrical shock when these checks are performed.*

1   If the ignition system is the suspected cause of poor engine performance or failure to start, a number of checks can be made to isolate the problem.

2   Make sure the ignition stop switch is in the Run or On position.

Engine will not start

3   Remove the fuel tank (see Chapter 4). Disconnect one of the spark plug wires, connect the wire to a spare spark plug and lay the plug on the engine with the threads contacting the engine. If it's necessary to hold the spark plug, use an insulated tool **(see illustration)**. Crank the engine over and make sure a well-defined, blue spark occurs between the spark plug electrodes. **Warning**: *DO NOT remove one of the spark plugs from the engine to perform this check - atomized fuel being pumped out of the open spark plug hole could ignite, causing severe injury!*

4   If no spark occurs, the following checks should be made:

5   Unscrew a spark plug cap from a plug wire and check the cap resistance with an ohmmeter **(see illustration)**. If the resistance is infi-

nite, replace it with a new one. Repeat this check on the other plug cap.

6   Make sure all electrical connectors are clean and tight. Refer to the wiring diagrams at the end of this book and check all wires for shorts, opens and correct installation.

7   Check the battery voltage with a voltmeter and the specific gravity with a hydrometer (see Chapter 1). If the voltage is less than 12-volts or if the specific gravity is low, recharge the battery.

8   Check the ignition fuse and the fuse connections. If the fuse is blown, replace it with a new one; if the connections are loose or corroded, clean or repair them.

9   Refer to Section 3 and check the ignition coil primary and secondary resistance.

10   Refer to Section 4 and check the pickup coil resistance.

11   If the preceding checks produce positive results but there is still no spark at the plug, have the IC igniter checked by a Kawasaki dealer service department or other repair shop equipped with the special tester required.

Engine starts but misfires

12   If the engine starts but misfires, make the following checks before deciding that the ignition system is at fault.

13   The ignition system must be able to produce a spark across a seven millimeter (1/4-inch) gap (minimum). A simple test fixture **(see illustration)** can be constructed to make sure the minimum spark gap

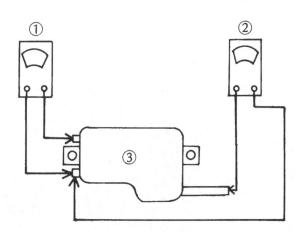

3.10a The right-hand ignition coil is mounted to the frame just behind the downtube

3.4 Ignition coil test

1) Measure primary winding resistance
2) Measure secondary winding resistance
3) Ignition coil

3.10b The left-hand ignition coil wires and mounting bolts are accessible from below

can be jumped. Make sure the fixture electrodes are positioned seven millimeters apart.

14   Connect one of the spark plug wires to the protruding test fixture electrode, then attach the fixture's alligator clip to a good engine ground/earth **(see illustration)**.

15   Crank the engine over (it may start and run on the remaining cylinder) and see if well-defined, blue sparks occur between the test fixture electrodes. If the minimum spark gap test is positive, the ignition coil for that cylinder is functioning properly. Repeat the check on the spark plug wire that is connected to the other coil. If the spark will not jump the gap during either test, or if it is weak (orange colored), refer to Steps 5 through 11 of this Section and perform the component checks described.

---

3   Ignition coils - check, removal and installation

Check

Refer to illustration 3.4

1   In order to determine conclusively that the ignition coils are defective, they should be tested by an authorized Kawasaki dealer service department which is equipped with the special electrical tester required for this check.

2   However, the coils can be checked visually (for cracks and other damage) and the primary and secondary coil resistances can be measured with an ohmmeter. If the coils are undamaged, and if the resistances are as specified, they are probably capable of proper operation.

3   To check the coils for physical damage, they must be removed (see Step 9). To check the resistances, simply remove the fuel tank (see Chapter 4), unplug the primary circuit electrical connectors from the coil(s) and remove the spark plug wire from the plug that is connected to the coil being checked. Mark the locations of all wires before disconnecting them.

4   To check the coil primary resistance, attach one ohmmeter lead to one of the primary terminals and the other ohmmeter lead to the other primary terminal **(see illustration)**.

5   Place the ohmmeter selector switch in the Rx1 position and compare the measured resistance to the value listed in this Chapter's Specifications.

6   If the coil primary resistance is as specified, check the coil secondary resistance by disconnecting the meter leads from the primary terminals and attaching one of them to the spark plug wire terminal and the other to either of the primary terminals **(see illustration 3.4)**.

7   Place the ohmmeter selector switch in the Rx100 position and compare the measured resistance to the values listed in this Chapter's Specifications.

8   If the resistances are not as specified, unscrew the spark plug wire retainers from the coil, detach the wires and check the resistance again. If it is now within specifications, one or both of the wires are bad. If it's still not as specified, the coil is probably defective and should be replaced with a new one.

Removal and installation

Refer to illustrations 3.10a and 3.10b

9   To remove the coils, refer to Chapter 4 and remove the fuel tank, then disconnect the spark plug wires from the plugs. After labeling them with tape to aid in reinstallation, unplug the coil primary circuit electrical connectors.

10   Support the coil with one hand and remove the coil mounting bolts **(see illustrations)**, then withdraw the coil from its bracket. If necessary, detach the bracket from the frame.

11   Installation is the reverse of removal. If a new coil is being installed, disconnect the spark plug wire terminal from the coil, disconnect the wire and transfer it to the new coil. Make sure the primary circuit electrical connectors are attached to the proper terminals. Just in case you forgot to mark the wires, the black and red wires connect to the right-hand ignition coil (red to positive, black to negative) and the red and green wires attach to the left-hand coil (red to positive, green to negative).

5

4.1 The pickup coil wiring harness leaves the alternator cover at this grommet (arrow); follow the harness to the connector (apply silicone sealer to the grommet whenever it's removed and reinstalled)

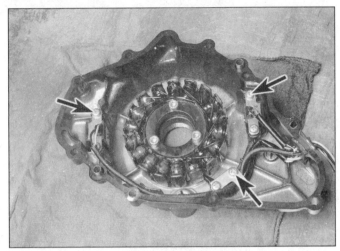

4.6 To remove the pickup coils (upper arrows), remove the mounting screws; also remove the screws that secure the harness clip (lower arrow)

electrical connector. The meter should read infinity.
4   If the pickup coils fail either of the above tests, they must be replaced.

Removal

Refer to illustration 4.6

5   Remove the alternator cover (see Chapter 9).
6   Unscrew the pickup coil mounting screws and remove the pickup coils **(see illustration)**. Remove the wiring harness retainer, slip the grommet out of its slot and remove the pickup coils together with their wiring harness.

Installation

7   Position the pickup coils in the alternator cover and install the screws, tightening them securely. Apply a small amount of silicone sealant to the grommet on the wiring harness and seat the grommet securely in the notch in the alternator cover **(see illustration 4.1)**.
8   Install the alternator cover and connect the electrical connector.

5.2 The IC igniter is mounted on the right-hand side behind the air box

---

5   IC igniter - removal, check and installation

Refer to illustration 5.2

Removal

1   Remove the right side cover.
2   Disconnect the electrical connector and remove the igniter mounting bolts **(see illustration)**. Take the igniter out.

Check

3   A special tester is required to accurately measure the resistance values across the various terminals of the IC igniter. Take the unit to a Kawasaki dealer service department or other repair shop equipped with this tester.

Installation

4   Installation is the reverse of the removal steps.

---

4   Pick-up coils - check, removal and installation

Refer to illustration 4.1

Check

1   Follow the pickup coil wiring harness from the point where it leaves the alternator cover to the electrical connector, then disconnect the connector for the pickup coils **(see illustration)**.
2   Probe each pair of terminals in the pickup coil connector with an ohmmeter (the black and yellow wire terminals, then the blue and black/white wire terminals) and compare the resistance reading with the value listed in this Chapter's Specifications.
3   Set the ohmmeter on the highest resistance range. Measure the resistance between a good ground/earth and each terminal in the

Chapter 6 Frame, suspension and final drive

Contents

Specifications

Fork spring length
Standard .... 20.34 inch (516.7 mm)
Minimum .... 19.92 inch (506 mm)
Rear spring preload
    Standard setting.. Compressed to 0.669 inch (17 mm) less than free length
    Usable range .... 0.275 inch (7 mm) to 1.06 inch (27 mm) less than free length

Sprockets
Rear sprocket runout (maximum) .... 0.020 in (0.5 mm)
Engine sprocket diameter (16 teeth)
    Standard... 2.795 to 2.803 inch (71.01 to 71.21 mm)
    Minimum... 2.767 inch (70.3 mm)
Rear sprocket diameter (42 teeth)
    Standard... 7.965 to 7.985 inch (202.32 to 202.82 mm)
    Minimum... 7.953 inch (202 mm)

Torque specifications
Handlebar grip-to-upright bolts... 16.5 ft-lbs (23 Nm)
Handlebar upright-to-upper triple clamp bolts................... 16.5 ft-lbs (23 Nm)
Damper rod bolt.. 22 ft-lbs (29 Nm)
Steering stem bolt .... 35 ft-lbs (47 Nm)
Steering stem locknut... 65 in-lbs (7.4 Nm)
Fork upper triple clamp bolts .... 14.5 ft-lbs (20 Nm)
Fork lower triple clamp bolts .... 22 ft-lbs (29 Nm)
Rear shock absorber mounting bolts/nuts........................ 36 ft-lbs (49 Nm)
Tie-rod-to-rocker arm and swingarm bolt/nut................... 36 ft-lbs (49 Nm)
Rocker arm pivot shaft nut... 36 ft-lbs (49 Nm)
Swingarm pivot shaft nut.. 65 ft-lbs (88 Nm)
Rear sprocket-to-wheel coupling nuts.............................. 54 ft-lbs (74 Nm)
Engine sprocket holding plate bolts .... 87 in-lbs (9.8 Nm)

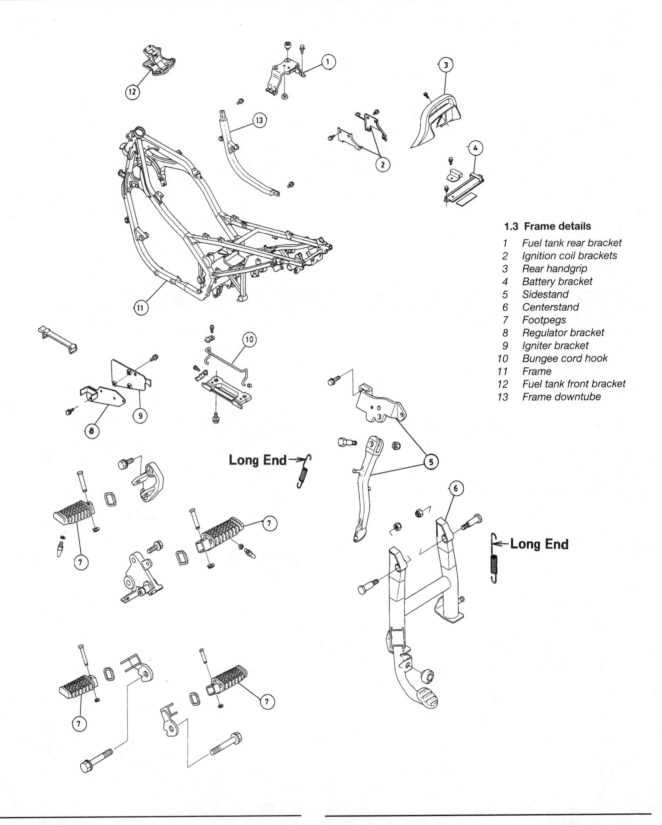

1.3 Frame details

1   Fuel tank rear bracket
2   Ignition coil brackets
3   Rear handgrip
4   Battery bracket
5   Sidestand
6   Centerstand
7   Footpegs
8   Regulator bracket
9   Igniter bracket
10   Bungee cord hook
11   Frame
12   Fuel tank front bracket
13   Frame downtube

Long End →

←**Long End**

---

1   General information

Refer to illustration 1.3

The machines covered by this manual use a full cradle frame, constructed of steel square tubing. The right downtube is detachable, which allows for easy engine removal.

The front forks are of the conventional coil spring, hydraulically-

damped telescopic type.

The rear suspension is Kawasaki's Uni-trak design, which consists of a single shock absorber, a rocker arm, two tie-rods and a square-section aluminum swingarm **(see illustration)**.

The final drive uses an endless chain (which means it doesn't have a master link). A rubber damper is installed between the rear wheel coupling and the wheel.

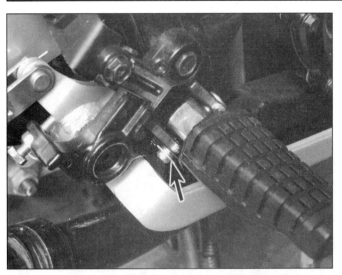

3.1 The footpegs are secured to their brackets by C-clips (rider's right footpeg shown)

3.8 The rider's left side footpeg bracket is secured by two bolts (arrows)

2 Frame - inspection and repair

1   The frame should not require attention unless accident damage has occurred. In most cases, frame replacement is the only satisfactory remedy for such damage. A few frame specialists have the jigs and other equipment necessary for straightening the frame to the required standard of accuracy, but even then there is no simple way of assessing to what extent the frame may have been over stressed.

2   After the machine has accumulated a lot of miles, the frame should be examined closely for signs of cracking or splitting at the welded joints **(see illustration 1.3)**. Rust can also cause weakness at these joints. Loose engine mount bolts can cause ovaling or fracturing of the mounting tabs. Minor damage can often be repaired by welding, depending on the extent and nature of the damage.

3   Remember that a frame which is out of alignment will cause handling problems. If misalignment is suspected as the result of an accident, it will be necessary to strip the machine completely so the frame can be thoroughly checked.

3 Footpegs and brackets - removal and installation

Rider's right side

Refer to illustration 3.1

1   If it's only necessary to detach the footpeg from the bracket, pry the C-clip off the pivot pin **(see illustration)**, slide out the pin and detach the footpeg from the bracket. Be careful not to lose the spring. Installation is the reverse of removal, but be sure to install the spring correctly.

2   If it's necessary to remove the entire bracket from the frame, unplug the electrical connector for the rear brake light switch.

3   Remove the cotter pin (split pin) from the clevis pin that attaches the brake pedal to the brake rod, then remove the clevis pin (see Chapter 7).

4   Remove the bolts that secure the bracket to the frame, then detach the footpeg and bracket.

5   Installation is the reverse of removal.

Rider's left side

Refer to illustration 3.8

6   If it's only necessary to detach the footpeg from the bracket, pry the C-clip off the pivot pin **(see illustration 3.1)**, slide out the pin and detach the footpeg from the bracket.

7   If it's necessary to remove the entire bracket from the frame, remove the shift lever (see Chapter 2).

4.1 The centerstand is secured by pivot bolts (arrow); the long end of the spring is installed toward the pivot bolt

8   Remove the bracket bolts **(see illustration)** and remove the bracket from the frame.

9   Installation is the basically the reverse of removal. Apply a thin coat of grease to the shift pedal pivot bolt, and be sure to line up the matchmarks on the shift lever and shift shaft. The link rod should be parallel to the shift pedal.

Passenger footpegs and brackets (either side)

10   If it's only necessary to detach the footpeg from the bracket, pry the C-clip off the pivot pin **(see illustration 3.1)**, slide out the pin and detach the footpeg from the bracket.

11   If it's necessary to remove the entire bracket, unscrew the bolt and detach the bracket from the frame.

12   Installation is the reverse of removal.

4 Side and centerstand - maintenance

Refer to illustrations 4.1 and 4.3

1   The centerstand pivots on two bolts attached to the frame **(see illustration)**. Periodically, remove the pivot bolts and grease them thoroughly to avoid excessive wear.

2   Make sure the return spring is in good condition. A broken or weak spring is an obvious safety hazard.

6

4.3 The sidestand is secured by two bolts (arrows); the long end of the spring is upward when the stand is down

5.1a To remove an upright, remove the plugs (right arrow) and the bolts beneath them (left arrow). . .

5.1b . . .and lift the upright off

5.2a To detach a handlebar grip, remove the plug (arrow). . .

5.2b . . .and remove the bolt behind it

3   The sidestand is bolted to the frame **(see illustration)**. An extension spring anchored to the bracket ensures that the stand is held in the retracted position.

4   Make sure the pivot bolt is tight and the extension spring is in good condition and not over stretched. An accident is almost certain to occur if the stand extends while the machine is in motion.

5   Handlebars - removal and installation

Refer to illustrations 5.1a, 5.1b, 5.2a and 5.2b

1   The handlebars are individual assemblies that slip over the tops of the fork tubes, each being retained to the triple clamp by two Allen-head bolts. If the handlebars must be removed for access to other components, such as the forks or the steering head, simply remove the bolts and slip the handlebar(s) off the fork tubes **(see illustrations)**. It's not necessary to disconnect the cables, wires or hoses, but it is a good idea to support the assembly with a piece of wire or rope, to avoid unnecessary strain on the cables, wires and (on the right side) the brake hose.

2   To remove the grip portion of the handlebar, refer to Chapter 7 for the master cylinder removal procedure and Chapter 4 for the throttle cable/switch housing and choke cable/switch housing removal procedures. Remove the plug and the bolt behind it **(see illustrations)**, then detach the grip from the handlebar upright.

3   Check the handlebars for cracks and distortion and replace them if any undesirable conditions are found.

4   Installation is the reverse of the removal steps. Tighten the bolts to the torques listed in this Chapter's Specifications.

6.9a Remove the upper triple clamp bolts (arrow) . . .

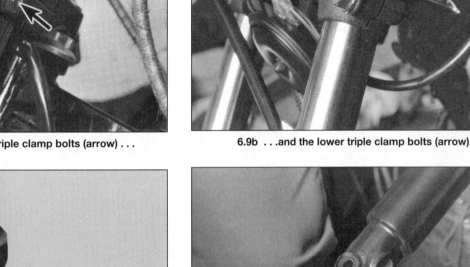

6.9b . . .and the lower triple clamp bolts (arrow)

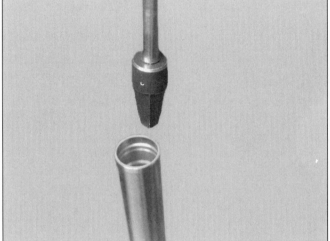

7.4a This is the Kawasaki tool that keeps the damper rod from turning - the corners of the tapered section bite into the round hole in the damper rod to hold it

7.4b Hold the damper rod and remove the screw with an Allen wrench

6   Forks - removal and installation

Refer to illustrations 6.9a and 6.9b

Removal

1   Set the bike on its centerstand.
2   Remove the fuel tank (see Chapter 4)
3   Remove the upper fairing (see Chapter 8).
4   If you're removing the left fork leg, remove the brake caliper and hang it from the bike with a piece of rope or wire (see Chapter 7).
5   Remove the wheel (see Chapter 7).
6   Remove the front fender (see Chapter 8).
7   Remove the handlebars (see Section 5). Support them so the cables, wires and brake hose aren't strained or kinked.
8   Remove any wiring harness clamps or straps from the fork tubes.
9   Loosen the fork upper and lower triple clamp bolts **(see illustrations)**, then twist the fork tubes and slide them downward and out of the triple clamps.

Installation

10   Slide each fork leg into the lower triple clamp.
11   Slide the fork legs up, installing the tops of the tubes into the upper triple clamp.

12   The remainder of installation is the reverse of the removal procedure. Be sure to tighten the triple clamp bolts to the torque listed in this Chapter's Specifications. Tighten the caliper mounting bolts to the torque listed in the Chapter 7 Specifications.
13   Pump the front brake lever several times to bring the pads into contact with the discs.

7   Forks - disassembly, inspection and reassembly

Disassembly

Refer to illustrations 7.4a, 7.4b, 7.4c, 7.4d, 7.5, 7.6, 7.7a, 7.7b, 7.9 and 7.10

1   Remove the forks following the procedure in Section 6. Work on one fork leg at a time to avoid mixing up the parts.
2   Remove the retaining ring, top plug and fork spring (see in Chapter 1, Section 29).
3   Invert the fork assembly over a container and allow the oil to drain out.
4   Prevent the damper rod from turning using a holding handle (Kawasaki tool no. 57001-183) and adapter (Kawasaki tool no. 57001-1057) or equivalents **(see illustration)**. Unscrew the Allen bolt at the bottom of the outer tube and retrieve the copper washer **(see illustration)**. **Note**: *If you don't have access to these special tools, you can*

6

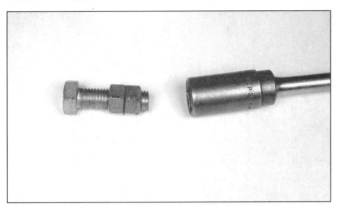

7.4c To make a damper rod holder, thread two nuts onto a bolt with a head that will wedge inside the damper rod and tighten the nuts against each other. . .

7.4d . . .then install the nut-end into a socket (connected to a long extension) and tape it into place

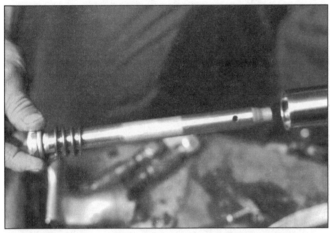

7.5 Remove the damper rod and rebound spring from the inner tube

7.6 Pry the dust seal out of the outer tube with a small screwdriver

7.7a Pry the retaining ring (arrow) out of its groove. . .

7.7b . . .and slide it off the inner fork tube

fabricate your own using a bolt with a head that fits inside the damper rod, two nuts, a socket (to fit on the nuts), a long extension and a ratchet. Thread the two nuts onto the bolt and tighten them against each other **(see illustration)**. Insert the assembly into the socket and tape it into place **(see illustration)**. Now, insert the tool into the fork tube and engage the bolt head (or the special Kawasaki tool) into the round hole in the damper rod.

5   Pull out the damper rod and the rebound spring **(see illustration)**. Don't remove the Teflon ring from the damper rod; the damper

rod is sold as an assembly, so if the ring is worn, you'll need a new damper rod.

6   Pry the dust seal from the outer tube **(see illustration)**.

7   Pry the retaining ring from its groove in the outer tube **(see illustrations)**. Remove the ring and the washer that's present underneath it.

8   Hold the outer tube and yank the inner tube upward, repeatedly (like a slide hammer), until the seal and outer tube guide bushing pop loose.

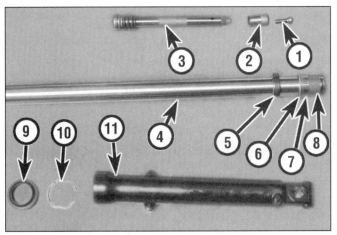

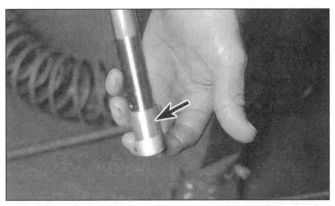

7.10 Dump the damper rod base (arrow) out of the fork tube and put it back on the damper rod

7.9 Fork details

1	Damper rod screw	7	Inner fork tube bushing
2	Damper rod base	8	Outer fork tube bushing
3	Damper rod	9	Dust seal
4	Inner fork tube	10	Oil seal retainer
5	Oil seal	11	Outer fork tube
6	Washer		

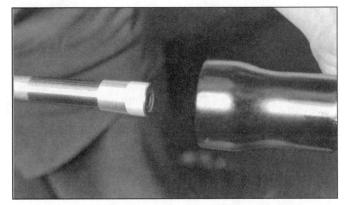

7.17a ...then install the assembly into the outer fork tube...

7.16 Assemble the damper rod into the inner fork tube...

9   Slide the seal, washer and outer tube guide bushing from the inner tube **(see illustration)**.

10   Invert the outer tube and remove the damper rod base **(see illustration)**.

Inspection

11   Clean all parts in solvent and blow them dry with compressed air, if available. Check the inner and outer fork tubes, the guide bushings and the damper rod for score marks, scratches, flaking of the chrome and excessive or abnormal wear. Look for dents in the tubes and replace them if any are found. Check the fork seal seat for nicks, gouges and scratches. If damage is evident, leaks will occur around the seal-to-outer tube junction. Replace worn or defective parts with new ones.

12   Have the fork inner tube checked for runout at a dealer service department or other repair shop. **Warning:** *If it is bent, it should not be straightened; replace it with a new one.*

13   Measure the overall length of the long spring and check it for cracks and other damage. Compare the length to the minimum length listed in this Chapter's Specifications. If it's defective or sagged, replace both fork springs with new ones. Never replace only one spring.

Reassembly

Refer to illustrations 7.16, 7.17a, 7.17b, 7.17c, 7.18a, 7.18b, 7.20a, 7.20b, 7.20c and 7.21

14   If it's necessary to replace the inner guide bushing (the one that won't come off that's on the bottom of the inner tube), pry it apart at the slit and slide it off. Make sure the new one seats properly.

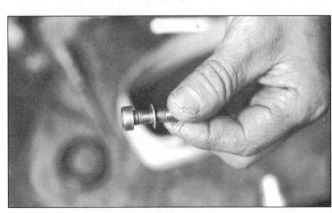

7.17b ...place a new washer on the damper rod bolt...

15   Place the rebound spring over the damper rod and slide the rod assembly into the inner fork tube until it protrudes from the lower end of the tube.

16   Install the damper rod base onto the end of the damper rod **(see illustration)**.

17   Insert the inner tube/damper rod assembly into the outer tube **(see illustration)** until the Allen-head bolt (with copper washer) can be threaded into the damper rod from the lower end of the outer tube **(see illustrations)**. **Note:** *Apply a non-permanent thread locking compound to the threads of the bolt. Keep the two tubes fairly horizontal so the damper rod base doesn't fall off. Using the tool described in Step 4, hold the damper rod and tighten the Allen bolt to the torque listed in this Chapter's Specifications.*

6

7.17c . . .and thread it into the damper rod (arrow)

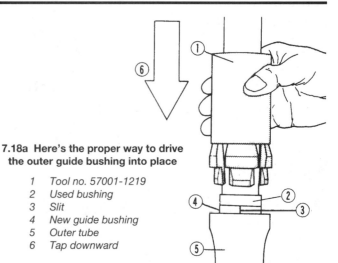

**7.18a Here's the proper way to drive
the outer guide bushing into place**

1   Tool no. 57001-1219
2   Used bushing
3   Slit
4   New guide bushing
5   Outer tube
6   Tap downward

**7.18b If you don't have the proper tool, a section of pipe can be
used the same way the special tool would be used - as a slide
hammer (be sure to tape the ends of the pipe so it doesn't scratch
the fork tube)**

**7.20a Slide the oil seal down the fork tube as far as you can
with fingers. . .**

18   Slide the outer guide bushing down the inner tube. The slit in the
bushing must point to the left or right - not to the front or rear. Using a
special bushing driver (Kawasaki tool no. 57001-1219) or equivalent
and a used guide bushing placed on top of the guide bushing being installed, drive the bushing into place until it is fully seated **(see illustration)**. If you don't have access to one of these tools, it is highly recommended that you take the assembly to a Kawasaki dealer service
department or other motorcycle repair shop to have this done. It is
possible, however, to drive the bushing into place using a section of
tubing and an old guide bushing **(see illustration)**. Wrap tape around
the ends of the tubing to prevent it from scratching the fork tube.
19   Slide the washer down the inner tube, into position over the guide
bushing.
20   Lubricate the lips and the outer diameter of the fork seal with the
recommended fork oil (see Chapter 1) and slide it down the inner tube,
with the lips facing down **(see illustration)**. Drive the seal into place
with a special seal driver (Kawasaki tool no. 57001-1091 **(see illustrations)**. If you don't have access to one of these, it is recommended
that you take the assembly to a Kawasaki dealer service department
or other motorcycle repair shop to have the seal driven in. If you are
very careful, the seal can be driven in with a hammer and a drift punch.
Work around the circumference of the seal, tapping gently on the outer
edge of the seal until it's seated. Be careful - if you distort the seal,
you'll have to disassemble the fork again and end up taking it to a
dealer anyway!

**7.20b . . .slide the driver (this is Kawasaki special tool no. 57001-
1091) over the inner fork tube and position it against the seal. . .**

21   Install the washer and the retaining ring, making sure the ring is
completely seated in its groove **(see illustration)**.
22   Install the dust seal, making sure it seats completely.
23   Install the drain screw and a new gasket, if it was removed.

7.20c ...and tap the driver against the seal to seat it in the outer fork tube

7.21 Install the retaining ring

8.6a Remove the steering stem bolt...

8.6b ...and the upper triple clamp

8.9a Remove the washer and upper bearing race...

8.9b ...and the 19 ball bearings

24 Compress the fork fully and add the recommended type and quantity of fork oil (see Chapter 1).
25 Install the fork spring, with the small-diameter end at the bottom. Install the top plug and secure it with the retaining ring (see Chapter 1).
26 Install the fork by following the procedure outlined in Section 6. If you won't be installing the fork right away, store it in an upright position to prevent leakage.

8 Steering head bearings - replacement

Refer to illustrations 8.6a, 8.6b, 8.9a, 8.9b, 8.10, 8.12, 8.14a, 8.14b, 8.15, 8.18, 8.19 and 8.20

1 If the steering head bearing check/adjustment (see Chapter 1) does not remedy excessive play or roughness in the steering head

bearings, the entire front end must be disassembled and the bearings and races replaced with new ones.
2 Remove the fuel tank (see Chapter 4).
3 Remove the upper fairing (and lower fairing, if equipped). (See Chapter 8).
4 Remove the front forks (see Section 6).
5 Unbolt the horn bracket from the steering head (see Chapter 9).
6 Remove the steering stem bolt **(see illustration)**, then lift off the upper triple clamp (sometimes called the fork bridge or crown) **(see illustration)**.
7 Support the steering stem from the bottom so it doesn't fall out of the frame during the next steps.
8 Remove the steering stem locknut with a spanner wrench (see in Chapter 1).
9 Remove the washer and upper race from the upper bearing, then remove the 19 ball bearings **(see illustrations)**.

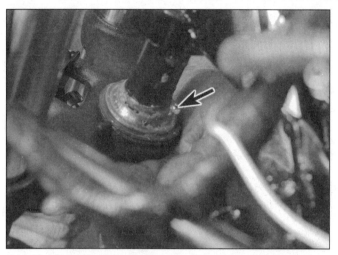

8.10 When you lower the steering stem, some ball bearings (arrow) will fall out, so be ready to catch them

8.12 Check the lower bearing race on the steering stem (arrow); don't remove it unless it or the grease seal below it needs to be replaced

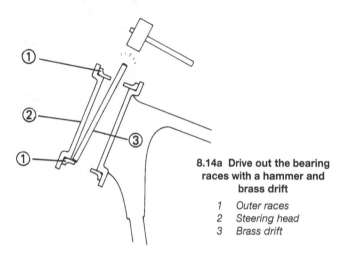

8.14a Drive out the bearing races with a hammer and brass drift

1   *Outer races*
2   *Steering head*
3   *Brass drift*

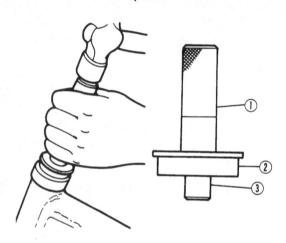

8.14b Drive in the bearing races with a bearing driver or a socket the same diameter as the bearing race

1   *Bearing driver handle*   3   *Bearing driver*
2   *Bearing driver*

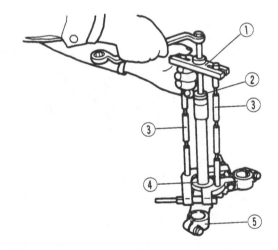

8.15 Remove the steering stem bearing with a puller like this one (or have it pressed off by a Kawasaki dealer or machine shop)

1   *Bearing puller*   3   *Post (Kawasaki part*
    (Kawasaki tool   *no. 57001-1190)*
    no. 57001-158)   4   *Lower bearing race*
2   *Adapter (Kawasaki tool*   5   *Lower triple clamp and*
    no. 57001-317)   *steering stem*

10   Lower the steering stem and lower triple clamp just far enough to expose the lower ball bearing **(see illustration)**. If it's stuck, gently tap on the top of the steering stem with a plastic mallet or a hammer and a wood block. **Note**: *Ball bearings may fall out when the steering stem is lowered. Position your hands so you can catch them. There are 20 ball bearings in the lower bearing.*

Inspection

11   Clean all the parts with solvent and dry them thoroughly, using compressed air, if available. Wipe the old grease out of the frame steering head and bearing races.
12   Examine the races on the steering stem and in the steering head for cracks, dents, and pits **(see illustration)**. If even the slightest amount of wear or damage is evident, the races should be replaced with new ones.
13   Check the ball bearings for wear. Replace any defective parts with new ones. If a new bearing is required, replace both of them as a set.
14   To remove the races, drive them out of the steering head with a brass drift **(see illustration)**. A slide hammer with the proper internal-jaw puller will also work. Since the races are an interference fit in the frame, installation will be easier if the new races are left overnight in a freezer. This will cause them to contract and slip into place in the

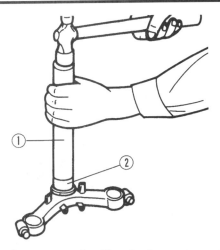

8.18 Drive the grease seal and bearing lower race on with a hollow driver (or an equivalent piece of pipe) - these are the Kawasaki special tools

1 *Stem bearing driver (tool no. 57001-137)*
2 *Adapter (tool no. 57001-294)*

8.20 Stick 20 steel balls into place in the grease

8.19 Smear a thick layer of grease onto the lower race to hold the ball bearings in place

9.3a Loosen the upper nut (arrow) and bolt, but don't remove them at first

frame with very little effort. When installing the races, coat them with oil and tap them gently into place with a bearing driver **(see illustration)** or a hammer and punch or a large socket. Do not strike the bearing surface or the race will be damaged.

15   To remove the lower bearing from the steering stem, use a bearing puller (Kawasaki tool no. 57001-158 or equivalent, combined with adapter no. 57001-317 and post no. 57001-1190) **(see illustration)**. Don't remove this bearing unless it, or the grease seal underneath, must be replaced.

16   Check the grease seal under the lower bearing and replace it with a new one if necessary.

17   Inspect the steering stem/lower triple clamp for cracks and other damage. Do not attempt to repair any steering components. Replace them with new parts if defects are found.

Installation

18   Install the grease seal and lower bearing race onto the steering stem (if they were removed). Coat the race with oil and drive it onto the steering stem using Kawasaki stem bearing driver no. 57001-137 and adapter no. 57001-294 **(see illustration)**. If you don't have access to these tools, a section of pipe with a diameter the same as the inner race of the bearing can be used. Drive the bearing race on until it is fully seated.

19   Coat the lower bearing race in the steering stem with a thick layer of grease **(see illustration)**.

20   Coat 20 ball bearings with grease and stick them to the lower bearing race in the steering head **(see illustration)**.

21   Carefully insert the steering stem/lower triple clamp into the frame head, making sure you don't displace any of the ball bearings.

22   Install 19 ball bearings in the upper bearing **(see illustration 8.9b)**. Install the upper race and washer. Install the locknut, chamfered side down.

23   Using a spanner wrench, tighten the locknut to the torque listed in this Chapter's Specifications.

24   Turn the lower triple clamp back and forth. It should turn easily (without binding and without looseness).

25   Install the upper triple clamp on the steering stem. Install the bolt, tightening it to the torque listed in this Chapter's Specifications.

26   The remainder of installation is the reverse of removal.

27   After all parts are installed, recheck steering head bearing adjustment and correct it if necessary (see Chapter 1).

6

---

9   Rear shock absorber - removal, adjustment and installation

Removal

Refer to illustrations 9.3a, 9.3b and 9.4

1   Set the bike on its centerstand.

2   Remove the side covers.

3   Loosen the shock absorber upper nut **(see illustrations)**. Don't remove it yet.

9.3b Rear suspension - exploded view

1 Rocker arm
2 Bushing
3 Sleeve
4 O-ring
5 Nut
6 Seal
7 Sleeve
8 Bushing
9 Nut
10 Right-hand tie rod
11 Bolt
12 O-ring
13 Bushing
14 Sleeve
15 Nut
16 Left-hand tie rod
17 Rear shock absorber and fasteners
18 Swingarm pivot shaft
19 Seal
20 Sleeve
21 Bearing
22 Swingarm
23 Chain guard
24 Bearing
25 Seal
26 Nut

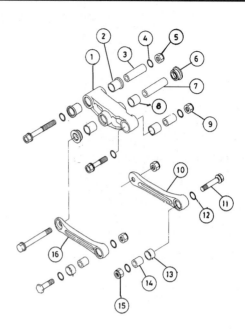

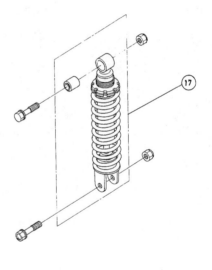

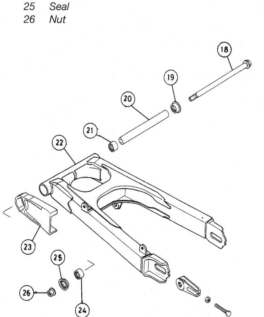

4   Remove the shock absorber lower nut and bolt and the tie-rod lower nut and bolt **(see illustration)**.
5   Remove the upper nut and bolt. Pull the tie-rods back and lower the shock absorber to the ground.

Adjustment

Refer to illustration 9.6

6   The shock absorber is adjusted by turning the adjusting nut at the top **(see illustration)**. Compressing the spring (turning the adjusting nut down) increases the preload, while turning the nut upward decreases it. Compare preload with the values listed in this Chapter's Specifications and adjust as needed.

Installation

7   Installation is the reverse of the removal procedure. Tighten the shock absorber and tie-rod nuts to the torque values listed in this Chapter's Specifications.

10   Rear suspension linkage - removal, check and installation

1   Set the bike on its centerstand.

Tie-rod(s)

Refer to illustrations 10.3 and 10.4

2   Remove the tie-rod lower nut and bolt **(see illustration 9.4)**.

9.4 Remove the shock absorber lower nut and bolt (left arrow) and tie rod nut and bolt (right arrow)

9.6 Spring preload can be adjusted by turning this nut (arrow)

10.3 Remove the tie rod upper bolts (arrows) and nuts

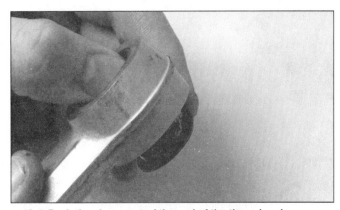

10.4 Push the sleeve out of the end of the tie-rod and remove the O-rings

rings for cracking and general deterioration and replace them if necessary. Check the bushing in the tie-rod and the outer surface of the sleeve for wear, replacing them if necessary. **Note:** *A bushing driver will be required if the bushing is to be replaced.*

5   Apply a thin coat of moly-based grease to the bushing and sleeve and install the sleeve in the bushing. Press the O-rings into place around the sleeve.

6   Installation is the reverse of the removal steps.

7   Tighten the nuts and bolts to the torque listed in this Chapter's Specifications.

Rocker arm

Refer to illustrations 10.10, 10.15a, 10.15b, 10.16a and 10.16b

8   Remove the lower shock absorber and tie rod nuts, but not the bolts **(see illustration 9.4)**.

9   Support the swingarm with a jack and remove the shock absorber and tie rod bolts.

10   Loosen the rocker arm nut **(see illustration)**, but don't remove the bolt yet.

11   Support the bike with a temporary stand, such as a section of large wooden beam, so the centerstand can be retracted and the exhaust system can be removed. **Warning:** *Whatever you use to support the bike must be stable enough so the machine can't fall on you during this procedure. It's a good idea to have an assistant ready to steady the bike.*

12   Retract the centerstand.

13   Remove the exhaust pipes (see Chapter 4).

14   Remove the nut and pull out the rocker arm pivot bolt **(see illustration 10.10)**. Detach the rocker arm from the frame.

10.10 Loosen the rocker arm pivot bolt nut, but don't remove it at first

3   Remove the nut(s) and bolt(s) that secure the tie-rods to the swingarm and remove the tie-rod(s) **(see illustration)**.

4   Push the sleeve out of the tie-rod **(see illustration)**. Check the O-

6

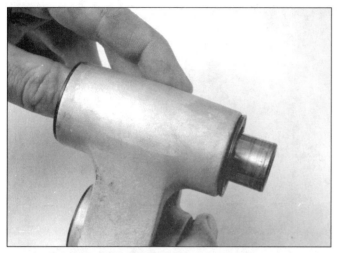

10.15a To check the condition of the bushings, push the sleeves out of the rocker arm

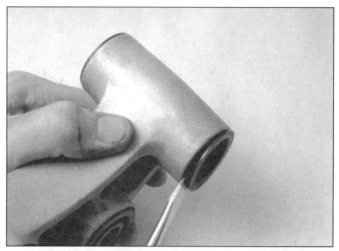

10.15b Pry out the grease seals for access to the bushings

10.16a To replace the bushings, knock them out with a hammer and punch. . .

10.16b . . .then drive the new ones in with a socket that just fits into the bore of the rocker arm

15   Push the sleeves out of the rocker arm **(see illustration)**. Check the bushings for dryness and discoloration. If necessary, pry out the grease seals **(see illustration)**, clean the bushings with solvent, dry and repack them with moly-based grease.

16   If the bushings are deteriorated, drive them out of the rocker arm with a hammer and punch **(see illustration)**. Install new bushings by driving them in with a hammer and a socket of the appropriate size **(see illustration)**.

17   Coat the bearings with grease, install the grease seals and slide the bushings into place.

18   The remainder of installation is the reverse of the removal procedure.

19   Tighten the nut of the rocker arm pivot bolt, the shock absorber-to-rocker arm bolt/nut and the tie-rod-to-rocker arm bolt/nut to the torque values listed in this Chapter's Specifications.

11 Swingarm bearings - check

1   Refer to Chapter 7 and remove the rear wheel, then refer to Section 9 and remove the rear shock absorber.

2   Grasp the rear of the swingarm with one hand and place your other hand at the junction of the swingarm and the frame. Try to move the rear of the from side-to-side. Any wear (play) in the bearings should be felt as movement between the swingarm and the frame at the front. The swingarm will actually be felt to move forward and back-

ward at the front (not from side-to-side). If any play is noted, the bearings should be replaced with new ones (see Section 13).

3   Next, move the swingarm up and down through its full travel. It should move freely, without any binding or rough spots. If it does not move freely, refer to Section 13 for servicing procedures.

12 Swingarm - removal and installation

Refer to illustrations 12.4a, 12.4b, 12.6 and 12.7

1   Raise the bike and set it on its centerstand.

2   Remove the rear wheel (see Chapter 7).

3   Detach the brake torque link from the swingarm (see Chapter 7).

4   Remove the swingarm pivot nut **(see illustrations)**. Don't remove the pivot shaft yet.

5   Support the swingarm with a jack and detach the tie-rods and the shock absorber from the rocker arm **(see illustration 9.4)**.

6   Support the swingarm and pull the pivot shaft out **(see illustration)**. Remove the swingarm. If necessary, remove the bolts and detach the tie-rods from the swingarm.

7   Check the pivot bearings in the swingarm for dryness or deterioration **(see illustration)**. If they're in need of lubrication or replacement, refer to Section 13.

8   Installation is the reverse of the removal procedure, with the following additions:

a) Be sure the bearing seals are in position before installing the

12.4a Remove the plastic cap from the pivot shaft head. . .

12.4b . . .and the pivot shaft nut

12.6 Pull the pivot shaft out

12.7 There's a needle bearing in each side of the swingarm (sleeve and seal removed for clarity)

13.3 Slide the sleeve out of the front of the swingarm

13.4 Pry the seals out with a screwdriver

pivot shaft.

b) Tighten the pivot shaft nut and the shock absorber and tie-rod lower mounting bolts/nuts to the torque values listed in this Chapter's Specifications.

c) Adjust the chain as described in Chapter 1.

13 Swingarm bearings - replacement

Refer to illustrations 13.3 and 13.4

1 Bearing replacement isn't complicated, but it requires a blind hole (expanding) puller, a slide hammer and a hydraulic press. The puller and slide hammer can be rented if you don't have them, and you may be able to devise a substitute for a hydraulic press, but compare the cost of having the bearings replaced by a Kawasaki dealer to that of renting the equipment before you proceed. It may be cheaper, and it will probably be easier, to have the bearings replaced by the dealer. You can save money by removing the swingarm from the bike yourself.

2 Remove the swingarm (see Section 12).

3 Slide the sleeve out **(see illustration)**.

4 Pry out the seals **(see illustration)**.

5 Remove the bearings with a blind hole (expanding) puller and slide hammer.

6 Press new bearings into the swingarm.

6

14.2 Remove the screws (arrows) and detach the chain guard

14.3 Unbolt the engine sprocket cover (arrow) and take it off

15.4 Check the runout of the rear sprocket with a dial indicator

15.7 Measure the diameter of the rear sprocket and replace it, the engine sprocket and the chain if it has worn past the minimum diameter

14 Drive chain - removal, cleaning and installation

Refer to illustrations 14.2 and 14.3

Removal

1   Remove the shift lever (see Chapter 2).
2   Remove the chain guard **(see illustration)**.
3   Remove the bolts securing the engine sprocket cover to the engine case **(see illustration)**. Slide the sprocket cover off.
4   Remove the rear wheel (see Chapter 7).
5   Lift the chain off the engine sprocket.
6   Detach the swingarm from the frame by following the first few Steps of Section 12. Pull the swingarm back far enough to allow the chain to slip between the frame and the front of the swingarm.

Cleaning

7   Soak the chain in kerosene (paraffin) or diesel fuel for approximately five or six minutes. **Caution:** *Don't use gasoline (petrol) or other cleaning fluids. Remove the chain, wipe it off then blow dry it with compressed air immediately. The entire process shouldn't take longer than ten minutes - if it does, the O-rings in the chain rollers could be damaged.*

Installation

8   Installation is the reverse of the removal procedure, with the following additions:

a) Tighten the suspension fasteners to the torque values listed in this Chapter's Specifications.
b) Tighten the rear axle nut to the torque listed in the Chapter 7 Specifications.
c) Lubricate the chain following the procedure described in Chapter 1.

15 Sprockets - check and replacement

Refer to illustrations 15.4, 15.7, 15.8, 15.9, 15.10a, 15.10b and 15.11
1   Set the bike on its centerstand.
2   Whenever the drive chain is inspected, the sprockets should be inspected also. If you are replacing the chain, replace the sprockets as well. Likewise, if the sprockets are in need of replacement, install a new chain also.
3   Remove the engine sprocket cover following the procedure outlined in the previous Section.
4   Attach a dial indicator to the swingarm, with the plunger of the indicator touching the sprocket near its outer diameter **(see illustration)**. Turn the wheel and measure the runout. If the runout exceeds the maximum runout listed in this Chapter's Specifications, replace the rear sprocket. As stated before, it's a good idea to replace the chain and the sprockets as a set.
5   Check the wear pattern on the sprockets (see Chapter 1). If the sprocket teeth are worn excessively, replace the chain and sprockets.

15.8 Remove these nuts to separate the sprocket from the coupling

15.9 Remove the engine sprocket holding plate bolts

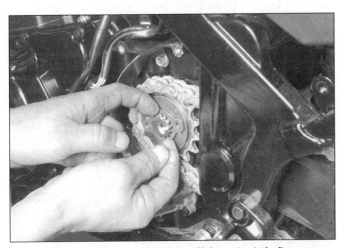

15.10a Pull the holding plate off the output shaft...

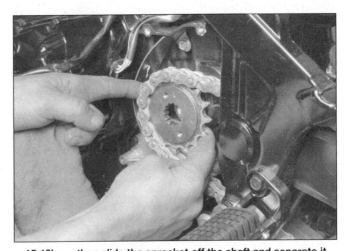

15.10b ...then slide the sprocket off the shaft and separate it from the chain

15.11 If necessary, unbolt and remove the front chain guard

6   Remove the rear wheel (see Chapter 7).

7   Using vernier calipers, measure the diameter of the rear sprocket **(see illustration)**. If the diameter of the sprocket is less than the minimum diameter listed in this Chapter's Specifications, replace the chain and sprockets.

8   To replace the rear sprocket, unscrew the nuts holding it to the wheel coupling and lift the sprocket off **(see illustration)**. When in-

stalling the sprocket, apply a non-hardening thread locking compound to the threads of the studs. Tighten the nuts to the torque listed in this Chapter's Specifications. Also, check the condition of the rubber damper under the rear wheel coupling (see Section 16).

9   To replace the engine sprocket, begin by installing the chain and rear wheel. With the chain now in place, have an assistant apply the rear brake. Loosen the holding plate bolts on the engine sprocket **(see illustration)**.

10   Remove the holding plate and pull the engine sprocket and chain off the shaft, then separate the sprocket from the chain **(see illustrations)**.

11   If necessary, unbolt the front chain guard and remove it from the engine **(see illustration)**.

12   When installing the engine sprocket, engage it with the chain, making sure the IN mark, or recess, faces the engine case. Install the holding plate, apply a non-hardening thread locking compound to the bolts, then tighten the bolts to the torque listed in this Chapter's Specifications.

13   Install the engine sprocket cover and shift lever (see Section 14).

6

16   Rear wheel coupling/rubber damper - check and replacement

Refer to illustrations 16.2, 16.3a, 16.3b and 16.5

1   Remove the rear wheel (see Chapter 7).

16.2 Lift the sprocket and coupling from the rear wheel

16.3a Pull the damper out of the recesses. . .

16.3b . . .and separate it from the wheel

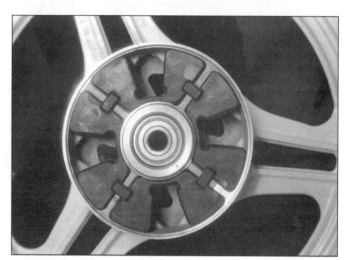

16.5 The damper should look like this when it's installed

2   Lift the collar and rear sprocket/rear wheel coupling from the wheel **(see illustration)**.
3   Lift the rubber damper from the wheel **(see illustrations)** and check it for cracks, hardening and general deterioration. Replace it with a new one if necessary.

4   Checking and replacement procedures for the coupling bearing are similar to those described for the wheel bearings. Refer to Chapter 7, Section 13.
5   Installation is the reverse of the removal procedure **(see illustration)**.

Chapter 7   Brakes, wheels and tires

Contents

Specifications

Brakes

Brake fluid type..	See Chapter 1
Brake pad minimum thickness	See Chapter 1
Disc thickness	
Standard..	0.150 to 0.153 inch (3.8 to 3.9 mm)
Minimum*...	0.138 inch (3.5 mm)

* Refer to marks stamped into the disc (they supersede information printed here)

Disc runout (maximum...	0.012 inch (0.3 mm)
Rear brake lining thickness	
Standard..	0.177 inch (4.5 mm)
Minimum..	0.039 inch (1 mm)
Brake drum diameter	
Standard..	6.299 to 6.305 inch (160.00 to 160.16 mm)
Maximum..	6.238 inch (160.75 mm)
Brake cam diameter	
Standard..	0.667 to 0.668 inch (16.975 to 16.984 mm)
Minimum..	0.665 inch (16.88 mm)
Cam hole diameter in brake panel	
Standard..	0.669 to 0.670 inch (17.00 to 17.03 mm)
Maximum..	0.675 inch (17.15 mm)

Wheels and tires

Wheel runout
    Axial (side-to-side) .... 0.020 in (0.5 mm)
    Radial (out-of-round) .... 0.031 in (0.8 mm)
Rear axle runout .... 0.007 in (0.2 mm) per 3.94 inch (100 mm) of axle length
Tire pressures .... See Chapter 1
Tire sizes
    Front 110/90-16 54H
    Rear 120/90-16 63H

Torque specifications

Caliper mounting bolts .... 24 ft-lbs (32 Nm)
Banjo fitting bolts... 18 ft-lbs (25 Nm)
Brake disc-to-wheel bolts .... 16.5 ft-lbs (23 Nm)
Master cylinder mounting bolts .... 95 in-lbs (11 Nm)
Brake lever pivot pin locknut .... 52 in-lbs (5.9 Nm)
Front axle nut.. 65 ft-lbs (88 Nm)
Front axle clamp bolt... 22 ft-lbs (29 Nm)
Rear axle nut... 80 ft-lbs (110 Nm)

2.2 Remove the caliper mounting bolts (arrows) and support the caliper so it doesn't hang by the brake hose

1   General information

    The models covered by this manual are equipped with a hydraulic disc brake on the front and a mechanical drum brake on the rear. The front brake uses a dual piston caliper.
    All models are equipped with cast aluminum wheels, which require very little maintenance and allow tubeless tires to be used.
Caution: *Disc brake components rarely require disassembly. Do not disassemble components unless absolutely necessary. If any hydraulic brake line connection in the system is loosened, the entire system should be disassembled, drained, cleaned and then properly filled and bled upon reassembly. Do not use solvents on internal brake components. Solvents will cause seals to swell and distort. Use only clean brake fluid or alcohol for cleaning. Use care when working with brake fluid as it can injure your eyes and it will damage painted surfaces and plastic parts.*

2   Brake pads - replacement

Refer to illustrations 2.2, 2.4, 2.5, 2.6 and 2.7
Warning: *The dust created by the brake system may contain asbestos, which is harmful to your health. Never blow it out with compressed air and don't inhale any of it. An approved filtering mask should be worn when working on the brakes.*
1   Set the bike on its centerstand.
2   Remove the caliper mounting bolts **(see illustration)**. Slide the caliper and pads off the disc.
3   Support the caliper with rope or wire so it doesn't hang by the

2.4 Slide the caliper bracket toward the pistons so it clears the inner pad, then remove the pad

2.5 Disengage the clips on the outer pad from the caliper and remove the pad

brake hose.
4   Push the caliper bracket in (toward the piston) until the pins on the bracket clear the holes in the pad backing plate, then remove the inner pad **(see illustration)**.
5   Remove the outer brake pad from the caliper **(see illustration)**.

2.6 Remove the anti-rattle spring

banjo fitting bolt - there's a sealing washer on each side of the fitting

6   Remove the anti-rattle spring (see illustration). If it appears damaged, replace it.
7   Check the pad support clips on the caliper bracket (see illustration). If they are missing or distorted, replace them.
8   Check the condition of the brake disc (see Section 4). If it is in need of machining or replacement, follow the procedure in that Section to remove it. If it is okay, deglaze it with sandpaper or emery cloth, using a swirling motion.
9   Remove the cap from the master cylinder reservoir and siphon out some fluid. Push the piston into the caliper as far as possible, while checking the master cylinder reservoir to make sure it doesn't overflow. If you can't depress the piston with thumb pressure, try using a C-clamp (G-clamp). If the piston sticks, remove the caliper and overhaul it as described in Section 3.
10   Install the anti-rattle spring in the caliper.
11   Install both pads in the caliper and pull the caliper bracket out, so the pins on the bracket engage with the holes in the pad backing plate.
12   Install the caliper, tightening the mounting bolts to the torque listed in this Chapter's Specifications.
13   Refill the master cylinder reservoir (see Chapter 1) and install the diaphragm and cap.
14   Operate the brake lever or pedal several times to bring the pads into contact with the disc. Check the operation of the brakes carefully before riding the motorcycle.

---

3   Brake caliper - removal, overhaul and installation

Warning: If a caliper indicates the need for an overhaul (usually due to leaking fluid or sticky operation), all old brake fluid should be flushed

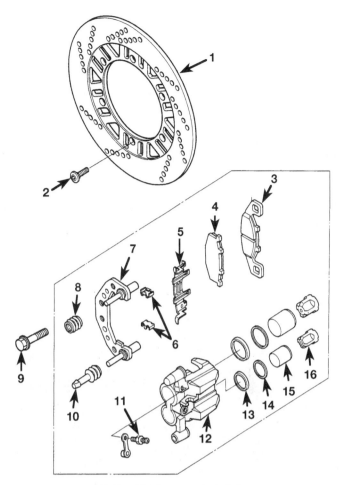

2.7 Front brakes - exploded view

1	Brake disc	9	Caliper mounting bolt
2	Allen bolt	10	Boot
3	Inner pad	11	Bleed valve and cap
4	Outer pad	12	Caliper
5	Anti-rattle spring	13	Piston seals
6	Pad support clips	14	Dust seals
7	Caliper bracket	15	Pistons
8	Boot	16	Piston inserts

3.2 Remove the caliper hose

from the system. Also, the dust created by the brake system may contain asbestos, which is harmful to your health. Never blow it out with compressed air and don't inhale any of it. An approved filtering mask should be worn when working on the brakes. Do not, under any circumstances, use petroleum-based solvents to clean brake parts. Use clean brake fluid, brake cleaner or denatured alcohol only!
Note: If you are removing the caliper only to replace or inspect the brake pads, don't disconnect the hose from the caliper.

Removal

Refer to illustration 3.2

1   Place the bike on its centerstand. Note: If you're planning to overhaul the caliper and don't have a source of compressed air to blow out the pistons, use the bike's hydraulic system instead. To do this, remove the pads (see Section 2) and squeeze the brake lever to force the pistons out of the cylinder.
2   Remove the brake hose banjo fitting bolt and separate the hose from the caliper (see illustration). Discard the sealing washers. Plug the end of the hose or wrap a plastic bag tightly around it to prevent excessive fluid loss and contamination.
3   Remove the caliper (see Section 2).

3.5 Remove the insert from each piston

3.9 The dust seal should be removed with a plastic or wooden tool to avoid damage to the bore and seal groove (a pencil works well) - remove the piston seal the same way

3.16 Install the slider pin boots

3.17 Apply a thin coat of the specified grease to the slider pins on the caliper bracket

Overhaul

Refer to illustrations 3.5, 3.9, 3.16 and 3.17

4   Remove the brake pads and anti-rattle spring from the caliper (see Section 2, if necessary).

5   Remove the caliper piston inserts **(see illustration)**.

6   Clean the exterior of the caliper with denatured alcohol or brake system cleaner.

7   Remove the caliper bracket and the slider pin boots from the caliper **(see illustration 2.7)**.

8   If you didn't blow out the pistons with the bike's hydraulic system in Step 1, place a few rags between the piston and the caliper frame to act as a cushion, then use compressed air, directed into the fluid inlet, to remove the pistons. Use only enough air pressure to ease the pistons out of the bore. If a piston is blown out, even with the cushion in place, it may be damaged. **Warning**: *Never place your fingers in front of the piston in an attempt to catch or protect it when applying compressed air, as serious injury could occur.*

9   Using a wood or plastic tool, remove the dust seals **(see illustration)**. Metal tools may cause bore damage.

10   Using a wood or plastic tool, remove the piston seal from the groove in each caliper bore.

11   Clean the pistons and the bores with denatured alcohol, clean brake fluid or brake system cleaner and blow dry them with filtered, unlubricated compressed air. Inspect the surfaces of the pistons for nicks and burrs and loss of plating. Check the caliper bores, too. If surface defects are present, the caliper must be replaced. If the caliper is in bad shape, the master cylinder should also be checked.

12   Temporarily reinstall the caliper bracket. Make sure it slides smoothly in-and-out of the caliper. If it doesn't, check the slider pins for burrs or excessive wear. Also check the slider pin bores in the caliper for wear and scoring. Replace the caliper bracket, the caliper, or both if necessary.

13   Lubricate the piston seals with clean brake fluid and install them in their grooves in the caliper bore. Make sure they seat completely and aren't twisted.

14   Lubricate the dust seals with clean brake fluid and install them in their grooves, making sure they seat correctly.

15   Lubricate the pistons with clean brake fluid and install them in the caliper bores. Using your thumbs, push the pistons all the way in, making sure they don't get cocked in the bore.

16   Install the slider pin boots **(see illustration)**.

17   Apply a thin coat of PBC (poly butyl cuprysil) grease, or silicone grease designed for high-temperature brake applications, to the slider pins on the caliper bracket **(see illustration)**. Install the caliper bracket to the caliper and seat the boots over the lips on the bracket.

Installation

Refer to illustration 3.18

18   Install the piston inserts **(see illustration)**.

19   Install the anti-rattle spring and the brake pads (see Section 2).

20   Install the caliper, tightening the mounting bolts to the torque listed in this Chapter's Specifications.

21   Connect the brake hose to the caliper, using new sealing washers

3.18 Install the piston inserts (arrows) so they seat in the pistons

4.4 The minimum allowable thickness is stamped into the disc

4   The disc must not be machined or allowed to wear down to a thickness less than the minimum allowable thickness listed in this Chapter's Specifications. The thickness of the disc can be checked with a micrometer. If the thickness of the disc is less than the minimum allowable, it must be replaced. The minimum thickness is also stamped into the disc **(see illustration)**.

Removal

Refer to illustration 4.6

5   Remove the wheel (see Section 11). **Caution:** *Don't lay the wheel down and allow it to rest on the disc - the disc could become warped. Set the wheel on wood blocks so the disc doesn't support the weight of the wheel.*
6   Mark the relationship of the disc to the wheel, so it can be installed in the same position. Remove the Allen bolts that retain the disc to the wheel **(see illustration)**. Loosen the bolts a little at a time, in a criss-cross pattern, to avoid distorting the disc.
7   Take note of any paper shims that may be present where the disc mates to the wheel. If there are any, mark their position and be sure to include them when installing the disc.

Installation

8   Position the disc on the wheel, aligning the previously applied matchmarks (if you're reinstalling the original disc). Make sure the arrow (stamped on the disc) marking the direction of rotation is pointing in the proper direction.
9   Apply a non-hardening thread locking compound to the threads of the bolts. Install the bolts, tightening them a little at a time, in a criss-cross pattern, until the torque listed in this Chapter's Specifications is reached. Clean off all grease from the brake disc using acetone or brake system cleaner.
10   Install the wheel.
11   Operate the brake lever several times to bring the pads into contact with the disc. Check the operation of the brakes carefully before riding the motorcycle.

4.6 Loosen the disc retaining bolts a little at a time to prevent distortion

on each side of the fitting. Tighten the banjo fitting bolt to the torque listed in this Chapter's Specifications.
22   Fill the master cylinder with the recommended brake fluid (see Chapter 1) and bleed the system (see Section 8). Check for leaks.
23   Check the operation of the brakes carefully before riding the motorcycle.

---

4   Brake disc(s) - inspection, removal and installation

Inspection

Refer to illustration 4.4

1   Set the bike on its centerstand.
2   Visually inspect the surface of the disc(s) for score marks and other damage. Light scratches are normal after use and won't affect brake operation, but deep grooves and heavy score marks will reduce braking efficiency and accelerate pad wear. If the discs are badly grooved they must be machined or replaced.
3   To check disc runout, mount a dial indicator to a fork leg with the plunger on the indicator touching the surface of the disc about 1/2-inch from the outer edge. Slowly turn the wheel (have an assistant sit on the seat to raise the front wheel off the ground) and watch the indicator needle, comparing your reading with the limit listed in this Chapter's Specifications. If the runout is greater than allowed, check the hub bearings for play (see Chapter 1). If the bearings are worn, replace them and repeat this check. If the disc runout is still excessive, it will have to be replaced.

---

5   Front brake master cylinder - removal, overhaul and installation

1   If the master cylinder is leaking fluid, or if the lever does not produce a firm feel when the brake is applied, and bleeding the brakes does not help, master cylinder overhaul is recommended. Before disassembling the master cylinder, read through the entire procedure and make sure that you have the correct rebuild kit. Also, you will need some new, clean brake fluid of the recommended type, some clean rags and internal snap-ring pliers. **Note:** *To prevent damage to the paint from spilled brake fluid, always cover the fuel tank when working on the master cylinder.*

7

5.4 Pull back the cover and remove the master cylinder banjo fitting bolt - use a six-point box wrench, and expect some leakage

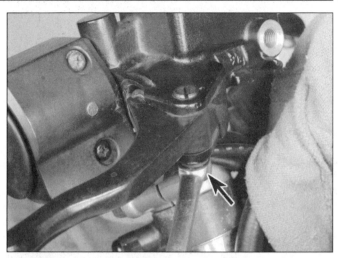

5.5 Remove the locknut, then unscrew the brake lever pivot bolt

5.6 Remove the master cylinder mounting bolts, unplug the electrical connectors and remove the master cylinder

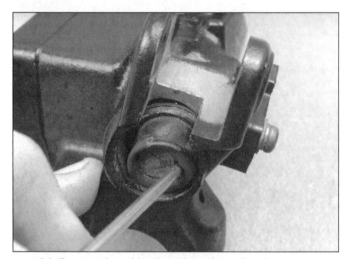

5.9 Remove the rubber boot from the end of the master cylinder piston. . .

5.10a . . .then depress the piston and remove the snap-ring with a pair of snap-ring pliers

2   **Caution**: *Disassembly, overhaul and reassembly of the brake master cylinder must be done in a spotlessly clean work area to avoid contamination and possible failure of the brake hydraulic system components.*

Removal

Refer to illustrations 5.4, 5.5 and 5.6

3   Loosen, but do not remove, the screws holding the reservoir cover in place.

4   Pull back the rubber boot, loosen the banjo fitting bolt **(see illustration)** and separate the brake hose from the master cylinder. Wrap the end of the hose in a clean rag and suspend the hose in an upright position or bend it down carefully and place the open end in a clean container. The objective is to prevent excess loss of brake fluid, fluid spills and system contamination.

5   Remove the locknut from the underside of the lever pivot bolt, then unscrew the bolt **(see illustration)**.

6   Remove the master cylinder mounting bolts **(see illustration)** and separate the master cylinder from the handlebar. **Caution**: *Do not tip the master cylinder upside down or brake fluid will run out.*

7   Disconnect the electrical connectors from the brake light switch.

Overhaul

Refer to illustrations 5.9, 5.10a, 5.10b and 5.12

8   Detach the top cover and the rubber diaphragm, then drain the brake fluid into a suitable container. Wipe any remaining fluid out of the reservoir with a clean rag.

9   Carefully remove the rubber dust boot from the end of the piston **(see illustration)**.

10   Using snap-ring pliers, remove the snap-ring **(see illustrations)** and slide out the piston, the cup seals and the spring. Lay the parts

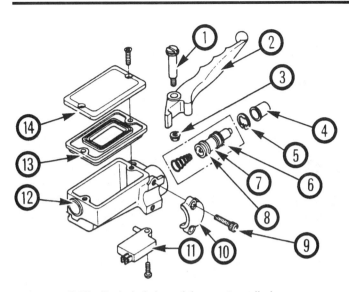

5.10b Exploded view of the master cylinder

1	Pivot bolt	8	Primary cup
2	Brake lever	9	Bolt
3	Locknut	10	Clamp
4	Dust boot	11	Brake light switch
5	Snap-ring	12	Master cylinder body
6	Secondary cup	13	Diaphragm
7	Piston	14	Cover

6.3 The brake shoes are mounted on a panel that fits into the rear wheel

out in the proper order to prevent confusion during reassembly.

11   Clean all of the parts with brake system cleaner (available at auto parts stores), denatured alcohol or clean brake fluid. **Caution:** *Do not, under any circumstances, use a petroleum-based solvent to clean brake parts. If compressed air is available, use it to dry the parts thoroughly (make sure it's filtered and unlubricated). Check the master cylinder bore for corrosion, scratches, nicks and score marks. If damage is evident, the master cylinder must be replaced with a new one. If the master cylinder is in poor condition, then the caliper should be checked as well.*

12   Remove the old cup seals from the piston and spring and install the new ones. Make sure the lips face away from the lever end of the piston **(see illustration)**. If a new piston is included in the rebuild kit, use it regardless of the condition of the old one.

13   Before reassembling the master cylinder, soak the piston and the rubber cup seals in clean brake fluid for ten to fifteen minutes. Lubricate the master cylinder bore with clean brake fluid, then carefully insert the piston and related parts in the reverse order of disassembly.

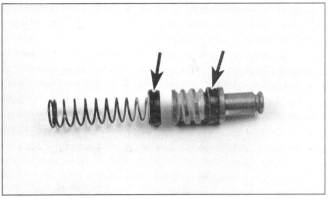

5.12 Make sure the lips of the piston cups (arrows) are facing away from the lever end of the piston

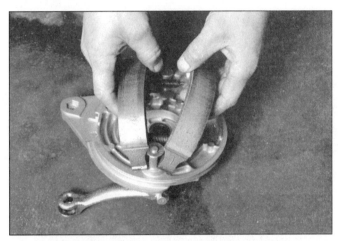

6.4 Fold the shoes off the panel to remove them

Make sure the lips on the cup seals do not turn inside out when they are slipped into the bore.

14   Depress the piston, then install the snap-ring (make sure the snap-ring is properly seated in the groove with the sharp edge facing out). Install the rubber dust boot (make sure the lip is seated properly in the piston groove).

Installation

15   Attach the master cylinder to the handlebar with the arrow and the word "up" on the master cylinder clamp pointing up. Tighten the bolts to the torque listed in this Chapter's Specifications. **Note:** *Tighten the upper bolt first, then the lower bolt. There will be a gap at the bottom between the clamp and master cylinder body.*

16   Install the brake lever and tighten the pivot bolt locknut.

17   Connect the brake hose to the master cylinder, using new sealing washers. Tighten the banjo fitting bolt to the torque listed in this Chapter's Specifications. Refer to Section 8 and bleed the air from the system.

6   Rear drum brakes - removal, inspection and installation

Removal

Refer to illustrations 6.3 and 6.4

1   Before you start, inspect the rear brake wear indicator (see Chapter 1).

2   Remove the rear wheel (see Section 12).

3   Lift the brake panel out of the wheel **(see illustration)**.

4   Fold the shoes toward each other to release the spring tension **(see illustration)**. Remove the shoes and springs from the brake panel.

7

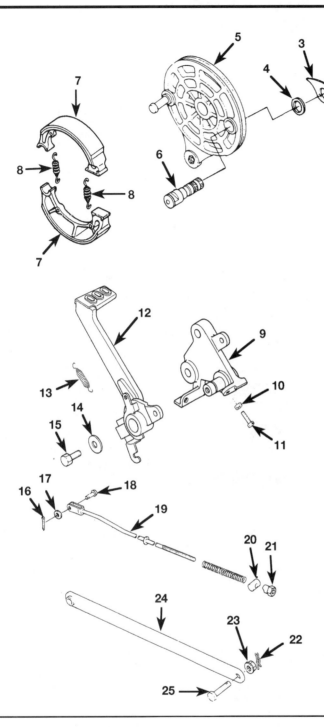

6.8 Exploded view of the rear brake

  1   Pinch bolt
  2   Brake cam lever
  3   Wear indicator pointer
  4   Seal
  5   Brake panel
  6   Brake cam
  7   Brake shoes
  8   Brake springs
  9   Pedal bracket
 10   Locknut
 11   Adjusting bolt
 12   Brake pedal
 13   Spring
 14   Washer
 15   Bolt
 16   Cotter pin (split pin)
 17   Washer
 18   Clevis pin
 19   Brake rod
 20   Brake rod pin
 21   Brake rod nut
 22   Clip
 23   Nut
 24   Torque link
 25   Bolt

Inspection

Refer to illustration 6.8

5   Check the linings for wear, damage, and signs of contamination from road dirt or water. If the linings are visibly defective, replace them.

6   Measure the thickness of the lining material (just the lining material, not the metal backing) and compare with the value listed in this Chapter's Specifications. Replace the shoes if the material is worn to less than the minimum.

7   Check the ends of the shoes where they contact the brake cam and pivot post. Replace the shoes if there's visible wear.

8   Check the brake cam and pivot post for wear and damage. If necessary, make match marks on the cam and cam lever, then remove the pinch bolt, lever, wear indicator pointer, seal and cam **(see illustration)**.

9   Check the brake drum (inside the wheel) for wear or damage. Measure the diameter at several points with a brake drum micrometer (or have this done by a Kawasaki dealer). If the measurements are uneven (indicating that the drum is out-of-round) or if there are scratches deep enough to snag a fingernail, have the drum turned (skimmed) by a dealer to correct the surface. If the drum has to be turned (skimmed) beyond the wear limit to remove the defects, replace it.

10   Check the brake cam for looseness in the brake panel hole. If it feels loose, measure the diameter of the cam and hole and compare them with those listed in this Chapter's Specifications. Replace worn parts.

Installation

11   Apply high temperature brake grease to the ends of the springs, the cam and the anchor pin.

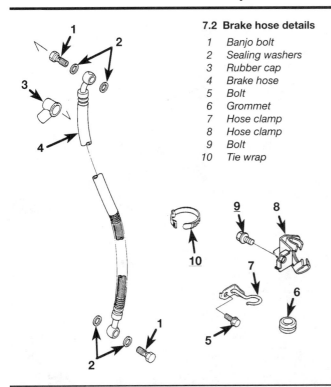

7.2 Brake hose details

1   Banjo bolt
2   Sealing washers
3   Rubber cap
4   Brake hose
5   Bolt
6   Grommet
7   Hose clamp
8   Hose clamp
9   Bolt
10 Tie wrap

8.5 Remove the bleed valve cap and fit a length of tubing over it; place the other end in a clean glass jar and place a wrench on the bleed valve

12   Hook the springs to the shoes. Position the shoes in a V on the brake panel, then fold them down into position **(see illustration 6.4)**. Make sure the ends of the shoes fit correctly in the cam and on the anchor pin.
13   The remainder of installation is the reverse of the removal steps.
14   Check the position of the brake pedal (see Chapter 1) and adjust it if necessary. Check the operation of the brakes carefully before riding the motorcycle.

7   Brake hoses and lines - inspection and replacement

Inspection

Refer to illustration 7.2
1   Once a week, or if the motorcycle is used less frequently, before every ride, check the condition of the brake hose.
2   Twist and flex the rubber hose **(see illustration)** while looking for cracks, bulges and seeping fluid. Check extra carefully around the areas where the hose connects to the banjo fittings, as these are common areas for hose failure.

Replacement

3   The brake hose has banjo fittings on each end. Cover the surrounding area with plenty of rags and unscrew the banjo bolts on either end of the hose. Detach the hose from the clips and remove the hose.
4   Position the new hose, making sure it isn't twisted or otherwise strained, between the two components. Install the banjo bolts, using new sealing washers on both sides of the fittings, and tighten them to the torque listed in this Chapter's Specifications.
5   Flush the old brake fluid from the system, refill the system with the recommended fluid (see Chapter 1) and bleed the air from the system (see Section 8). Check the operation of the brakes carefully before riding the motorcycle.

8   Brake system bleeding

Refer to illustration 8.5
1   Bleeding the brake is simply the process of removing all the air

bubbles from the brake fluid reservoir, the lines and the brake caliper. Bleeding is necessary whenever a brake system hydraulic connection is loosened, when a component or hose is replaced, or when the master cylinder or caliper is overhauled. Leaks in the system may also allow air to enter, but leaking brake fluid will reveal their presence and warn you of the need for repair.
2   To bleed the brake, you will need some new, clean brake fluid of the recommended type (see Chapter 1), a length of clear vinyl or plastic tubing, a small container partially filled with clean brake fluid, some rags and a wrench to fit the brake caliper bleed valve.
3   Cover the fuel tank and other painted components to prevent damage in the event that brake fluid is spilled.
4   Remove the reservoir cap or cover and slowly pump the brake lever a few times, until no air bubbles can be seen floating up from the holes at the bottom of the reservoir. Doing this bleeds the air from the master cylinder end of the line. Reinstall the reservoir cap or cover.
5   Attach one end of the clear vinyl or plastic tubing to the brake caliper bleeder valve and submerge the other end in the brake fluid in the container **(see illustration)**.
6   Remove the reservoir cap or cover and check the fluid level. Do not allow the fluid level to drop below the lower mark during the bleeding process.
7   Carefully pump the brake lever three or four times and hold it while opening the caliper bleeder valve. When the valve is opened, brake fluid will flow out of the caliper into the clear tubing and the lever will move toward the handlebar.
8   Retighten the bleeder valve, then release the brake lever gradually. Repeat the process until no air bubbles are visible in the brake fluid leaving the caliper and the lever is firm when applied. Remember to add fluid to the reservoir as the level drops. Use only new, clean brake fluid of the recommended type. Never reuse the fluid lost during bleeding; it absorbs moisture from the air, which can lead to brake failure.
9   Replace the reservoir cover, wipe up any spilled brake fluid and check the entire system for leaks. **Note**: *If bleeding is difficult, it may be necessary to let the brake fluid in the system stabilize for a few hours (it may be aerated). Repeat the bleeding procedure when the tiny bubbles in the system have settled out.*

9   Wheels - inspection and repair

1   Place the motorcycle on the centerstand, then clean the wheels thoroughly to remove mud and dirt that may interfere with the inspection procedure or mask defects. Make a general check of the wheels and tires as described in Chapter 1.
2   With the motorcycle on the centerstand and the wheel in the air, attach a dial indicator to the fork slider or the swingarm and position

7

11.2 Remove the nut from the end of the axle

11.3 Unscrew the speedometer cable nut

the pointer against the side of the rim. Spin the wheel slowly and check the side-to-side (axial) runout of the rim, then compare your readings with the value listed in this Chapter's Specifications. In order to accurately check radial runout with the dial indicator, the wheel would have to be removed from the machine and the tire removed from the wheel. With the axle clamped in a vise, the wheel can be rotated to check the runout.

3   An easier, though slightly less accurate, method is to attach a stiff wire pointer to the fork slider or the swingarm and position the end a fraction of an inch from the wheel (where the wheel and tire join). If the wheel is true, the distance from the pointer to the rim will be constant as the wheel is rotated. Repeat the procedure to check the runout of the rear wheel. **Note**: *If wheel runout is excessive, refer to the appropriate Section in this Chapter and check the wheel bearings very carefully before replacing the wheel.*

4   The wheels should also be visually inspected for cracks, flat spots on the rim and other damage. Since tubeless tires are involved, look very closely for dents in the area where the tire bead contacts the rim. Dents in this area may prevent complete sealing of the tire against the rim, which leads to deflation of the tire over a period of time.

5   If damage is evident, or if runout in either direction is excessive, the wheel will have to be replaced with a new one. Never attempt to repair a damaged cast aluminum wheel.

10   Wheels - alignment check

1   Misalignment of the wheels, which may be due to a cocked rear wheel or a bent frame or triple clamps, can cause strange and possibly serious handling problems. If the frame or triple clamps are at fault, repair by a frame specialist or replacement with new parts are the only alternatives.

2   To check the alignment you will need an assistant, a length of string or a perfectly straight piece of wood and a ruler graduated in 1/64 inch increments. A plumb bob or other suitable weight will also be required.

3   Place the motorcycle on the centerstand, then measure the width of both tires at their widest points. Subtract the smaller measurement from the larger measurement, then divide the difference by two. The result is the amount of offset that should exist between the front and rear tires on both sides.

4   If a string is used, have your assistant hold one end of it about half way between the floor and the rear axle, touching the rear sidewall of the tire.

5   Run the other end of the string forward and pull it tight so that it is roughly parallel to the floor. Slowly bring the string into contact with the front sidewall of the rear tire, then turn the front wheel until it is parallel with the string. Measure the distance from the front tire sidewall to the string.

6   Repeat the procedure on the other side of the motorcycle. The distance from the front tire sidewall to the string should be equal on both sides.

7   As was previously pointed out, a perfectly straight length of wood

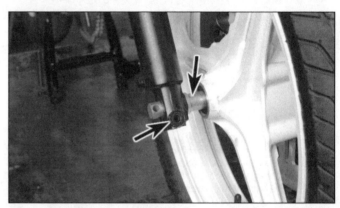

11.4 The axle clamp bolt (left arrow) goes in this hole; remove the collar (right arrow) as the axle is pulled out

may be substituted for the string. The procedure is the same.

8   If the distance between the string and tire is greater on one side, or if the rear wheel appears to be cocked, refer to Chapter 6, Swingarm bearings - check, and make sure the swingarm is tight. Also refer to the chain adjustment procedure in Chapter 1 and make sure the adjusters are set evenly.

9   If the front-to-back alignment is correct, the wheels still may be out of alignment vertically.

10   Using the plumb bob, or other suitable weight, and a length of string, check the rear wheel to make sure it is vertical. To do this, hold the string against the tire upper sidewall and allow the weight to settle just off the floor. When the string touches both the upper and lower tire sidewalls and is perfectly straight, the wheel is vertical. If it is not, place thin spacers under one leg of the centerstand.

11   Once the rear wheel is vertical, check the front wheel in the same manner. If both wheels are not perfectly vertical, the frame and/or major suspension components are bent.

11   Front wheel - removal and installation

Refer to illustrations 11.2, 11.3 and 11.4

Removal

1   Remove the lower fairing (if equipped) (see Chapter 8). Place the motorcycle on the centerstand, then raise the front wheel off the ground by placing a floor jack, with a wood block on the jack head, under the engine.

2   Remove the axle nut on the left side **(see illustration)**.

3   Disconnect the speedometer cable from the drive unit **(see illustration)**.

4   Loosen the right side axle clamp bolt **(see illustration)**.

5   Support the wheel, then pull out the axle and collar **(see illustration 11.4)** and carefully lower the wheel until the brake disc clears the

12.2 Remove the cotter pin (split pin) from the axle nut

12.3 Loosen the locknut on each chain adjuster (arrow), then loosen the adjuster bolts all the way

12.4 Remove the nut from the brake rod, then slip the rod out of the pin

12.6a Note the location of the spacer (left arrow) on each side of the wheel, then remove the axle nut. . .

caliper. It will probably be necessary to tilt the wheel to one side to allow removal. Don't lose the spacer that fits into the right side of the hub. **Caution:** *Don't lay the wheel down and allow it to rest on the disc - the disc could become warped. Set the wheel on wood blocks so the disc doesn't support the weight of the wheel. If the axle is corroded, remove the corrosion with fine emery cloth.* **Note:** *Do not operate the front brake lever with the wheel removed. To prevent accidental operation of the brake, slip a piece of wood between the brake pads.*

6   Check the condition of the wheel bearings (see Section 13).

Installation

7   Installation is the reverse of removal. Apply a thin coat of grease to the seal lip, then slide the collar into the right side of the hub. Position the speedometer drive unit in place in the left side of the hub (if it was removed), then slide the wheel into place. Make sure the notches in the speedometer drive housing line up with the lugs in the wheel. If the disc will not slide between the brake pads, remove the wheel and carefully pry them apart with a piece of wood.

8   Slip the axle into place, then tighten the axle nut to the torque listed in this Chapter's Specifications. Tighten the right side axle clamp bolt to the torque listed in this Chapter's Specifications.

9   Apply the front brake, pump the forks up and down several times and check for binding and proper brake operation.

---

12   Rear wheel - removal and installation

Refer to illustrations 12.2, 12.3, 12.4, 12.6a, 12.6b and 12.7

Removal

1   Set the bike on its centerstand.

2   Remove the cotter pin (split pin) from the axle nut and loosen the nut **(see illustration)**.

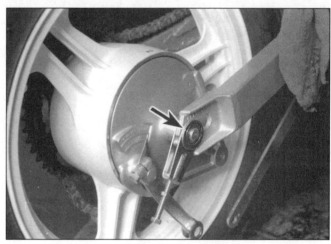

12.6b . . .and the washer

3   Loosen the chain adjusting bolt locknuts and fully loosen both adjusting bolts **(see illustration)**.

4   Unscrew the brake pedal adjusting nut from the shaft **(see illustration)**. Slide out the pin and disconnect the brake rod from the cam lever. Remove the cotter pin (split pin) from the torque link nut, then remove the nut and disconnect the torque link from the brake panel (see Section 6 if necessary).

5   Push the rear wheel as far forward as possible. Lift the top of the chain up off the rear sprocket and pull it to the left while rotating the wheel backwards. This will disengage the chain from the sprocket. **Warning**: *Don't let your fingers slip between the chain and the sprocket.*

6   Remove the axle nut and the washer **(see illustrations)**. Note the

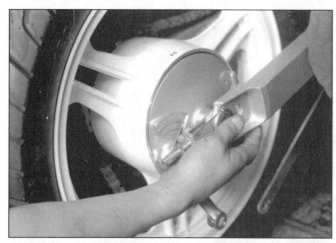

12.7 Slide the wheel rearward, set the chain adjuster down and pull the wheel the rest of the way out

12.11 Position the left chain adjuster, washer and axle so the axle can be pushed in as soon as the wheel is in position

location of the spacer on each side of the wheel.

7   Support the wheel and slide the axle out. Lower the wheel and remove it from the swingarm, being careful not to lose the spacers on either side of the hub **(see illustration)**. **Caution**: *Don't lay the wheel down and allow it to rest on the sprocket - it could become warped. Set the wheel on wood blocks so the sprocket doesn't support the weight of the wheel.*

Inspection

Refer to illustration 12.8

8   Before installing the wheel, check the axle for straightness. If the axle is corroded, first remove the corrosion with fine emery cloth. Set the axle on V-blocks and check it for runout using a dial indicator **(see illustration)**. If the axle exceeds the maximum allowable runout limit listed in this Chapter's Specifications, it must be replaced.

9   Check the condition of the wheel bearings (see Section 13).

Installation

Refer to illustration 12.11

10   Apply a thin coat of grease to the seal lips, then slide the spacers into their proper positions on the sides of the hub.

11   Place the axle, washer and chain adjuster in the left side of the swingarm so they're ready to go when the wheel is in position **(see illustration)**.

12   Slide the wheel and spacers into place.

13   Pull the chain up over the sprocket, raise the wheel and install the axle and axle nut. Don't tighten the axle nut at this time.

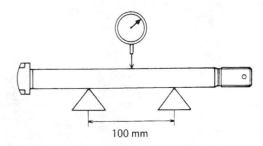

12.8 Check the axle for runout using a dial indicator and V-blocks

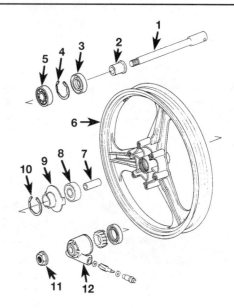

13.4 Front wheel bearing and hub details

1	Axle	8	Bearing
2	Collar	9	Speedometer drive
3	Seal	10	Snap-ring
4	Snap-ring	11	Nut
5	Bearing	12	Speedometer gear and
6	Wheel		housing
7	Spacer		

14   Adjust the chain slack (see Chapter 1) and tighten the adjuster locknuts.

15   Tighten the axle nut to the torque listed in this Chapter's Specifications. Install a new cotter pin (split pin), tightening the axle nut an additional amount, if necessary, to align the hole in the axle with the castellations on the nut.

16   Tighten the torque link nut to the torque listed in this Chapter's Specifications and install a new cotter pin (split pin).

17   The remainder of installation is the reverse of the removal steps.

18   Check the operation of the brakes carefully before riding the motorcycle.

13   Wheel bearings - inspection and maintenance

1   The front wheel uses two ball bearings, which are permanently lubricated and sealed on both sides. The rear wheel hub uses two ball bearings, which are sealed on the outer side. The sprocket coupling uses one unsealed ball bearing.

2   Set the bike on its centerstand and remove the wheel (see Section 11 or 12).

3   Set the wheel on blocks so as not to allow the weight of the wheel to rest on the brake disc or sprocket.

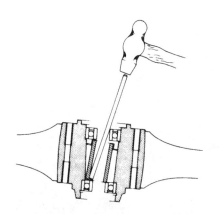

13.6 Once the snap-rings have been removed, drive the bearings from the hub with a metal rod and hammer

13.12a Remove the coupling sleeve. . .

13.12b . . .and coupling collar

Front wheel bearings

Refer to illustration 13.4

4   Remove the speedometer gear housing and collar, brake disc (see Section 4), snap-ring and speedometer drive **(see illustration)**.

5   Turn the wheel over and pry out the grease seal.

6   Insert a brass drift from the right side of the hub and tap evenly around the inner race of the opposite bearing to remove it **(see illustration)**. Remove the bearing spacer, then remove the remaining bearing in the same way.

7   Thoroughly clean the inside of the hub with high-flash point solvent and blow it out with compressed air, if available.

8   Drive in the new bearings with a bearing driver or a socket the same diameter as the bearing outer race. Don't forget to install the spacer after you've installed the first bearing.

9   Install a new circlip on the right-hand side and make sure it seats securely in its groove.

10   Tap in a new grease seal evenly, using a bearing driver or a socket the same diameter as the seal, until it stops at the circlip.

11   The remainder of installation is the reverse of the removal steps.

Sprocket coupling bearing

Refer to illustrations 13.12a, 13.12b, 13.13, 13.14, 13.15, 13.17 and 13.19

12   Lift off the coupling sleeve, rear wheel coupling and coupling collar **(see illustrations)**.

13   Pry the grease seal out of the coupling to expose the bearing and

13.13 Pry the grease seal out to expose the snap-ring and bearing

snap-ring **(see illustration)**.

14   Remove the snap-ring **(see illustration)**.

15   Tap against the back side of the bearing with a bearing driver or a socket to drive it out of the coupling **(see illustration)**.

16   Thoroughly clean the bearing with solvent. Blow it dry with compressed air, if available, but don't spin the bearing with compressed air

13.14 Remove the snap-ring

13.15 Drive the bearing out from this side

7

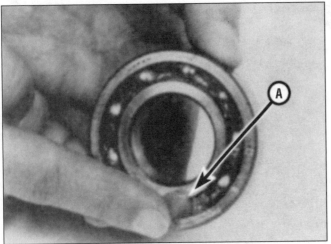

13.17 Pack grease (A) into the bearing until it's full

13.19 Tap a new grease seal in evenly

13.21a Remove the snap-ring

13.22 Insert a drift into the hub and tap evenly around the opposite bearing to drive it out

while it's dry. Hold the inner race with fingers and spin the outer race. If the bearing feels rough, loose, or makes noise (more than a slight whirring), replace it.

17   Pack the bearing with grease **(see illustration)**.

18   Drive the bearing into the coupling with a bearing driver or a socket the same diameter as the outer race.

19   Tap in a new oil seal with a brass or plastic mallet **(see illustration)**. Tap evenly so the seal doesn't tilt. If necessary, lay a block of wood across the seal so the hammer's force will be spread evenly.

Rear wheel bearings

Refer to illustrations 13.21a, 13.21b and 13.22

20   If you haven't already done so, lift the sprocket coupling out of the hub.

21   Remove the snap-ring from the right-hand bearing **(see illustrations)**.

22   Insert a brass drift into the hub and place it against the opposite bearing **(see illustration)**. Tap evenly around the inner race to drive

13.21b Rear hub and wheel bearing details

    1   Axle
    2   Collar
    3   Bearing
    4   Spacer
    5   Wheel
    6   Bearing
    7   Snap-ring
    8   Collar
    9   Nut
    10   Cotter pin (split pin)

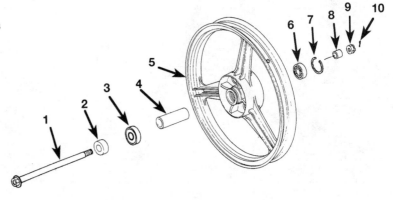

Tyre changing sequence — tubeless tyres

Deflate tyre. After releasing beads, push tyre bead into well of rim at point opposite valve. Insert lever adjacent to valve and work bead over edge or rim.

Use two levers to work bead over edge of rim. Note use of rim protectors.

When first bead is clear, remove tyre as shown.

Before fitting, ensure that tyre is suitable for wheel. Take note of any sidewall markings such as direction of rotation arrows.

Work first bead over the rim flange.

Use a tyre lever to work the second bead over rim flange.

the bearing from the hub. The bearing spacer will also come out.

23   Lay the wheel on its other side and remove the remaining bearing using the same technique.

24   Refer to Step 16 and inspect the bearings.

25   If the bearings check out okay and will be reused, wash them in solvent once again and dry them, then pack the bearings from the open side with high-quality bearing grease **(see illustration 13.17)**.

26   Thoroughly clean the hub area of the wheel. Install the right-hand bearing into the recess in the hub, with the marked or shielded side facing out. Using a bearing driver or a socket large enough to contact the outer race of the bearing, drive it in until the snap-ring groove is visible. Install the snap-ring.

27   Turn the wheel over and install the bearing spacer and bearing, driving the bearing into place as described in Step 26.

28   Press a little grease into the bearing in the rear wheel coupling (if you haven't just repacked it). Install the coupling to the wheel, making sure the coupling collar is located in the inside of the inner race (between the wheel and the coupling).

29   The remainder of installation is the reverse of the removal steps.

14   Tubeless tires - general information

1   Tubeless tires are used as standard equipment on this motorcycle. They are generally safer than tube-type tires but if problems do occur they require special repair techniques.

2   The force required to break the seal between the rim and the bead of the tire is substantial, and is usually beyond the capabilities of an individual working with normal tire irons.

3   Also, repair of the punctured tire and replacement on the wheel rim requires special tools, skills and experience that the average do-it-yourselfer lacks.

4   For these reasons, if a puncture or flat occurs with a tubeless tire, the wheel should be removed from the motorcycle and taken to a dealer service department or a motorcycle repair shop for repair or replacement of the tire.

The accompanying illustration can be used as a guide for tire replacement in an emergency.

Chapter 8 Fairing and bodywork

Contents

8

1   General information

Refer to illustration 1.1

This Chapter covers the procedures necessary to remove and install the fairing and other body parts **(see illustration)**. Since many service and repair operations on these motorcycles require removal of the fairing and/or other body parts, the procedures are grouped here and referred to from other Chapters.

In the case of damage to the fairing or other body part, it is usually necessary to remove the broken component and replace it with a new (or used) one. The material that the fairing and other body parts is composed of doesn't lend itself to conventional repair techniques. There are, however, some shops that specialize in "plastic welding", so it would be advantageous to check around first before throwing the damaged part away.

1.1 Bodywork details

1   Windshield
2   Upper fairing
3   Inner fairing
4   Steering lock
5   Rearview mirror
6   Fairing stay
7   Seat
8   Tailpiece
9   Seat latch
10 Reflectors
11 Side covers
12 Taillight bracket
13 Front fender/mudguard
14 Rear fender/mudguard
    (rear section)
15 Rear fender/mudguard
    (front section)
16 Front fender/mudguard brace
17 Lower fairing brackets
18 Lower fairing

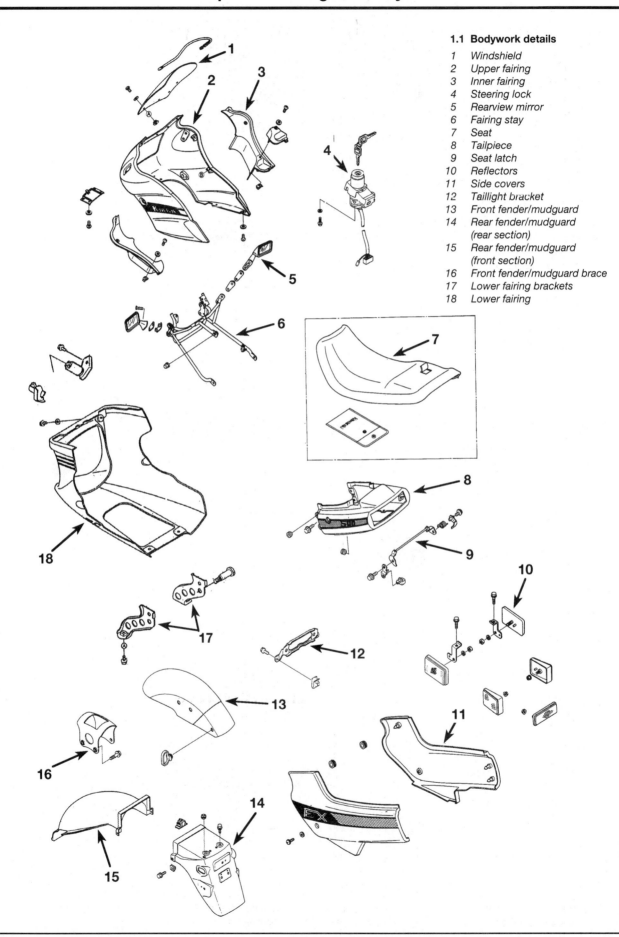

3.3 Remove the screws (arrows) and detach the inner fairing on each side of the motorcycle

3.4 Pull back the rubber cover and remove the mirror mounting screws

3.6 Remove the screw from under the fairing on each side (arrow)

3.7a Spread the fairing slightly and carefully work it forward to clear the fairing stay

2 Lower fairing - removal and installation

1   Set the bike on its centerstand.
2   Support the lower fairing and remove the mounting screws **(see illustration 1.1).**
3   Carefully maneuver the fairing out from under the bike.
4   Installation is the reverse of removal.

3 Upper fairing - removal and installation

Refer to illustrations 3.3, 3.4, 3.6, 3.7a and 3.7b

1   Set the bike on its centerstand.
2   Remove the seat. Remove the fuel tank (see Chapter 4).
3   Remove the inner fairing from each side of the bike **(see illustration)**.
4   Remove the rearview mirrors **(see illustration)**.
5   Disconnect the front turn signal wiring connectors.
6   Remove the screws from the underside of the fairing **(see illustration)**.
7   Spread the fairing slightly and pull it forward to clear the fairing stays, then pull it off **(see illustration)**. **Note:** *If you're removing the*

3.7b If you only need access to other components, you can prop the fairing away from the sides of the bike with blocks of wood

fairing partially for access to other components, prop the rear ends away from the bike with blocks of wood **(see illustration)**.
8   Installation is the reverse of removal.

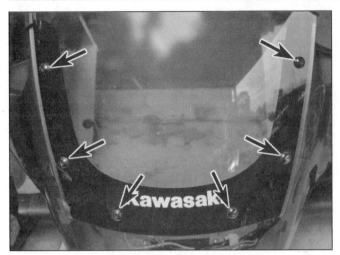

4.1 Windshield mounting screws

7.2 Remove the side cover mounting screw on each side (arrow)

4   Windshield - removal and installation

Refer to illustration 4.1

1   Remove the screws securing the windshield to the fairing **(see illustration)**.

2   Carefully separate the windshield from the fairing. If it sticks, don't attempt to pry it off - just keep applying steady pressure with your fingers.

3   Installation is the reverse of the removal procedure. Be sure each screw has a plastic washer under its head. Tighten the screws securely, but be careful not to overtighten them, as the windshield might crack.

5   Rear view mirrors - removal and installation

Refer to Section 3, Step 4 - removing the rear view mirrors is part of the upper fairing removal procedure.

6   Fairing stay - removal and installation

1   Remove the fairing (see Section 3).

2   Remove the headlight assembly and instrument cluster (see Chapter 9).

3   Carefully note how the wiring harness are routed in the area of the fairing stay.

4   Remove the bolts and nut and take the fairing stay off the bike **(see illustration 1.1).**

5   Installation is the reverse of the removal steps.

6   Adjust the headlight aim (see Chapter 9).

7   Side covers - removal and installation

Refer to illustrations 7.2 and 7.3

1   Remove the seat.

2   Remove the side cover mounting screw from each side of the motorcycle **(see illustration)**.

3   Carefully pull the securing lugs out of the grommets **(see illustration)** and lift the cover off. Caution: Don't use force; some models may be attached by screws. If the cover won't come off with a light pull, make sure all fasteners have been removed.

4   Installation is the reverse of the removal procedure.

8   Front fender/mudguard - removal and installation

Refer to illustration 8.3

1   Set the bike on its centerstand.

2   Disconnect the speedometer cable from the speedometer drive.

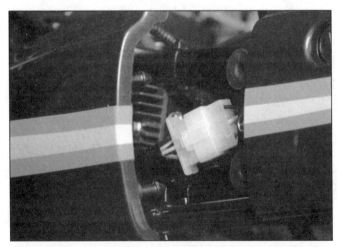

7.3 Pull the lugs out of the grommets; if they won't come with a light pull, make sure all fasteners have been removed

8.3 The fender/mudguard mounting bolts are accessible from inside the fender/mudguard

9.2 Remove the grab rail mounting bolts

9.3 Remove the bolt on each side of the tailpiece (arrow) and slide it rearward

3   Remove the bolts from inside the fender/mudguard **(see illustration)**.
4   Installation is the reverse of removal.

9   Tailpiece - remo

val and installation

Refer to illustrations 9.2 and 9.3
1   Remove the side covers (see Section 7).
2   Unbolt the grab rail and take it off **(see illustration)**.
3   Remove the tailpiece bolt on each side **(see illustration)**.
4   Disconnect the electrical connector for taillights. Slide the tailpiece to the rear until the projections on the tailpiece separate from the grommets in the frame, then remove it.
5   Installation is the reverse of removal.

10   Rear fender/mudguard - removal and installation

Rear section
1   Set the bike on its centerstand.
2   Remove the seat. Remove the tailpiece (see Section 9).
3   Unplug the electrical connectors for the turn signal lights.
4   Remove the mounting bolts and remove the rear section of the rear fender **(see illustration 1.1)**.
5   Installation is the reverse of the removal procedure.

Front section
6   Remove the rear section (see above).
7   Lift the front section out toward the rear.
8   Installation is the reverse of removal. Be sure to route the brake fluid reservoir hose between the fender/mudguard and the frame tube.

NOTES

Chapter 9 Electrical system

Contents

Specifications

Battery

Type	12 volt, 14Ah (amp hours)
Specific gravity	See Chapter 1

Charging system

Charging system output	14 to 15 volts DC at 4000 rpm
Alternator output	60 volts AC at 4000 rpm
Stator coil resistance	0.3 to 0.6 ohms

Starter motor

Brush length	
Standard	15/32 to 31/64 inch (12 to 12.5 mm)
Minimum	15/64 in (6 mm)
Commutator diameter	
Standard	1-7/64 in (28 mm)
Minimum	1-1/16 in (27 mm)

Circuit fuse ratings

Taillight	10A
Accessory	10A
Headlight relay	10A
Main fuse	30A

Bulb wattages

Headlight	12V, 60/55W
Taillight	
US models	12V, 8/27W x 2
UK models	12V, 5/21W x 2
License plate light	
US models	12V, 8W
UK models	12V, 5W
Turn signals	
US models	12V, 23W x 4
UK models	12V, 21W x 4
Instrument cluster lights	12V, 3.4W

Torque specifications

Alternator rotor bolt	51 ft-lbs (69 Nm)
Alternator stator screws	104 in-lbs (12 Nm)
Alternator cover bolts	Not specified
Oil pressure switch	11 ft-lbs (15 Nm)
Starter clutch bolts	25 ft-lbs (34 Nm)

9

1   General information

The machines covered by this manual are equipped with a 12-volt electrical system. The components include a crankshaft mounted permanent magnet alternator and a solid state voltage regulator/rectifier unit.

The regulator maintains the charging system output within the specified range to prevent overcharging. The rectifier converts the AC (alternating current) output of the alternator to DC (direct current) to power the lights and other components and to charge the battery.

The alternator consists of a multi-coil stator (bolted to the right-hand engine case) and a permanent magnet rotor.

An electric starter mounted to the engine case behind the cylinders is standard equipment. The starting system includes the motor, the battery, the solenoid, the starter circuit relay (part of the junction box) and the various wires and switches. If the engine stop switch and the main key switch are both in the On position, the circuit relay allows the starter motor to operate only if the transmission is in Neutral (Neutral switch on) or the clutch lever is pulled to the handlebar (clutch switch on) and the sidestand is up (sidestand switch on). **Note:** *Keep in mind that electrical parts, once purchased, can't be returned. To avoid unnecessary expense, make very sure the faulty component has been positively identified before buying a replacement part.*

2   Electrical troubleshooting

A typical electrical circuit consists of an electrical component, the switches, relays, etc. related to that component and the wiring and connectors that hook the component to both the battery and the frame. To aid in locating a problem in any electrical circuit, complete wiring diagrams of each model are included at the end of this Chapter.

Before tackling any troublesome electrical circuit, first study the appropriate diagrams thoroughly to get a complete picture of what makes up that individual circuit. Trouble spots, for instance, can often be narrowed down by noting if other components related to that circuit are operating properly or not. If several components or circuits fail at one time, chances are the fault lies in the fuse or ground connection, as several circuits often are routed through the same fuse and ground connections.

Electrical problems often stem from simple causes, such as loose or corroded connections or a blown fuse. Prior to any electrical troubleshooting, always visually check the condition of the fuse, wires and connections in the problem circuit.

If testing instruments are going to be utilized, use the diagrams to plan where you will make the necessary connections in order to accurately pinpoint the trouble spot.

The basic tools needed for electrical troubleshooting include a test light or voltmeter, a continuity tester (which includes a bulb, battery and set of test leads) and a jumper wire, preferably with a circuit breaker incorporated, which can be used to bypass electrical components. Specific checks described later in this Chapter may also require an ohmmeter.

Voltage checks should be performed if a circuit is not functioning properly. Connect one lead of a test light or voltmeter to either the negative battery terminal or a known good ground. Connect the other lead to a connector in the circuit being tested, preferably nearest to the battery or fuse. If the bulb lights, voltage is reaching that point, which means the part of the circuit between that connector and the battery is problem-free. Continue checking the remainder of the circuit in the same manner. When you reach a point where no voltage is present, the problem lies between there and the last good test point. Most of the time the problem is due to a loose connection. Keep in mind that some circuits only receive voltage when the ignition key is in the On position.

One method of finding short circuits is to remove the fuse and connect a test light or voltmeter in its place to the fuse terminals. There should be no load in the circuit. Move the wiring harness from side-to-side while watching the test light. If the bulb lights, there is a short to ground somewhere in that area, probably where insulation has

rubbed off a wire. The same test can be performed on other components in the circuit, including the switch.

A ground/earth check should be done to see if a component is grounded (earthed) properly. Disconnect the battery and connect one lead of a self-powered test light (continuity tester) to a known good ground/earth. Connect the other lead to the wire or ground/earth connection being tested. If the bulb lights, the ground/earth is good. If the bulb does not light, the ground/earth is not good.

A continuity check is performed to see if a circuit, section of circuit or individual component is capable of passing electricity through it. Disconnect the battery and connect one lead of a self-powered test light (continuity tester) to one end of the circuit being tested and the other lead to the other end of the circuit. If the bulb lights, there is continuity, which means the circuit is passing electricity through it properly. Switches can be checked in the same way.

Remember that all electrical circuits are designed to conduct electricity from the battery, through the wires, switches, relays, etc. to the electrical component (light bulb, motor, etc.). From there it is directed to the frame (ground/earth) where it is passed back to the battery. Electrical problems are basically an interruption in the flow of electricity from the battery or back to it.

3   Battery - inspection and maintenance

1   Most battery damage is caused by heat, vibration, and/or low electrolyte levels, so keep the battery securely mounted, check the electrolyte level frequently and make sure the charging system is functioning properly.

2   Refer to Chapter 1 for electrolyte level and specific gravity checking procedures.

3   Check around the base inside of the battery for sediment, which is the result of sulfation caused by low electrolyte levels. These deposits will cause internal short circuits, which can quickly discharge the battery. Look for cracks in the case and replace the battery if either of these conditions is found.

4   Check the battery terminals and cable ends for tightness and corrosion. If corrosion is evident, remove the cables from the battery and clean the terminals and cable ends with a wire brush or knife and emery paper. Reconnect the cables and apply a thin coat of petroleum jelly to the connections to slow further corrosion.

5   The battery case should be kept clean to prevent current leakage, which can discharge the battery over a period of time (especially when it sits unused). Wash the outside of the case with a solution of baking soda and water. Do not get any baking soda solution in the battery cells. Rinse the battery thoroughly, then dry it.

6   If acid has been spilled on the frame or battery box, neutralize it with the baking soda and water solution, dry it thoroughly, then touch up any damaged paint. Make sure the battery vent tube is directed away from the frame and is not kinked or pinched.

7   If the motorcycle sits unused for long periods of time, disconnect the cables from the battery terminals. Refer to Section 4 and charge the battery approximately once every month.

4   Battery - charging

1   If the machine sits idle for extended periods or if the charging system malfunctions, the battery can be charged from an external source.

2   To properly charge the battery, you will need a charger of the correct rating, a hydrometer, a clean rag and a syringe for adding distilled water to the battery cells.

3   The maximum charging rate for any battery is 1/10 of the rated amp/hour capacity. As an example, the maximum charging rate for a 14 amp/hour battery would be 1.4 amps. If the battery is charged at a higher rate, it could be damaged.

4   Do not allow the battery to be subjected to a so-called quick charge (high rate of charge over a short period of time) unless you are prepared to buy a new battery.

5.1a Most of the fuses, including the spares, are located on the junction box. . .

5.1b . . .the main fuse is located on the starter relay (arrow)

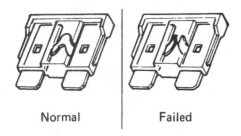

| Normal | Failed |

5.3 A blown fuse can be identified by a broken element - be sure to replace a blown fuse with one of the same amperage rating

5   When charging the battery, always remove it from the machine and be sure to check the electrolyte level before hooking up the charger. Add distilled water to any cells that are low.

6   Loosen the cell caps, hook up the battery charger leads (red to positive, black to negative), cover the top of the battery with a clean rag, then, and only then, plug in the battery charger. **Warning**: *Remember, the gas escaping from a charging battery is explosive, so keep open flames and sparks well away from the area. If the gas ignites, the entire battery can explode and spray acid. Also, the electrolyte is extremely corrosive and will damage anything it comes in contact with.*

7   Allow the battery to charge until the specific gravity is as specified (refer to Chapter 1 for specific gravity checking procedures). The charger must be unplugged and disconnected from the battery when making specific gravity checks. If the battery overheats or gases excessively, the charging rate is too high. Either disconnect the charger or lower the charging rate to prevent damage to the battery.

8   If one or more of the cells do not show an increase in specific gravity after a long slow charge, or if the battery as a whole does not seem to want to take a charge, it is time for a new battery.

9   When the battery is fully charged, unplug the charger first, then disconnect the leads from the battery. Install the cell caps and wipe any electrolyte off the outside of the battery case.

5   Fuses - check and replacement

Refer to illustrations 5.1a, 5.1b and 5.3

1   All of the fuses except the main fuse are located under the seat, on the junction box **(see illustration)**. The main fuse is located on the

starter relay **(see illustration)**. The fuses on the junction box are protected by a plastic cover, which snaps into place. It contains fuses (and spares) which protect the main, headlight, taillight and accessory circuit wiring and components from damage caused by short circuits.

2   If you have a test light, the fuses can be checked without removing them. Turn the ignition to the On position, connect one end of the test light to a good ground, then probe each terminal on top of the fuse. If the fuse is good, there will be voltage available at both terminals. If the fuse is blown, there will only be voltage present at one of the terminals.

3   The fuses can be removed and checked visually. If you can't pull the fuse out with your fingertips, use a pair of needle-nose pliers. A blown fuse is easily identified by a break in the element **(see illustration)**.

4   If a fuse blows, be sure to check the wiring harnesses very carefully for evidence of a short circuit. Look for bare wires and chafed, melted or burned insulation. If a fuse is replaced before the cause is located, the new fuse will blow immediately.

5   Never, under any circumstances, use a higher rated fuse or bridge the fuse block terminals, as damage to the electrical system - including melted wires, ruined components, and fire - could result.

6   Occasionally a fuse will blow or cause an open circuit for no obvious reason. Corrosion of the fuse ends and fuse block terminals may occur and cause poor fuse contact. If this happens, remove the corrosion with a wire brush or emery paper, then spray the fuse end and terminals with electrical contact cleaner.

6   Junction box - check

1   Aside from serving as the fuse block, the junction box also houses three relays - the fan relay (early models only), the starter circuit relay (not the starter relay) and the headlight relay (US and Canada only). If one of these relays fails, the junction box must be replaced.

2   In addition to the relay checks, the fuse circuits and diode circuits should be checked also, to rule out the possibility of an open circuit condition or blown diode within the junction block as the cause of an electrical problem. Schematics of the junction box can be found in the Wiring diagrams at the end of this Chapter.

Fuse circuit check

Refer to illustration 6.4

3   Remove the junction box by sliding it out of its holder. Unplug the electrical connectors from the box.

4   If the terminals are dirty or bent, clean and straighten them. Using the accompanying table as a guide, check the continuity across the indicated terminals with an ohmmeter - some should have no resistance

Fuse Circuit Inspection

Meter Connection	Meter Reading (Ω)
1 — 2	0
1 — 3	0
6 — 7	0
6 — 17	0
1 — 7	∞
3A — 8	∞
8 — 17	∞

6.4 Using an ohmmeter, check the conductivity across the indicated pairs of terminals

	Meter Connection	Battery Connection + −	Meter Reading (Ω)
Fan[1]	2 — 5	2 — 4	0
Headlight[2]	7 — 8	9 — 13	0
Starter	11 — 13	11 — 12	0

6.10b Use jumper wires to connect battery voltage to the indicated terminals, then check the conductivity across the indicated terminals - the resistance should be zero

1   Early models (single wire fan switch) only
2   US and Canadian models only

and others should have infinite resistance **(see illustration)**.
5   If the resistance values are not as specified, replace the junction box.

Diode circuit check

6   Remove the junction box by sliding it out of its holder. Unplug the electrical connectors from the box.
7   Using an ohmmeter, check the resistance across the following pairs of terminals, then write down the readings.
     Here are the terminal pairs to be checked:
     13 and 8 (US and Canadian models only)
     13 and 9 (US and Canadian models only)
     12 and 14
     15 and 14
     16 and 14
8   Now, reverse the ohmmeter leads and check the resistances again, writing down the readings. The resistances should be low in one direction and more than ten times as much in the other direction. If the readings for any pair of terminals are low or high in both directions, a diode is defective and the junction box must be replaced.

Relay checks

Refer to illustrations 6.10a and 6.10b

9   Remove the junction box by sliding it out of its holder. Unplug the electrical connectors from the box.
10   Using an ohmmeter, check the conductivity across the terminals indicated in the accompanying table **(see illustration)**. Then, energize each relay by applying battery voltage across the indicated terminals and check the conductivity across the corresponding terminals shown on the table **(see illustration)**.
11   If the junction box fails any of these tests, it must be replaced.

---

7   Lighting system - check

---

1   The battery provides power for operation of the headlight, taillight, brake light, license plate light and instrument cluster lights. If none of the lights operate, always check battery voltage before pro-

	Meter Connection	Meter Reading (Ω)
Fan Relay[1]	2 — 5	∞
	4 — 5	∞
Headlight Relay[2]	7 — 8	∞
	7 — 13	∞
Starter Relay	11 — 13	∞
	12 — 13	∞

6.10a With the junction box unplugged, there should be infinite resistance between the indicated terminals

1   Early models (single wire fan switch) only
2   US and Canadian models only

7.3 The reserve lighting device is mounted behind the shock absorber

ceeding. Low battery voltage indicates either a faulty battery, low battery electrolyte level or a defective charging system. Refer to Chapter 1 for battery checks and Sections 28 through 32 for charging system tests. Also, check the condition of the fuses and replace any blown fuses with new ones.

Headlight

Refer to illustration 7.3

2   If the headlight is out when the engine is running, check the fuse first with the key On (see Section 5), then unplug the electrical connector for the headlight and use jumper wires to connect the bulb directly to the battery terminals. If the light comes on, the problem lies in the wiring or one of the switches in the circuit. Refer to Sections 19 and 20 for the switch testing procedures, and also the wiring diagrams at the end of this Chapter.
3   US and Canadian models use an additional relay in the system, called the reserve lighting device. On these models, the headlight doesn't come on when the ignition switch is first turned on, but comes on when the starter button is pressed and stays on until the ignition is turned off. The light will go out whenever the starter is operated after the engine has stalled (this prevents excessive strain on the battery). The reserve lighting device is located behind the shock absorber **(see illustration)**.

Taillight/license plate light

4   If the taillight fails to work, check the bulbs and the bulb terminals first, then check for battery voltage at the red wire in the taillight. If voltage is present, check the ground circuit for an open or poor connection.

8.1 The headlight assembly is secured by two screws on either side (arrows)

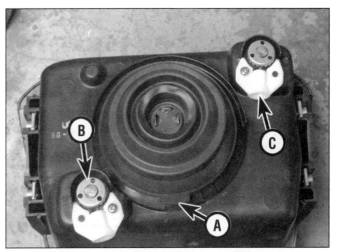

8.2 Pull up on the tab to lift the dust cover away from the headlight

A Tab	C Vertical adjuster
B Horizontal adjuster	

8.3 The bulb holder is held in place by this retaining clip

8.4 Pull the bulb holder out of the socket

5   If no voltage is indicated, check the wiring between the taillight and the main (key) switch, then check the switch.

Brake light

6   See Section 14 for the brake light circuit checking procedure.

Neutral indicator light

7   If the neutral light fails to operate when the transmission is in Neutral, check the fuses and the bulb (see Section 17 for bulb removal procedures). If the bulb and fuses are in good condition, check for battery voltage at the light green wire attached to the neutral switch on the left side of the engine. If battery voltage is present, refer to Section 22 for the neutral switch check and replacement procedures.

8   If no voltage is indicated, check the wires between the junction box and the bulb, the junction box and the switch and between the switch and the bulb for open circuits and poor connections.

Oil pressure warning light

9   See Section 18 for the oil pressure warning light circuit check.

8   Headlight bulb - replacement

Refer to illustrations 8.1, 8.2, 8.3 and 8.4

1   If it's necessary for access, remove the headlight assembly securing screws, disconnect the electrical connector and remove the as-

sembly **(see illustration)**.

2   Pull up the tab and remove the dust cover **(see illustration)**.

3   Lift up the retaining clip and swing it out of the way **(see illustration)**. **Warning**: *If the headlight has just been on, let the bulb cool before you continue. It will be hot to enough to cause burns.*

4   Remove the bulb holder **(see illustration)**.

5   When installing the new bulb, reverse the removal procedure. Be sure not to touch the bulb with your fingers - oil from your skin will cause the bulb to overheat and fail prematurely. If you do touch the bulb, wipe it off with a clean rag dampened with rubbing alcohol.

9   Headlight assembly - removal and installation

1   Remove the upper fairing (see Chapter 8).

2   Remove the screws holding the headlight assembly to the fairing **(see illustration 8.1)**. Separate the headlight assembly from the fairing.

3   Installation is the reverse of removal. Be sure to adjust the headlight aim (see Section 10).

9

10   Headlight aim - check and adjustment

1   An improperly adjusted headlight may cause problems for on-

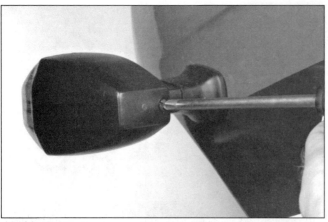

11.2 Remove the screws securing the turn signal lens-reflector assembly to the turn signal housing, then pull the lens/reflector assembly out

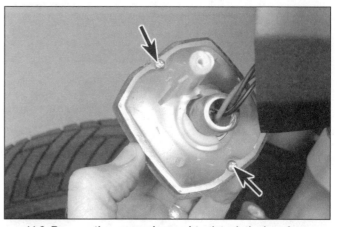

11.3 Remove the screws (arrows) to detach the lens from the reflector

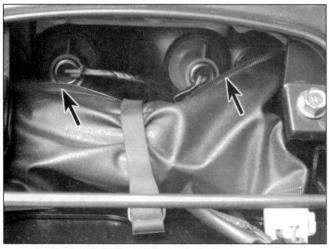

11.8a Unhook the rubber strap and remove the tool bag to gain access to the bulb holders. . .

11.8b . . .then rotate the holders and pull them out of their sockets

coming traffic or provide poor, unsafe illumination of the road ahead. Before adjusting the headlight, be sure to consult with local traffic laws and regulations.

2   The headlight beam can be adjusted both vertically and horizontally. Before performing the adjustment, make sure the fuel tank has at least a half tank of fuel, and have an assistant sit on the seat.

3   Insert a Phillips screwdriver into the horizontal adjuster guide **(see illustration 8.2)**, then turn the adjuster as necessary to center the beam.

4   To adjust the vertical position of the beam, insert the screwdriver into the vertical adjuster guide and turn the adjuster as necessary to raise or lower the beam.

---

11   Turn signal and taillight bulbs - replacement

Turn signal bulbs

Refer to illustrations 11.2 and 11.3

1   Bulb replacement for the turn signals is the same for the front and rear.

2   Remove the screw that holds the lens/reflector assembly to the turn signal housing **(see illustration)**. Pull out the lens/reflector assembly.

3   Remove the screws securing the lens to the reflector **(see illustration)**.

4   Push the bulb in and turn it counterclockwise (anticlockwise) to

remove it. Check the socket terminals for corrosion and clean them if necessary. Line up the pins on the new bulb with the slots in the socket, push in and turn the bulb clockwise until it locks in place. **Note**: *The pins on the bulb are offset so it can only be installed one way. It is a good idea to use a paper towel or dry cloth when handling the new bulb to prevent injury if the bulb should break and to increase bulb life.*

5   Position the lens on the reflector and install the screws. Be careful not to overtighten them.

6   Place the lens/reflector assembly into the housing and install the screw, tightening it securely.

Taillight bulbs

Refer to illustrations 11.8a and 11.8b

7   To remove the taillight bulbs, remove the seat.

8   Turn the bulb holders counterclockwise (anticlockwise) **(see illustration)** until they stop, then pull straight out to remove them from the taillight housing **(see illustration)**. The bulbs can be removed from the holders by turning them counterclockwise (anticlockwise) and pulling straight out.

9   Check the socket terminals for corrosion and clean them if necessary. Line up the pins on the new bulb with the slots in the socket, push in and turn the bulb clockwise until it locks in place. **Note**: *The pins on the bulb are offset so it can only be installed one way. It is a good idea to use a paper towel or dry cloth when handling the new bulb to prevent injury if the bulb should break and to increase bulb life.*

10   Make sure the rubber gaskets are in place and in good condition, then line up the tabs on the holder with the slots in the housing and

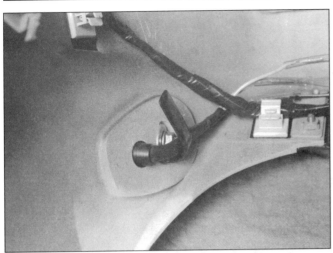

12.3 The turn signals are secured by a nut inside the fender or fairing

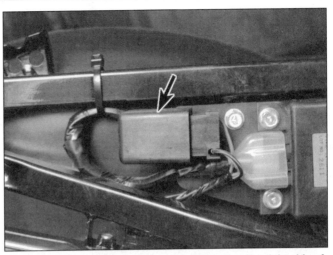

13.3 The turn signal flasher (arrow) is located on the right side of the frame, behind the side cover

14.6 The brake light switch mounted on the brake lever is retained by a screw

push the holder into the mounting hole. Turn it clockwise until it stops to lock it in place. **Note**: *The tabs and slots are two different sizes so the holders can only be installed one way.*

11   Reinstall the seat.

12   Turn signal assemblies - removal and installation

Refer to illustration 12.3

1   The turn signal assemblies can be removed individually in the event of damage or failure.

2   To remove a turn signal assembly, first follow the wiring harness from the turn signal to its electrical connectors. Mark the wires with pieces of numbered tape then unplug the electrical connectors.

3   Unscrew the nut that secures the turn signal to the fairing or rear fender **(see illustration)**.

4   Detach the turn signal from the fairing or fender. If you're installing a new turn signal, separate the stalk trim from the old stalk and transfer it to the new one.

5   Installation is the reverse of the removal procedure.

13   Turn signal circuit - check

Refer to illustration 13.3

1   The battery provides power for operation of the signal lights, so if

they do not operate, always check the battery voltage and specific gravity first. Low battery voltage indicates either a faulty battery, low electrolyte level or a defective charging system. Refer to Chapter 1 for battery checks and Sections 28 through 32 for charging system tests. Also, check the fuses (see Section 5).

2   Most turn signal problems are the result of a burned out bulb or corroded socket. This is especially true when the turn signals function properly in one direction, but fail to flash in the other direction. Check the bulbs and the sockets (see Section 11).

3   If the bulbs and sockets check out okay, refer to the wiring diagrams at the end of this Chapter and check for power at the turn signal flasher **(see illustration)** with the ignition On. If there's no power at the flasher, check the junction box (see Section 6) and the switch (see Section 21).

4   If the junction box and switch are okay, check the wiring between the turn signal flasher and the turn signal lights (see the wiring diagrams at the end of this Chapter).

5   If the wiring checks out okay, replace the turn signal flasher.

14   Brake light switches - check and replacement

Circuit check

1   Before checking any electrical circuit, check the fuses (see Section 5).

2   Using a test light connected to a good ground, check for voltage at the brown wire terminal in the electrical connector at the brake light switch. If there's no voltage present, check the brown wire between the switch and the junction box (see the wiring diagrams at the end of this Chapter).

3   If voltage is available, touch the probe of the test light to the other terminal of the switch, then pull the brake lever or depress the brake pedal - if the test light doesn't light up, replace the switch.

4   If the test light does light, check the wiring between the switch and the brake lights (see the wiring diagrams at the end of this Chapter).

Switch replacement
Brake lever switch

Refer to illustration 14.6

5   Unplug the electrical connectors from the switch.

6   Remove the mounting screw **(see illustration)** and detach the switch from the brake lever bracket/front master cylinder.

7   Installation is the reverse of the removal procedure. The brake lever switch isn't adjustable.

9

14.8 Location of the rear brake light switch connectors

14.9 You'll need a new tie wrap to replace this one (arrow)

14.10 Loosen the adjuster nut (arrow) and unscrew the switch

15.1 Location of the cluster electrical connectors

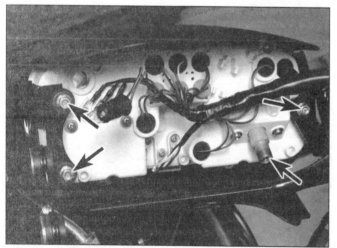

15.2 Disconnect the speedometer cable and remove the cluster mounting screws (arrows)

Brake pedal switch

Refer to illustrations 14.8, 14.9 and 14.10

8   Remove the side cover (see Chapter 8) and unplug the electrical connectors in the switch harness **(see illustration)**.

9   Cut the tie wrap that secures the brake light switch harness to the

frame **(see illustration)**.

10   Loosen the adjuster nut **(see illustration)** and unscrew the switch.

11   Install the switch by reversing the removal procedure (use a new tie wrap to secure the harness to the frame).

12   Adjust the switch by following the procedure described in Chapter 1.

---

15   Instrument cluster - removal and installation

Refer to illustrations 15.1 and 15.2

1   Remove the upper fairing (see Chapter 8) and disconnect the electrical connectors from the cluster harness **(see illustration)**.

2   Disconnect the speedometer cable and remove the instrument cluster mounting screws **(see illustration)**, then detach the cluster from the fairing stay. **Caution**: *Keep the cluster in an upright position while it's off the motorcycle or the gauges will be ruined.*

3   Installation is the reverse of the removal procedure.

---

16   Meters and gauges - check and replacement

Check

Temperature gauge

1   Refer to Chapter 3 for the temperature gauge checking procedure.

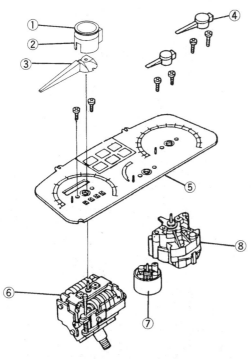

16.3 Exploded view of the instrument cluster

1	Retainer*	5	Dial
2	Cap*	6	Speedometer
3	Pointer*	7	Temperature gauge
4	Pointer	8	Tachometer

Supplied with replacement gauges

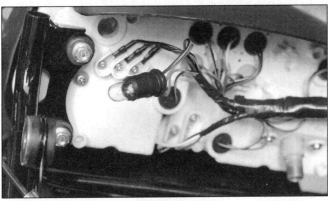

17.2 Pull the bulb socket out of the cluster, then pull the bulb out of the socket

Tachometer and speedometer

2   Special instruments are required to properly check the operation of these meters. Take the instrument cluster to a Kawasaki dealer service department or other qualified repair shop for diagnosis.

Gauge replacement

Refer to illustration 16.3

3   Remove the screws that secure the instrument cluster cover **(see illustration)**. Detach the cover. **Caution**: *Always store the cluster with the gauges facing up or the gauges will be ruined.*

4   Pull the indicator pointer off the gauge to be replaced.

5   Mark the positions of the wires and remove the small screws that secure the gauge to the cluster housing.

6   Detach the gauge from the housing, being careful not to disturb the other components.

7   Inspect the rubber dampers at the cluster screw attaching points. Replace them if they're cracked or brittle.

16.10 Speedometer cable lower connection

18.2 Location of the oil pressure switch

8   Installation is the reverse of the removal procedure, with the following addition: New gauges come with a cap and retainer that holds the pointer on.

Speedometer cable replacement

Refer to illustration 16.10

9   Disconnect the speedometer cable from the cluster **(see illustration 15.2)**.

10   Disconnect the lower end of the speedometer cable from the drive **(see illustration)**. Note carefully how the cable is routed, then remove it.

11   Installation is the reverse of the removal steps.

17   Instrument and warning light bulbs - replacement

Refer to illustration 17.2

1   Remove the fairing (see Chapter 8).

2   To replace a bulb, pull the appropriate rubber socket out of the back of the instrument cluster housing **(see illustration)**, then pull the bulb out of the socket. If the socket contacts are dirty or corroded, they should be scraped clean and sprayed with electrical contact cleaner before new bulbs are installed.

3   Carefully push the new bulb into position, then push the socket into the cluster housing.

4   Install the fairing.

18   Oil pressure switch - check and replacement

Refer to illustration 18.2

1   If the oil pressure warning light fails to operate properly, check the oil level and make sure it is correct.

2   If the oil level is correct, disconnect the wire from the oil pressure switch, which is located on the bottom of the engine **(see illustration)**.

9

	BR	W	Y	BL	R	W/BK	O/G
OFF, LOCK							
ON	O———	———	——O	O———	——O	O———	——O
P (Park)		O———	———	———	——O	O———	——O
						US, Canada	

19.2 Check the continuity of the ignition switch in the different switch positions across the indicated terminals

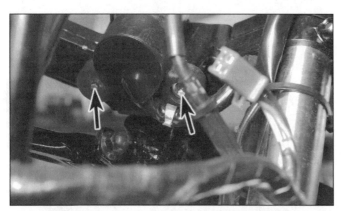

19.7 The shear-head bolts (arrows) must be carefully drilled and removed with a screw extractor or knocked in a counterclockwise direction with a hammer and punch

Turn the main switch On and ground/earth the end of the wire. If the light comes on, the oil pressure switch is defective and must be replaced with a new one (only after draining the engine oil).

3   If the light does not come on, check the oil pressure warning light bulb, the wiring between the oil pressure switch and the light, and between the light and the junction box (see the wiring diagrams at the end of this Chapter).

4   To replace the switch, drain the engine oil (see Chapter 1) and unscrew the switch from the case. Coat the threads of the new switch with a non-permanent thread locking agent (not sealant), then screw the unit into its hole, tightening it to the torque listed in this Chapter's Specifications.

5   Fill the crankcase with the recommended type and amount of oil (see Chapter 1) and check for leaks.

19   Ignition main (key) switch - check and replacement

Check

Refer to illustration 19.2

1   Remove the upper fairing (see Chapter 8). This isn't absolutely necessary, but it makes access to the switch electrical connector easier.

2   Using an ohmmeter, check the continuity of the terminal pairs indicated in the accompanying table **(see illustration)**. Continuity should exist between the terminals connected by a solid line when the switch is in the indicated position.

3   If the switch fails any of the tests, replace it.

Replacement

Refer to illustration 19.7

4   Remove the upper fairing, if you haven't already done so (see Chapter 8).

5   Remove the instrument cluster (see Section 15).

6   Unplug the switch electrical connector.

7   The switch is held to the upper clamp with two shear-head bolts **(see illustration)**. Using a hammer and a sharp punch, knock the shear-head bolts in a counterclockwise (anticlockwise) direction to un-

screw them. Ifthey're too tight and won't turn, carefully drill holes through the centers of the bolts and unscrew them using a screw extractor (E-Z Out). If necessary, remove the fairing mount for better access to the bolts. Detach the switch from the upper clamp.

8   Hold the new switch in position and install the new shear-head bolts. Tighten the bolts until the heads break off.

9   The remainder of installation is the reverse of the removal steps.

20   Handlebar switches - check

Refer to illustration 20.4

1   Generally speaking, the switches are reliable and trouble-free. Most troubles, when they do occur, are caused by dirty or corroded contacts, but wear and breakage of internal parts is a possibility that should not be overlooked. If breakage does occur, the entire switch and related wiring harness will have to be replaced with a new one, since individual parts are not usually available.

2   The switches can be checked for continuity with an ohmmeter or a continuity test light. Always disconnect the battery ground/earth cable, which will prevent the possibility of a short circuit, before making the checks.

3   Trace the wiring harness of the switch in question and unplug the electrical connectors.

4   Using the ohmmeter or test light, check for continuity between the terminals of the switch harness with the switch in the various positions **(see illustration)**. Continuity should exist between the terminals connected by a solid line when the switch is in the indicated position.

5   If the continuity check indicates a problem exists, refer to Section 21, disassemble the switch and spray the switch contacts with electrical contact cleaner. If they are accessible, the contacts can be scraped clean with a knife or polished with crocus cloth. If switch components are damaged or broken, it will be obvious when the switch is disassembled.

21   Handlebar switches - removal and installation

1   The handlebar switches are composed of two halves that clamp around the bars. They are easily removed for cleaning or inspection by taking out the clamp screws and pulling the switch halves away from the handlebars.

2   To completely remove the switches, the electrical connectors in the wiring harness should be unplugged. The right side switch must be separated from the throttle cables, also.

3   When installing the switches, make sure the wiring harnesses are properly routed to avoid pinching or stretching the wires.

22   Neutral switch - check and replacement

Refer to illustration 22.3

Check

1   Remove the shift pedal and linkage (see Chapter 2).

2   Remove the engine sprocket cover (see Chapter 6).

Starter Lockout Switch Connections

	BK/Y	BK	BK/R
When clutch lever is pulled in	O━━━O		
When clutch lever is released		O━━━O	O

Dimmer Switch Connections (US, Canada)

	BL/Y	BL/O	R/Y	R/BK
HI	O━━━━━━━━━━━━━━━O	O━━━O		
LO	O━━━━━━━O	O━━━━━━━O		

Engine Stop Switch Connections

	R	Y/R
OFF		
RUN	O━━━O	

Dimmer Switch Connections (Other than US, Canada)

	R/BK	BL/Y	R/Y
HI	O━━━O		
LO		O━━━O	

Starter Button Connections

		BK (BK/R)	BK (BK/R)
Free			
Push on		O━━━O	

Turn Signal Switch Connections

	GY	O	G
R	O━━━O		
N			
L		O━━━O	

Headlight Switch Connections (Other than US, Canada)

	R/W	R/BL	BL	BL/Y
OFF				
■		O━━━O		
ON	O━━━O		O━━━O	

Hazard Switch Connections

	GY	O	G
Off ▄			
On ▄	O━━━O	O━━━O	

Front Brake Light Switch Connections

		BR (BK)	BL or BL/R (BK)
When brake lever is pulled in		O━━━O	

Passing Button Connections (Other than US, Canada)

		BR	R/BK
Free			
Push on		O━━━O	

Horn Button Connections

		BK/W	BK/Y
Free			
Push on		O━━━O	

20.4 Continuity tables for the handlebar switches

9

22.3 Location of the neutral switch

23.6 The sidestand switch is located between the sidestand and the frame

through the switch (0 ohms). With the sidestand down, there should be no continuity (infinite resistance).
5   If the switch fails either of these tests, replace it.

Replacement

Refer to illustration 23.6

6   Remove the switch bolts and remove the sidestand **(see illustration)**.
7   Remove the switch.
8   Installation is the reverse of the removal procedure.

---

24   Horn - check, replacement and adjustment

Refer to illustration 24.1

Check

1   Unplug the electrical connectors from the horn **(see illustration)**. Using two jumper wires, apply battery voltage directly to the terminals on the horn. If the horn sounds, check the switch (see Section 20) and the wiring between the switch and the horn (see the wiring diagrams at the end of this Chapter).
2   If the horn doesn't sound, replace it. If it makes noise, but sounds "sick," try adjusting the tone as described below.

Replacement

3   Detach the electrical connectors and unbolt the horn bracket from the frame.
4   Unbolt the horn from the bracket and transfer the bracket to the new horn.
5   Installation is the reverse of removal.

Adjustment

6   Loosen the locknut on the adjustment screw. Have an assistant operate the horn. Turn the adjustment screw in or out until the tone is satisfactory. Tighten the locknut.

24.1 The horn is accessible from the front of the motorcycle

3   Disconnect the wire from the neutral switch **(see illustration)**. Connect one lead of an ohmmeter to a good ground and the other lead to the post on the switch.
4   When the transmission is in neutral, the ohmmeter should read 0 ohms - in any other gear, the meter should read infinite resistance.
5   If the switch doesn't check out as described, replace it. **Note:** *If the neutral light works intermittently, try removing the switch and reinstalling it temporarily without its sealing washer. If the light now works consistently, the switch plunger is worn and the switch should be replaced (don't just leave the old switch in position without the washer).*

Replacement

6   Unscrew the neutral switch from the case and remove the sealing washer.
7   Install the switch with a new sealing washer and tighten it securely.

---

23   Sidestand switch - check and replacement

Check

1   Place the bike on the centerstand.
2   Follow the wiring harness from the switch to the connector, then disconnect the connector.
3   Connect the leads of an ohmmeter to the black/red and black/yellow wire terminals.
4   With the sidestand in the up position, there should be continuity

---

25   Starter solenoid - check and replacement

Refer to illustration 25.2

Check

1   Remove the left side cover (see Chapter 8).
2   Disconnect the battery positive cable and the starter wire from the terminals on the starter solenoid **(see illustration)**. **Caution:** *Don't let the battery positive cable make contact with anything, as it would be a direct short to ground/earth.*

25.2 The battery positive cable and starter motor cable connections (arrow) are behind the wiring connector

26.3 Pull back the covers and disconnect the starter wires (arrows)

26.4a Remove the alternator cover bolts (arrows). . .

26.4b . . .and pull off the cover (pull firmly to overcome the pull of the rotor magnets, but don't force it)

3   Connect the leads of an ohmmeter to the terminals of the starter solenoid.
4   Turn the ignition switch to On and the engine stop switch to Run. Place the transmission in Neutral.
5   Press the starter button - the solenoid should click and the ohmmeter should indicate 0 ohms.
6   If the meter doesn't read 0 ohms or the solenoid doesn't click, replace it.

Replacement

7   Disconnect the cable from the negative terminal of the battery.
8   Detach the battery positive cable, the starter cable and electrical connector from the solenoid.
9   Pull the solenoid out.
10   Installation is the reverse of removal. Reconnect the negative battery cable after all the other electrical connections are made.

---

26   Starter motor - removal and installation

Refer to illustrations 26.3, 26.4a, 26.4b, 26.5, 26.6 and 26.7

Removal

1   Remove the lower fairing (if equipped) (see Chapter 8). Remove the fuel tank and carburetors (see Chapter 4).
2   Disconnect the cable from the negative terminal of the battery.

26.5 Remove the starter chain cover bolts (arrows)

3   Remove the nuts retaining the starter wires to the starter **(see illustration)**.
4   Remove the alternator cover bolts and pull off the cover **(see illustrations)**. **Note:** *The alternator magnets will hold the cover on. Pull firmly to remove it, but don't pry it off. If it won't come off with a firm two-hand pull, make sure you've removed all of the cover bolts.*
5   Remove the starter chain cover **(see illustration)**.

26.6 Remove the starter mounting bolts (arrows)

26.7 Lift the starter and disengage it from the chain

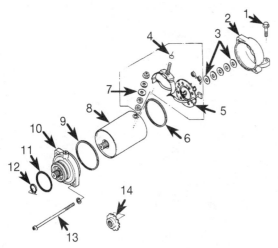

27.2 Exploded view of the starter motor

1	Starter mounting bolt	8	Yoke
2	End cover	9	O-ring
3	Washers	10	Reduction gear housing
4	Terminal bolt and nut	11	O-ring
5	Brush plate	12	Snap-ring
6	O-ring	13	Through-bolt
7	Terminal washers	14	Sprocket

27.4 Remove the brush plate from the housing

6   Remove the starter mounting bolts **(see illustration)**.
7   Lift the starter up a little bit and disengage the starter sprocket from the chain **(see illustration)**.
8   Check the condition of the O-ring on the end of the starter and replace it if necessary.

Installation

9   Apply a little engine oil to the O-ring and install the starter by reversing the removal procedure.

---

27   Starter motor - disassembly, inspection and reassembly

1   Remove the starter motor (see Section 26).

Disassembly

Refer to illustrations 27.2, 27.4 and 27.5

2   Mark the position of the housing to each end cover. Remove the two long screws and detach both end covers **(see illustration)**.
3   Pull the armature out of the housing (toward the pinion gear side).

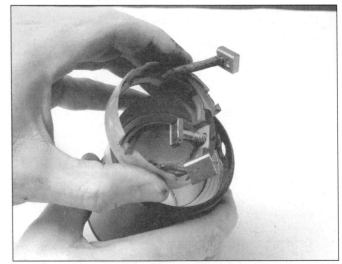

27.5 Push the terminal bolt through the housing and remove the plastic brush holder

4   Remove the brush plate from the housing **(see illustration)**.
5   Remove the nut and push the terminal bolt through the housing. Remove the two brushes with the plastic holder from the housing **(see illustration)**.

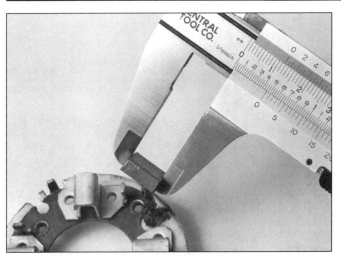

27.6 Measure the length of the brushes and compare the length of the shortest brush with the length listed in this Chapter's Specifications

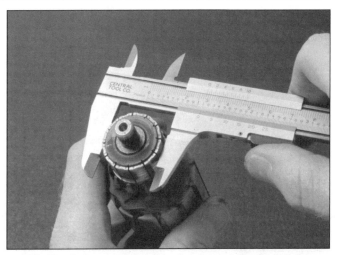

27.7 Check the commutator for cracks and discoloring, then measure the diameter and compare it with the minimum diameter listed in this Chapter's Specifications

27.8a Continuity should exist between the commutator bars

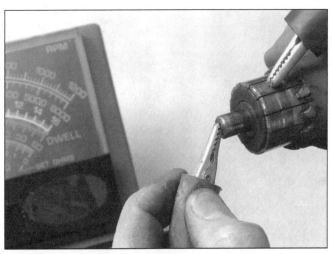

27.8b There should be no continuity between the commutator bars and the armature shaft

27.9 There should be almost no resistance (0 ohms) between the brushes and the brush plate

Inspection

Refer to illustrations 27.6, 27.7, 27.8a, 27.8b, 27.9 and 27.10

6   The parts of the starter motor that most likely will require attention are the brushes. Measure the length of the brushes and compare

the results to the brush length listed in this Chapter's Specifications **(see illustration)**. If any of the brushes are worn beyond the specified limits, replace the brush holder assembly with a new one. If the brushes are not worn excessively, cracked, chipped, or otherwise damaged, they may be reused.

7   Inspect the commutator **(see illustration)** for scoring, scratches and discoloration. The commutator can be cleaned and polished with crocus cloth, but do not use sandpaper or emery paper. After cleaning, wipe away any residue with a cloth soaked in an electrical system cleaner or denatured alcohol. Measure the commutator diameter and compare it to the diameter listed in this Chapter's Specifications. If it is less than the service limit, the motor must be replaced with a new one.

8   Using an ohmmeter or a continuity test light, check for continuity between the commutator bars **(see illustration)**. Continuity should exist between each bar and all of the others. Also, check for continuity between the commutator bars and the armature shaft **(see illustration)**. There should be no continuity between the commutator and the shaft. If the checks indicate otherwise, the armature is defective.

9   Check for continuity between the brush plate and the brushes **(see illustration)**. The meter should read close to 0 ohms. If it doesn't, the brush plate has an open and must be replaced.

10   Using the highest range on the ohmmeter, measure the resistance between the brush holders and the brush plate **(see illustration)**. The reading should be infinite. If there is any reading at all, replace the brush plate.

9

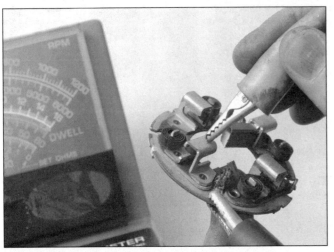

27.10 There should be no continuity between the brush plate and the brush holders (the resistance should be infinite)

27.12 Install the washers on the starter terminal as shown

27.13 When installing the brush plate, make sure the brush leads fit into the notches in the plate (arrow) - also, make sure the tongue on the plate fits into the notch in the housing (arrows)

27.14a Install each brush spring on the post in this position. . .

Reassembly

Refer to illustrations 27.12, 27.13, 27.14a and 27.14b

12   Install the plastic brush holder into the housing. Make sure the terminal bolt and washers are assembled correctly **(see illustration)**. Tighten the terminal nut securely.

13   Detach the brush springs from the brush plate (this will make armature installation much easier). Install the brush plate into the housing, routing the brush leads into the notches in the plate **(see illustration)**. Make sure the tongue on the brush plate fits into the notch in the housing.

14   Install the brushes into their holders and slide the armature into place. Install the brush springs **(see illustrations)**.

15   Install any washers that were present on the end of the armature shaft. Install the end covers, aligning the protrusions with the notches. Install the two long screws and tighten them securely.

27.14b . . .Then pull the end of the spring 1/2 turn clockwise and seat the end of it in the groove in the end of the brush

11   Check the starter reduction gears for worn, cracked, chipped and broken teeth. If the gears are damaged or worn, replace the starter motor.

28   Charging system testing - general information and precautions

1   If the performance of the charging system is suspect, the system as a whole should be checked first, followed by testing of the individual components (the alternator and the voltage regulator/rectifier). **Note**: *Before beginning the checks, make sure the battery is fully charged and that all system connections are clean and tight.*

2   Checking the output of the charging system and the performance

29.3 The regulator/rectifier and its connector (arrow) are located behind the left-hand side cover

of the various components within the charging system requires the use of special electrical test equipment. A voltmeter or a multimeter is the absolute minimum equipment required. In addition, an ohmmeter is generally required for checking the remainder of the system.

3   When making the checks, follow the procedures carefully to prevent incorrect connections or short circuits, as irreparable damage to electrical system components may result if short circuits occur. Because of the special tools and expertise required, it is recommended that the job of checking the charging system be left to a dealer service department or a reputable motorcycle repair shop.

29   Charging system - output test

Refer to illustration 29.3

Caution: *Never disconnect the battery cables from the battery while the engine is running. If the battery is disconnected, the alternator and regulator/rectifier will be damaged.*

1   To check the charging system output, you will need a voltmeter or a multimeter with a voltmeter function.

2   The battery must be fully charged (charge it from an external source if necessary) and the engine must be at normal operating temperature to obtain an accurate reading.

3   Remove the left-hand side cover and locate the regulator/rectifier connector **(see illustration)**.

4   Attach the positive (red) voltmeter lead to the white/red wire terminal and the negative lead to the black/yellow wire terminal. **Caution:** *The red/white wire is connected directly to the battery at all times, so don't allow the voltmeter to short this terminal to ground (don't let the voltmeter negative lead touch metal). The voltmeter selector switch (if so equipped) must be in a DC volt range greater than 15 volts.*

5   Start the engine. Run it at varying speeds up to 4,000 rpm, with headlight off and with it on (for US and Canadian models, disconnect the black/yellow wire at the headlight to turn it off with the engine running).

6   The charging system output should be within the range listed in this Chapter's Specifications. It should be at the low end of the range at low engine speeds and at the high end of the range at higher engine speeds.

7   If the output is as specified, the alternator is functioning properly. If the charging system as a whole is not performing as it should, refer to Section 32 and check the voltage regulator/rectifier.

8   Low voltage output may be the result of damaged windings in the alternator stator coils, loss of magnetism in the alternator rotor or wiring problems. Make sure all electrical connections are clean and tight, then refer to Sections 30 and 31 for specific alternator tests.

30   Alternator - output test

1   Follow the wiring harness from the alternator housing to the connector, then disconnect the connector.

2   Connect a voltmeter with a 250-volt AC scale to two of the yellow wire terminals in the alternator connector (at this point, you're measuring the alternator output before it has been rectified from alternating current to direct current, so the voltmeter must be able to measure AC).

3   Run the engine at 4,000 rpm and note the voltage reading.

4   Take three different measurements between different pairs of wires. In all cases, the voltage should be as listed in this Chapter's Specifications.

   a) If the voltage reading is correct, the rectifier/regulator is probably defective. Refer to Section 32 for test procedures.

   b) If the voltage reading is low, the alternator may be defective. Test the stator coils as described in Section 31.

31   Alternator stator coils - continuity test

1   If charging system output is low or non-existent, the alternator stator coil windings and leads should be checked for proper continuity. The test can be made with the stator in place on the machine.

2   Using an ohmmeter (preferred) or a continuity test light, check for continuity between each of the wires coming from the alternator stator (the same connector that was disconnected in Section 30 for the output test). Continuity should exist between any one wire and each of the others (Kawasaki actually specifies a resistance of 0.3 to 0.6 ohms).

3   Check for continuity between each of the wires and the engine. No continuity should exist between any of the wires and the case.

4   If there is no continuity between any two of the wires, or if there is continuity between the wires and an engine ground/earth, an open circuit or a short exists within the stator coils. Since repair of the stator is not feasible, it must be replaced with a new one.

32   Voltage regulator/rectifier - check and replacement

Refer to illustration 32.3

1   Remove the left side cover (see Chapter 8).

2   Remove the two bolts securing the regulator/rectifier to its bracket, then detach the electrical connector **(see illustration 29.3)**.

3   Using an ohmmeter, check the resistance across the terminals indicated in the accompanying table **(see illustration)**. If the meter readings are not as specified, replace the regulator.

4   This check, combined with the tests outlined in Sections 29 through 31, should diagnose most charging system problems. If the voltage regulator/rectifier passes the test described in Step 3, and the stator coil passes the test in Section 31, take the regulator/rectifier to a dealer service department or other repair shop for further checks, or substitute a known good unit and recheck the charging system output.

33   Alternator - removal and installation

Refer to illustrations 33.3 and 33.4

1   Disconnect the cable from the negative terminal of the battery.

2   Remove the starter (see Section 26).

3   Prevent the alternator rotor from turning by holding it with Kawasaki tool no. 57001-308, a strap wrench or a pin spanner wrench. Remove the rotor bolt **(see illustration)**. **Note**: *The bolt has left-hand threads (loosens in a clockwise direction).*

4   Hold the rotor from turning again, and using tool no. 57001-254 or 57001-1099, remove the rotor from the crankshaft **(see illustration)**.

5   If you're going to replace the rotor, remove the starter clutch (see Section 35).

9

Rectifier Circuit Inspection

Range ×100 Ω	Meter (+) Lead Connection					
Terminal	BK	BR	W/R	Y	Y	Y
BK		1 kΩ ~ 5 kΩ	400 Ω ~ 2 kΩ	200 Ω ~ 600 Ω	200 Ω ~ 600 Ω	200 Ω ~ 600 Ω
BR	10 kΩ ~ ∞		10 kΩ ~ ∞	10 kΩ ~ ∞	10 kΩ ~ ∞	100 kΩ ~ ∞
W/R	∞	∞		∞	∞	∞
Y	∞	∞	200 Ω ~ 600 Ω		∞	∞
Y	∞	∞	200 Ω ~ 600 Ω	∞		∞
Y	∞	∞	200 Ω ~ 600 Ω	∞	∞	

(Meter (−) Lead Connection — left column)

Regulator/Rectifier Terminal

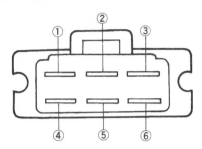

1. Brown Lead Terminal
2. White/Red Lead Terminal
3. Black Lead Terminal
4. Y_1
5. Y_2
6. Y_3

32.3 Rectifier circuit diode test table

33.3 The alternator rotor bolt has left-hand threads (turn it clockwise to loosen it)

33.4 This special tool is used to remove the alternator rotor

6   Clean all dirt from the crankshaft and the inside of the rotor with high flash point solvent.

7   Position the rotor on the engine and install the bolt, tightening it to the torque listed in this Chapter's Specifications.

8   The remainder of installation is the reverse of the removal steps. Before you install the housing, make sure the magnets haven't picked up any pieces of metal that could damage the alternator.

34   Alternator - stator coil replacement

Refer to illustration 34.2

1   Remove the alternator cover (see Section 26).

2   Remove the stator screws **(see illustration)**, remove the wiring harness retainer and lift the stator coils out of the alternator housing.

3   Installation is the reverse of the removal steps. Tighten the stator screws to the torque listed in this Chapter's Specifications.

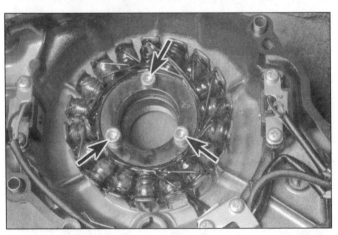

34.2 The stator coils are secured in the housing by three Allen screws (arrows)

35.3 Remove the washer and sprocket from the end of
the crankshaft

35.4a Compress the springs with a small screwdriver and remove
the rollers

35.4b Starter clutch details

35.8a Press the springs and caps into the holes. . .

35.8b . . .then install the rollers and release the springs

35   Starter clutch - removal and installation

1   The starter clutch is mounted on the back of the alternator rotor.

Removal

Refer to illustrations 35.3, 35.4a and 35.4b

2   Remove the alternator rotor (see Section 33).

3   Slide the washer and starter sprocket off the alternator shaft **(see illustration)**.

4   Pull the rollers out of the starter clutch, then remove the spring caps and springs **(see illustrations)**.

Inspection

5   Check all parts for wear and damage. Replace any worn or damaged parts.

6   If you're going to replace the starter clutch housing or rotor, remove the three Allen bolts and separate the starter clutch from the rotor.

Installation

Refer to illustrations 35.8a and 35.8b

7   If you removed the starter clutch from the rotor, bolt it back on. Use a non-permanent thread locking agent on the threads of the Allen bolts and tighten them to the torque listed in this Chapter's Specifications.

8   Place the spring caps on the springs. Place the springs in their holes, compress them with a screwdriver and install the rollers **(see illustrations)**.

9   Install the alternator rotor on the engine.

9

36   Wiring diagrams

Prior to troubleshooting a circuit, check the fuses to make sure they're in good condition. Make sure the battery is fully charged and check the cable connections.

When checking a circuit, make sure all connectors are clean, with no broken or loose terminals or wires. When unplugging a connector, don't pull on the wires - pull only on the connector housings themselves.

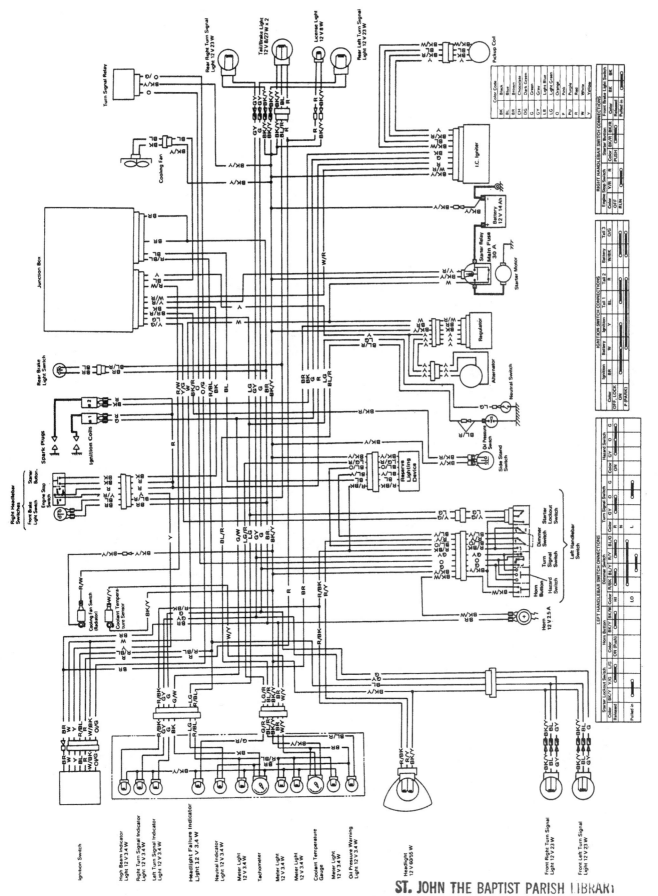

Wiring diagram – 1987 and 1988 US and Canadian models

9

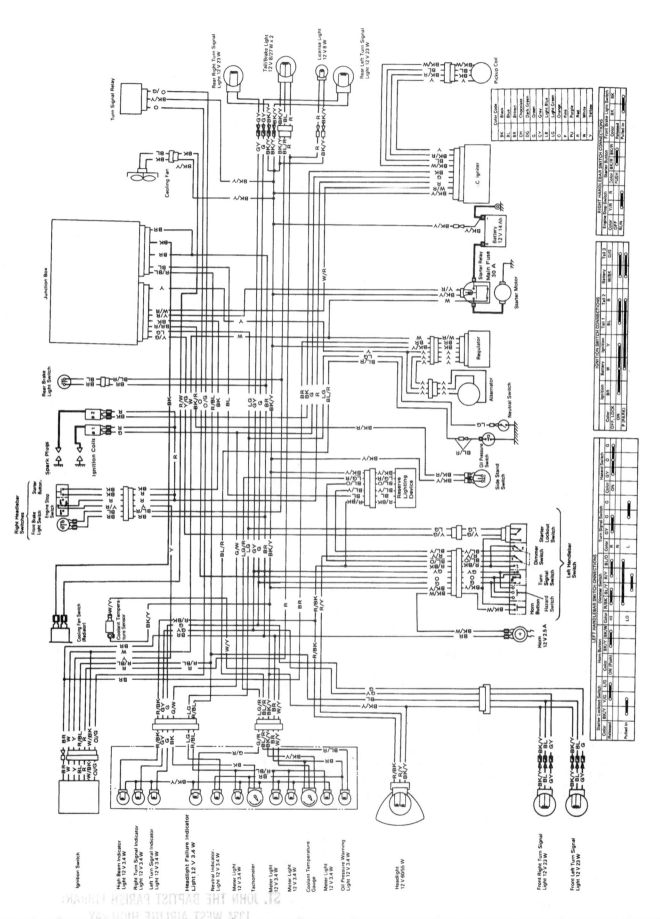

Wiring diagram – 1989 and later US and Canadian models

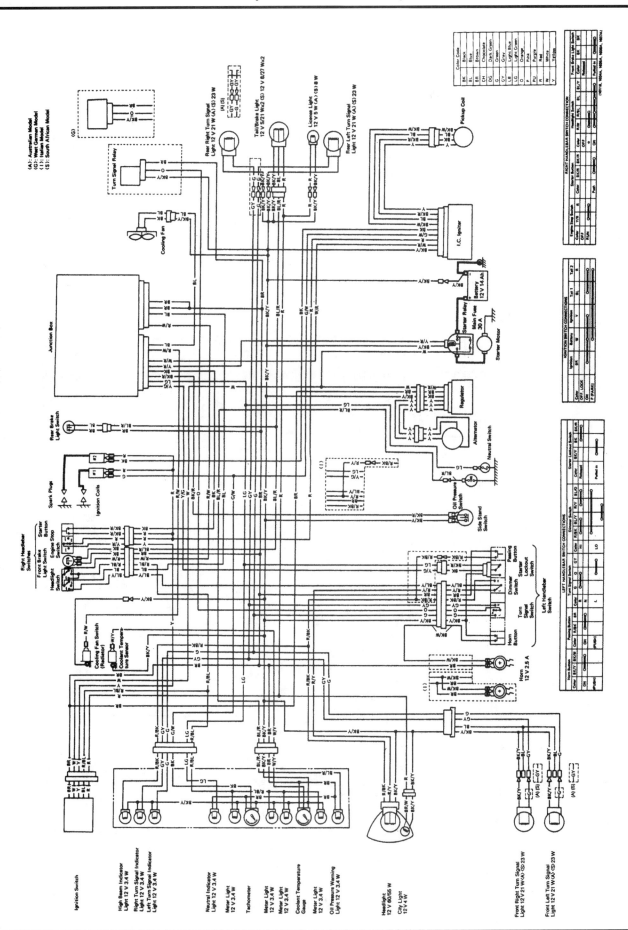

Wiring diagram - 1987 and 1988 models (UK and other markets except US and Canada)

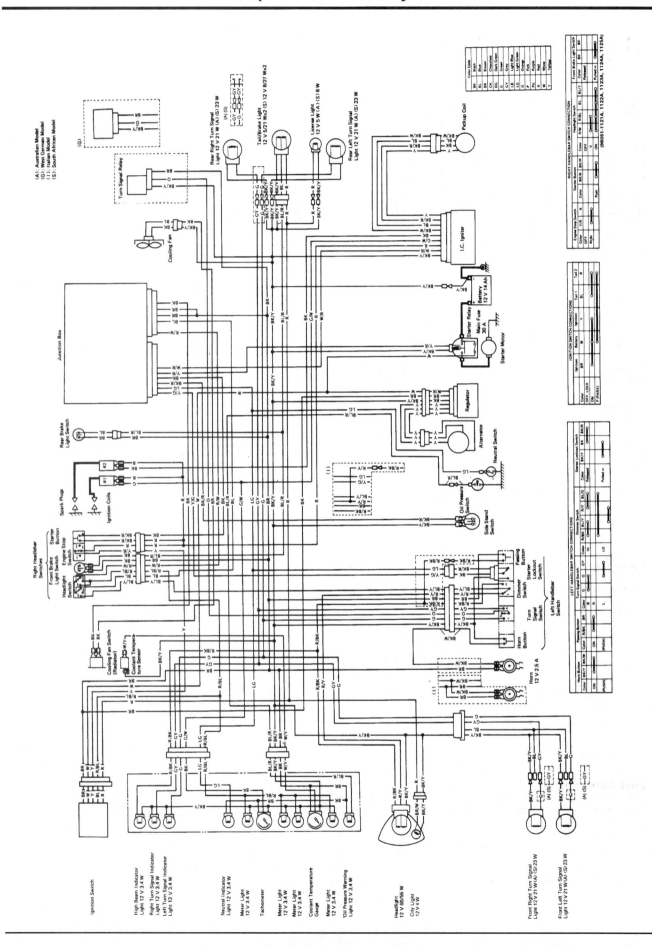

Wiring diagram – 1989 and later models (UK and other markets except US and Canada)

Conversion factors

Length (distance)
Inches (in)	X	25.4	= Millimetres (mm)	X 0.0394	= Inches (in)
Feet (ft)	X	0.305	= Metres (m)	X 3.281	= Feet (ft)
Miles	X	1.609	= Kilometres (km)	X 0.621	= Miles

Volume (capacity)
Cubic inches (cu in; in³)	X	16.387	= Cubic centimetres (cc; cm³)	X 0.061	= Cubic inches (cu in; in³)
Imperial pints (Imp pt)	X	0.568	= Litres (l)	X 1.76	= Imperial pints (Imp pt)
Imperial quarts (Imp qt)	X	1.137	= Litres (l)	X 0.88	= Imperial quarts (Imp qt)
Imperial quarts (Imp qt)	X	1.201	= US quarts (US qt)	X 0.833	= Imperial quarts (Imp qt)
US quarts (US qt)	X	0.946	= Litres (l)	X 1.057	= US quarts (US qt)
Imperial gallons (Imp gal)	X	4.546	= Litres (l)	X 0.22	= Imperial gallons (Imp gal)
Imperial gallons (Imp gal)	X	1.201	= US gallons (US gal)	X 0.833	= Imperial gallons (Imp gal)
US gallons (US gal)	X	3.785	= Litres (l)	X 0.264	= US gallons (US gal)

Mass (weight)
Ounces (oz)	X	28.35	= Grams (g)	X 0.035	Ounces (oz)
Pounds (lb)	X	0.454	= Kilograms (kg)	X 2.205	= Pounds (lb)

Force
Ounces-force (ozf; oz)	X	0.278	= Newtons (N)	X 3.6	= Ounces-force (ozf; oz)
Pounds-force (lbf; lb)	X	4.448	= Newtons (N)	X 0.225	= Pounds-force (lbf; lb)
Newtons (N)	X	0.1	= Kilograms-force (kgf; kg)	X 9.81	= Newtons (N)

Pressure
Pounds-force per square inch (psi; lbf/in²; lb/in²)	X	0.070	= Kilograms-force per square centimetre (kgf/cm²; kg/cm²)	X 14.223	= Pounds-force per square inch (psi; lbf/in²; lb/in²)
Pounds-force per square inch (psi; lbf/in²; lb/in²)	X	0.068	= Atmospheres (atm)	X 14.696	= Pounds-force per square inch (psi; lbf/in²; lb/in²)
Pounds-force per square inch (psi; lbf/in²; lb/in²)	X	0.069	= Bars	X 14.5	= Pounds-force per square inch (psi; lbf/in²; lb/in²)
Pounds-force per square inch (psi; lbf/in²; lb/in²)	X	6.895	= Kilopascals (kPa)	X 0.145	= Pounds-force per square inch (psi; lbf/in²; lb/in²)
Kilopascals (kPa)	X	0.01	= Kilograms-force per square centimetre (kgf/cm²; kg/cm²)	X 98.1	= Kilopascals (kPa)

Torque (moment of force)
Pounds-force inches (lbf in; lb in)	X	1.152	= Kilograms-force centimetre (kgf cm; kg cm)	X 0.868	= Pounds-force inches (lbf in; lb in)
Pounds-force inches (lbf in; lb in)	X	0.113	= Newton metres (Nm)	X 8.85	= Pounds-force inches (lbf in; lb in)
Pounds-force inches (lbf in; lb in)	X	0.083	= Pounds-force feet (lbf ft; lb ft)	X 12	= Pounds-force inches (lbf in; lb in)
Pounds-force feet (lbf ft; lb ft)	X	0.138	= Kilograms-force metres (kgf m; kg m)	X 7.233	= Pounds-force feet (lbf ft; lb ft)
Pounds-force feet (lbf ft; lb ft)	X	1.356	= Newton metres (Nm)	X 0.738	= Pounds-force feet (lbf ft; lb ft)
Newton metres (Nm)	X	0.102	= Kilograms-force metres (kgf m; kg m)	X 9.804	= Newton metres (Nm)

Power
Horsepower (hp)	X	745.7	= Watts (W)	X 0.0013	= Horsepower (hp)

Velocity (speed)
Miles per hour (miles/hr; mph)	X	1.609	= Kilometres per hour (km/hr; kph)	X 0.621	= Miles per hour (miles/hr; mph)

Fuel consumption*
Miles per gallon, Imperial (mpg)	X	0.354	= Kilometres per litre (km/l)	X 2.825	= Miles per gallon, Imperial (mpg)
Miles per gallon, US (mpg)	X	0.425	= Kilometres per litre (km/l)	X 2.352	= Miles per gallon, US (mpg)

Temperature
Degrees Fahrenheit = (°C x 1.8) + 32   Degrees Celsius (Degrees Centigrade; °C) = (°F - 32) x 0.56

*It is common practice to convert from miles per gallon (mpg) to litres/100 kilometres (l/100km), where mpg (Imperial) x l/100 km = 282 and mpg (US) x l/100 km = 235

NOTES

Index